# SPORTS & RECREATION FADS
Frank W. Hoffmann, PhD
William G. Bailey, MA

## SOME ADVANCE REVIEWS

"An encyclopedia of delight and information. From Hank Aaron's home run record chase to yo-yos, from Arnie's Army to WrestleMania, from artificial turf to volleyball, here are all the stories of the side shows and often main events of American Popular Culture. No sports buff or student of American life would want to be without this book either to read for simple enjoyment or to use for reference or further research."

**Robert J. Higgs, PhD**
Professor of English
East Tennessee State University

"Fads have always gripped and directed the attention of Americans, even with the fads that directed the lives — and the hates — of America's first puritans. Where did it all begin, and where will it end? Nobody knows the answer to either. But this [book] provides such a rich and instructive collection of the fads and foibles of American humankind that the reader really hopes the fad of fads never ends. Such an ending would terminate the fad of fun."

**Ray B. Brown, PhD**
Chair and Distinguished University Professor
Department of Popular Culture
Bowling Green State University
Secretary/Treasurer, Popular Culture Association

# Sports & Recreation Fads

*HAWORTH* Popular Culture
New, Recent, and Forthcoming Titles
Frank W. Hoffmann and William G. Bailey
Senior Co-Editors

*Arts & Entertainment Fads*

*Sports & Recreation Fads*

*Mind & Society Fads*

# Sports & Recreation Fads

Frank W. Hoffmann, PhD
William G. Bailey, MA

Harrington Park Press
New York • London • Sydney

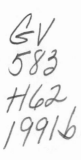
ISBN 0-918393-92-2

Published by

Harrington Park Press, 10 Alice Street, Binghamton, NY 13904-1580
EUROSPAN/Harrington, 3 Henrietta Street, London WC2E 8LU England
ASTAM/Haworth, 162-168 Parramatta Road, Stanmore (Sydney), N.S.W. 2048 Australia

Harrington Park Press is a subsidiary of The Haworth Press, Inc., 10 Alice Street, Binghamton, NY 13904-1580.

All photographs courtesy of the Library of Congress.

Cover art supplied by Steven Jenkins.

**Library of Congress Cataloging-in-Publication Data**

Hoffmann, Frank W., 1949–
    Sports & recreation fads / Frank W. Hoffmann, William G. Bailey.
      p.  cm.
    Simultaneously published: New York : Haworth Press, ©1991.
    Includes bibliographical references and index.
    ISBN 0-918393-92-2
    1. Sports–United States–History. 2. Recreation–United States–History. 3. Fads–United States–History. 4. United States–Popular culture–History. I. Bailey, William G., 1947– . II. Title. III. Title: Sports and recreation fads.
GV583.H62  1991b
796'.0973–dc20
                                           90-26592
                                              CIP

# CONTENTS

# ABOUT THE AUTHORS

**Frank W. Hoffmann, PhD, MLS,** is an associate professor in the School of Library Science, Sam Houston State University. His teaching responsibilities include library collection development, reference/information services, and a seminar of popular culture. His publications include *The Development of Collections of Sound Recordings in Libraries* (Marcel Dekker), *Popular Culture and Libraries* (Library Professional Publications), *The Literature of Rock* series (Scarecrow), and *The Cash Box* chart compilation series (Scarecrow). He received his doctorate from the University of Pittsburgh and his BA in History and MLS from Indiana University.

**William G. Bailey, MA, MLS,** has worked in the Information Services division of the Newton Gresham Library, Sam Houston State University, for the past 12 years. He is currently Head of the Reference Department. Due to his daily routine, he is constantly looking for new writing projects to fill information gaps. A fad encyclopedia appeals to his eclectic mind; he is already the editor/ compiler of books on such diverse topics as police, longevity, and Americans in Paris. He holds an MA degree in English and American literature from the University of Houston, and an MLS from the University of Texas at Austin.

# Introduction

Sports and recreation developed slowly in Colonial America. The Puritans who landed on Plymouth Rock in 1620 believed that luxury and pleasure were sinful. Work, God, and deserved rest were the trinity of their rigid lives. They had no time for frivolous activities such as their European brethren engaged in, and especially despised the games of the aristocracy. In Puritan America there would be no fox or boar hunts, falconry, dice and gambling, animal baiting and other blood sports. There was too much to accomplish in the new country to make it habitable and god fearing. They had left privilege and barbarism behind and never wanted to look back. Before we condemn the Puritans as a dull lot, a sample of English sporting history is in order.

In the shires of merry old England a favorite sport was bull-running. Each year near Christmas, the town butcher supplied a wild bull to let loose down main street. All shops closed for the morning and the townspeople, armed with bull clubs, pummeled the frightened beast as it tried to get away. The sport was to kill the bull with many small blows so everyone could get in on the fun—not that easy since iron clubs were disallowed. The townspeople had to chase the animal wherever it went and get close enough to whack it on the head. The reward came the next day when the butcher passed out beef steaks. During the chase there was a concern for civil liability. Posted guards warned travelers a bull-run was in progress so they could wait it out safely. With taverns locked in deference to the sport, one wonders how many travelers just dropped their bags and grabbed a non-iron club?

Another butcher story tells us about the first instance of bull-baiting (chaining the beast so it could not escape) which in turn fostered other forms of animal-baiting. The story is not historical fact but credible nevertheless. One day William, Earl of Warren, during the time of King John (1167?-1216), stood upon his castle wall in Stamford, observing a spectacle below. In the meadow two bulls were fighting over a cow. The butcher, seeing his prized bull about to get gored, sicced his mastiff on the lovesick combatants to stop the fight. The four animals created such a cacophony of barking, bellowing, and mooing that other dogs, great and small, raced to the meadow to join in. The motley pack of dogs tortured the two mad bulls by leaping at them and tearing their flesh. The butcher was not amused, but the Earl was. He gave the meadow to the town if once a year the butchers contributed an enraged bull for the continuance of the sport. That was in Stamford; in Tutbury a bull and mastiff bout was more perverse. Handlers sawed off the bull's horns, cropped his ears, shortened his tail, smeared his body with soap, and stuffed pepper in his nose—all to humiliate the proud beast. Once caught by human revelers, the bull was baited so dogs could concentrate their teasing, killing attack. Bull-baiting and bear-baiting appealed too much to the English people to be left in the meadow. Both blood sports became national pastimes by the 16th century, particularly after King Henry VIII sanctioned an office of Master of the Royal Game of Bears and Mastiff Dogs.

A more everyday recreation of our English ancestors was cock throwing. A farmer tied a fat cock to a post, then marked off a short distance from it. The sport was to hurl sharp sticks at the cock until a thrower pierced its heart and killed it. If the cock were only maimed it was propped up again. An offshoot of cock throwing challenged the player to break an earthen vessel containing a cock. The vessel suspended in the air allowed the cock's head and tail to protrude. Throwing distance increased and often the cock made it through unscathed. One folktale has it that mischiefmakers put an owl in a vessel with the severed head and tail of a cock showing as usual. When a burly bloke smashed the vessel, to everyone's amazement the flightless cock winged off in a hurry. Thereafter the townspeople persistently ridiculed the bloke for having lost his prize until he was forced to leave town—probably feeling as humiliated as the Tutbury bull. Another game using an owl was to tie the bird to the back of a duck. The owl, not liking its awkward position, started hooting. This scared the duck which dove in the water. The owl fought the duck to return to the surface. When both did, the hooting started the game over again until the owl drowned.

English sports and recreation were not all as brutal as these examples lead one to believe. The Dancing around the maypole at a festival shed no blood, but Puritans cringed at the thought of the pole's saturnalian association. Other recreation continued pagan rites. At a village in Oxfordshire, the Monday after Whitsun week, maidens with their thumbs tied behind their backs chased after a lamb. The girl who finally caught the lamb in her mouth and pinned it down was declared Lady of the Lamb. The next two days villagers celebrated in honor of all the maidens who had given chase. Tilting at the quintain (a revolving target mounted on a post), "Pale-Maille" (forerunner of croquet), and a variety of card games, were other fond amusements not based on blood.

The reason for reminiscing about these early English amusements is to present a clear picture of what repelled the Puritans. They crossed the Atlantic to escape every kind of indecency and that included — to their mind — barren and godless sports and recreation. They devoted their week to bettering humankind. Firmly set, they forbade participation in any Sabbath day play. Even a man who shot fowl on Sunday to feed his family did so at peril of being taken to court. Early church records of "sin" show that more people labored unnecessarily, drank, or traveled on Sunday than chanced indulging in amusements. Blood and erotic sports sickened the Puritans but were only one side of the coin. The other side, just as harmful to the individual and society, was incessant gambling that seemed to be part and parcel of every sport. Religious scripture condemned it. If left alone, gambling would surely become a plague destroying all those in its path. Seen today, the Puritans' stern mind-set was an overreaction to the ignoble character of English sports and recreation. But we also observe that the Puritian ethic locked out simple human needs and made for a humorless society. To recreate and test one another in games are childlike diversions one never outgrows. The Puritans, with their dogmatic faith in a grimly pious society, were able to hold sway just so long. The Dutch in New Amsterdam (1624) brought their sports and recreation with them. So, too, did other expatriate groups who knew the value of play. Here before the Puritans, American Indians engaged in all manner of skillful games, lacrosse being the most beloved. And the British in America still thought of themselves as British and saw no harm in animal-baiting, cock-fighting, rough-and-tumble fighting, and other such diversions.

What the foregoing has to do with fad history is that as sports and recreation developed slowly in America, crazes and manias materialized. The puritanical element in our culture fought the rise of sports and recreation because frivolous pursuits detracted from religious life. What if one day play assumed a more important role in daily living than obedience to God? And what about the sin of gambling? And what about corrupting youth? Often, as a result of the puritanical element, early Americans took to play feeling a little guilty. Yet, life was so hard for most of them that any emerging amusement generated faddish appeal. Just about every sport and recreation embraced from Colonial America to the present had its faddish aspects. For any one of them to have survived it had to face public approval, always a fickle thing. That fad enters into the creation of sports and recreation is to be expected. A few examples will clarify this notion. The first great sporting rage in America was horse racing. It had long been the private pleasure of the gentry before intoxicating the general public. From 1823 to 1845, a series of North/South horse races attracted every type of person, making for a truly Jacksonian gathering. The best horse from the South dared to stand up to the best horse from the North, or vice versa depending on one's loyalty. The gentry bred, trained, and raced the horses, but for once anyone who could afford a ticket attended the races. These Mason-Dixon clashes generated so much excitement no one thought of them as a passing fancy. Cornucopias of food and drink spilled forth and an orgy of gambling convinced promoters they could have run horses day and night to delight *t*.ie crowd. However, after the great race between Fashion and Peytona in 1845, the fad of North/South horse races was virtually over. The gentry had begun to suffer economic reversals in a downturn that affected all of America. That made it more difficult to continue the expensive business of breeding race horses. Also, the promotional gimmick of the North/South challenge — horses as ideology — had intensified quickly, then peaked. The fad demonstrated one thing for sure — horse racing stimulated the public and could draw enthusiastic crowds.

That was sport; now, an example from the world of recreation —

the game of bridge. This popular card game grew out of whist which in its day was also very fashionable. Bridge achieved fad status in the 1930s due to rule changes and the play of three men. Newly named, contract bridge featured vulnerability, high bonuses, and slams which reinvigorated the game. Harold S. Vanderbilt, Ely Culbertson, and Charles Goren were the three who ignited national interest in the game mainly because of their showmanship and enthusiasm. Before the 1930s people played bridge in a civil manner, much like hearts or gin rummy. Players did not take the game all that seriously. But during the 1930s bridge rapidly became a contest of wits that incited disputes with friends, confrontations with strangers, and family squabbles. Each person knew how to play bridge better than the next, for all of them had read and reread the best-selling books and had listened intently to radio programs on how to master the game. Local and national bridge tournaments mushroomed, turning the once simple recreation into battles royal. For a solid decade bridge preoccupied America. Movies, songs, and novels either focused on bridge or included the game as a "slice of life." Today, of course, bridge is still prominent. But it won its secure position in popular culture during the fad-ridden 1930s.

The importance of fad in the development of sports and recreation cannot be overlooked. Fad nourishes our most eminent pastimes. Take America's favorite sport—baseball—it has had its share of fads. All of which have renewed fan interest and attracted people usually unconcerned with bats, balls, and rounding bases. In fact, unless you are a baseball nut who recalls every player and game, the fads are what you do remember. Joe DiMaggio's consecutive game hitting streak, Babe Ruth calling his shot for a homer, the Maris-Mantle assault on the home run record, "Them Amazin' Mets," and the Pete Rose gambling scandal are baseball fads that got people talking. Daily baseball has needed, and will always need, something special to energize it that cannot last long—a season at most. Fad in all sports accomplishes this very thing. It lifts us into a larger-than-life dimension by concentrating our focus on a spectacular player, team, or manner of play to stir our hearts.

Before concluding this introduction we must revisit the 1890s. Then conservative factions in America disputed the value of what they called, "the athletic craze" and "the glorification of athletics." A hundred years ago, the guardians of youth were certain that collegiate sports were detrimental to acquiring an education. The prolific journalist, Ogden Rollo, sounded the alarm in *The Nation*, December 1, 1892:

> . . . the gambling mania [has] attached itself to college athletics with an excess and extravagance not seen earlier. Of course, the crowds and enthusiasm, the glory of the victors and the shame of the vanquished, the vulgarity and lawlessness of a lot of boys let loose in a great city, have all been greater than ever before. Greater, too we would add, has been the swamping throughout the entire year of all other undergraduate ideals by the one predominant and overmastering athletic ideal.

What could be done to save our young men and women? A daunting task since, "It seems to be the weakness of the American people to take nearly everything in 'crazes.'" And to worsen the situation, "It is a frequent remark of observant foreigners that the American young man of eighteen to twenty-five years is a singularly uninteresting being." No doubt, the athletic craze had already addled their brains. Fretful parents and educators prayed for an end to the fad of college spectacle sports and the licentious gambling they bred. Surely the loathsome fad would stumble and fall of its own volition once people awoke to its destructiveness. The puritanical element was at work again. Now, a century later, when a college or university—even a small one—drops a spectacle sport, particularly football, the news makes headlines and regents worry about losing enrollment. An inalienable right of every college student is to cheer on the dear old team. But there has been serious talk about more colleges and universities doing away with expensive athletic programs in favor of academics. Bereft students would transfer their sports loyalties to other teams at big-name institutions where the best players and coaches are anyway. However, at present the idea of such a sweeping change is clearly in the realm of faddish thinking.

# Hank Aaron Hits His 715th Home Run

During his early playing days, Hank Aaron was rarely considered a likely candidate to eclipse Babe Ruth's regular season career record of 714 home runs. Speculative pieces during the 1950s and 1960s devoted to the topic of who, among active players, might eventually overtake Ruth tended to like the chances of sluggers such as Mickey Mantle, Willie Mays, Eddie Mathews, and Harmon Killebrew more than those of Aaron.

While Aaron never had a season in which he hit more than forty-seven homers (in contrast, Ruth topped fifty-four in four different seasons), his career was extraordinary with respect to its combined longevity and consistency. By the early 1970s, it had become clear that Aaron's chances of surpassing Ruth were very good indeed; at the termination of the 1973 season—at which point Aaron had closed to 713—it appeared to be a virtual inevitability.

During the off-season, comparisons between Aaron and Ruth left no stone unturned as journalists and media personalities jostled each other for wider visibility. The relative advantages of each, as duly noted by the press, included:

*For Ruth*
- the absence of tiring cross-country plane trips, St. Louis being the western outpost of the major leagues in his day
- the absence of an endless stream of relievers with unorthodox deliveries and unusual pitches as in Aaron's era.
- indications that pitching in his day was generally considered to lack the overall quality and consistency characterizing the modern era; e.g., the cumulative batting average in the majors fell from .282 in Ruth's heyday to .252 in Aaron's
- the absence of night games
- a closer adherence to textbook mechanics as a hitter—Aaron

allegedly hit off the front foot (a flat-footed stance which ran contrary to established wisdom)
- an added insight because he broke into the majors as a pitcher in 1914
- a built-in advantage as a left-handed hitter in that there have always been far more right-handed than left-handed pitchers, and a lefty has a statistical batting edge against a right-hander
- the availability of closer fences: The right field fence of the Polo Grounds, where his team hosted opponents until 1923, had a right field line of only 254 feet while Yankee Stadium's was 296 feet—still one of the easiest targets in the game (the Milwaukee and Atlanta ballparks, while conducive to the long ball, measured 330 feet from home plate to the fences)
- the absence of pressure related to breaking a notable, long-standing record (Ruth held the career mark during the majority of his playing days, replacing Roger Connor as the all-time homer king when he hit number 138 in 1921)
- the absence of the intensified media scrutiny typifying modern-day coverage of sporting events

*For Aaron*
- the continued maintenance of prime physical condition which substantially prolonged his effectiveness as a player
- the opportunity to record nearly 3,000 more at bats (walks excluded) than Ruth over his career
- a career exclusively devoted to the art of hitting (i.e., no precious years lost to mastering the art of pitching with the obligatory days of rest between outings)
- a record to shoot for combined with a fierce pride rooted in his desire to overcome a host of racial inequities

On his first swing in the opening game of the 1974 season, Aaron promptly hit number 714. A controversy then ensued over the desire of his employers to have him break the record in Atlanta which resulted in his being benched on alien soil in Cincinnati. The commissioner of baseball, Bowie Kuhn, promptly responded by ordering the Braves to start Aaron on April 7 or face "serious penalties." To the relief of the Braves faithful, Aaron went homerless, setting the scene for the grand climax in Atlanta the following evening. One eyewitness, Joseph Durso, relates what happened:

> The stadium was packed with its largest crowd since the Braves left Milwaukee and brought major league baseball to the Deep South nine years ago. Pearl Bailey sang the national anthem; the Jonesboro High School band marched; balloons and fireworks filled the overcast sky before the game; Aaron's life was dramatized on a huge color map of the United States painted across the outfield grass, and Bad Henry was serenaded by the Atlanta Boy Choir, which now includes girls. . . . Gov. Jimmy Carter was there, along with Mayor Maynard Jackson, Sammy Davis, Jr. and broadcasters and writers from as far away as Japan, South America and Britain.
>
> To many Atlantans, it was like the city's festive premiere of "Gone With the Wind" during the 1930s. . . . The first time he batted, leading off the second inning, Aaron . . . took first base while the crowd hooted and booed because their home town hero had been walked. . . .
>
> Then came the fourth inning, with the Dodgers leading by 3-1 and the rain falling, with colored umbrellas raised in the stands and the crowd roaring every time Aaron appeared. Darrell Evans led off for Atlanta with a grounder behind second base that the shortstop, Bill Russell, juggled long enough for an error. And up came Henry for the eighth time this season and the second this evening. Downing pitched ball one inside, and Aaron watched impassively. Then came the second pitch, and this time Henry took his first cut of the night. The ball rose high toward left-center as the crowd came to its feet shouting, and as it dropped over the inside fence separating the outfield from the bullpen area, the skyrockets were fired and the scoreboard lights flashed in six-foot numerals: "715".

The game was halted for eleven minutes during the commotion that followed, which included a presentation of the home run ball (retrieved by Atlanta relief pitcher Tom House) as well as a plaque from team owner Bill Bartholomay. Following the game, Aaron reflected on his accomplishment as well as intimations that he might have been holding back in the Cincinnati series: "I have never gone out on a ball field and given less than my level best. When I hit it tonight, all I thought about was that I wanted to touch all the bases."

## BIBLIOGRAPHY

Aaron, Henry, with Furman Bisher. *Aaron*. Revised edition. Crowell, 1974.

Baldwin, S., and others. *Bad Henry*. Chilton, 1974.

"Braves' Owners Try For a Better Score." *Business Week*. (April 6, 1974) 23.

Buckley, T. "Packaging of a Home Run," *New York Times Magazine*. (March 31, 1974) 22ff.

Deegan, P.J. *Hank Aaron*. Creative Educ. Soc., 1974.

Durso, Joseph. "1974: 715: Move Over, Babe — Here Comes Henry!," In: *The Fireside Book of Baseball*, edited by Charles Einstein. Fourth Edition. New York: Simon & Schuster, 1987. pp. 106-107.

Fimrite, Ron. "End of the Glorious Ordeal," *Sports Illustrated*. 40 (April 15, 1974) 20-23.

Gulliver, H. "Women Behind Hank Aaron's Smashing Success," *Today's Health*. 52 (April 1974) 22-25ff.

"Hank Aaron Wastes No Time," *Newsweek*. 83 (April 15, 1974) 72.

Haskins, J. *Babe Ruth and Hank Aaron*. Lothrop, 1974.

"Home-Run Hysteria," *Time*. 103 (April 8, 1974) 57-58.

"It's Almost Over With," *Time*. 103 (April 15, 1974) 68.

Leggett, W. "Poised for the Golden Moment," *Sports Illustrated*. 40 (April 8, 1974) 46-48.

"Number 715; After the Ball Was Over," *Newsweek*. 83 (April 22, 1974) 69.

Plimpton, George. "Final Twist of the Drama," *Sports Illustrated*. 40 (April 22, 1974) 82-86ff.

Schlossberg, Dan. "Hank Aaron vs. Babe Ruth," In: *The Baseball Catalog*. Middle Village, New York: Jonathan David. pp. 120-124.

"That Home Run," *National Review*. 26 (April 26, 1974) 471-472.

# Arnie's Army

In 1962, Alfred Wright noted, "Seldom has any sport — and particularly this one — ever turned into the one-man show that golf has now become." During the first half of the 1960s, Arnold Palmer was that man. Win or lose — Palmer always seemed to be in the spotlight. Immediately prior to the 1962 PGA tournament, defending champion Jerry Barber observed, "They don't know anybody's here but Palmer." By "they" Barber meant everybody: the gallery, reporters, photographers, officials, and even the players themselves.

To understand Palmer's appeal, it is necessary to acknowledge that his skills were of the highest order. Beginning with his victory in the 1958 Masters, he began a run which by 1965 had resulted in four Masters crowns, two British Opens and one U.S. Open. However, beyond mere playing prowess, Palmer exhibited a devil-may-care, charging style which set him apart from the competition. In addition, he possessed a wealth of charisma, highlighted by pronounced displays of kindness and radiant bursts of personality while in the public eye.

But what rendered the Palmer phenomenon truly unique in the annals of golf was the devotion of his fans. Wright described these followers — dubbed "Arnie's Army" by the media — during his coverage of the 1962 PGA Championship:

> While Palmer and Nicklaus were playing together on Thursday and Friday, the gallery with them was, naturally, enormous. Virtually every other group, including a threesome of Sam Snead, Gary Player and Phil Rodgers, was contesting in privacy. . . . It was strictly a Palmer crowd, the fabled army. "Go Arnie," said a sign on the hat of one spectator. "Go Arnie," were the shouts every time it looked like he might get moving. Each time Palmer putted out his gallery would break

ranks in disorder and race for the next hole, not waiting or caring that Nicklaus or the other man in the threesome, Dave Marr, still had putts to make. The ground could have swallowed up Open Champion Nicklaus, and nobody would have known he was gone.

Friday morning at breakfast Nicklaus was asked if it wouldn't have been better to have had him and Palmer in separate threesomes so the gallery would be split up. "That wouldn't help," said Nicklaus. "There would still be 10,000 people following Palmer and about 10 people following me."

Although the victories dropped off significantly in the latter portion of the 1960s, Palmer's gallery remained overwhelming in its size and support for him. Eventually, Palmer joined the newly instituted Seniors Tour and played a large role in its success. His mass appeal rendered him a natural for commercials (e.g., Pennzoil, Hertz) and numerous business deals — all of which has made Palmer an extremely wealthy man. And amazingly, his boyish charm and humility have remained intact throughout all the years under the media spotlight.

## BIBLIOGRAPHY

McCormack, M.H. *Arnie*. New York: Simon & Schuster, 1967.

McDermott, B. "Where It Is Still 1960 and Hope Springs Eternal," *Sports Illustrated*. 40 (February 18, 1974) 73-76.

"Midas Swing," *Esquire*. 77 (April 1972) 142-144.

Wright, Alfred. "The Trouble With Leading an Army," *Sports Illustrated*. 17 (July 30, 1962) 16-21.

# Artificial Turf

The appearance of AstroTurf®, manufactured by Monsato Chemical Corporation, in 1964 ushered in a new era for outdoor sports. Within three years, no fewer than sixteen manufacturers were turning out some form of artificial turf for use at race tracks, baseball diamonds, football fields, and tennis courts.

The surface received its initial promotional windfall when installed as a last-minute solution after the lack of direct sunlight killed the natural grass in Houston's Astrodome in 1965. Over the next decade high school, college, and professional teams rushed to employ it. As noted by William Johnson, there were several apparent advantages intrinsic to any well-made artificial turf:

> Such surfaces do not get chewed up, pitted, scuffed, scarred or worn through to a hard dirt base. No matter how many raggedy high school games or thundering band parades or American Legion conventions or Bill Graham mass revival meetings may stamp and tramp across the turf, it simply doesn't do immediate damage to the uniformity of the surface . . . [University of] Wisconsin officials figure to save $20,000 a year in maintenance costs. (They can also salvage up to $10,000 on laundry since the deep dirt stains of mud and grass are no longer present.)

Perhaps the most significant general contribution offered by synthetic surfacing is the improved use of land — particularly in thickly populated and astronomically expensive sections of cities. For example, in Madison the land around the University of Wisconsin is valued at roughly $240,000 an acre. For years a five-acre section of it was earmarked for football practice fields. Now, with the advent of Tartan Turf in the stadium, the university is able to reoccupy nearly two acres (about

$450,000 worth) of the practice areas because the team can work out on the stadium Tartan itself much of the time.

In addition, artificial turf meant easy upkeep (when a section does wear out, it can be easily replaced) and rapid drainage (therefore allowing use even in rain). Some argued that it improved athletic performance (due in part to its reduction of the irregularities typifying natural playing fields) and cut down on potential injuries. Monsanto, in surveying 185 schools in the late 1960s on their incidence of knee and ankle injuries over the years, found that football teams playing on real sod suffered 9.6 such injuries each year while teams playing on AstroTurf® reported an average of 1.6.

Even allowing for traditionalists and those opposed to synthetic sod on merely aesthetic grounds, complaints were being heard almost from its first appearance. Many players suffered skid burns and abrasions. Some noted the difficulty experienced by visiting teams in adjusting to it, how it became slick when wet, and the intense heat the surface absorbed from the sun. Billy Cannon, then a tight end for the Oakland Raiders, said after playing in the Astrodome:

> Artificial turf is a joke. I can't understand why they'd build a beautiful stadium like that, then throw in a hard surface that has got to shorten the Oiler players' careers two and three years per man. It'd make a nice bowling alley.

Still others criticized its high price. In 1969 both AstroTurf® and its chief competition, 3M's Tartan Turf, cost about $31.50 a square yard, or roughly $200,000 per gridiron; well out of the means of most high schools and smaller colleges.

Growth in the use of artificial turf peaked sometime in the late 1970s; however, in the ensuing decade a substantial reaction against it set in. The growing perception that such surfaces contributed to a higher incidence of impact-related injuries, both in a short- and long-term sense, provided the chief point of contention for those opposing its use. Its increasing utilization by younger athletes, whose bodies had not yet completely matured, proved particularly alarming to some. The increased power of professional athletes — both through media pronouncements and as a lobbying force —

helped significantly in the development of this perception on the part of sports officials and fans. Consequently, stadium owners began approaching the issue of whether or not to switch to artificial turf with a far greater degree of caution than previously had been the case; a number of venues even reverted back to natural surfaces.

## BIBLIOGRAPHY

Johnson, William. "Goodbye to Three Yards and a Cloud of Dust," *Sports Illustrated*. 30 (January 27, 1969) 37-39.

"Mod Sod," *Time*. 89 (May 12, 1967) 57.

Pound, C.E. "Rug of Grass for Easy Maintenance; Use of AstroTurf for Westchester County Golf Courses," *Parks & Recreation*. 3 (May 1968) 25ff.

Whitaker, H.R. "Magic Carpet For All Outdoors," *Science Digest*. 66 (July 1969) 33-37.

# Charles Atlas and Dynamic Tension

Charles Atlas, dubbed "America's Most Perfectly Developed Man" by publisher Bernarr Macfadden, has been a household name in America throughout most of the twentieth century. During his heyday, three generations of comic books and pulp magazines carried his famous advertisement which featured him in a bikini bathing suit, legs planted firmly in hot, white sand, requesting only a five-day trial to turn any 97-pound weakling into a tower of strength.

Atlas invented the term "Dynamic Tension" in 1921, to describe his system of building muscles. Based upon the principle of pitting one muscle against another, his system falls into the category of exercise now known as isometrics.

Born in Italy on October 30, 1893 as Angelo Sicilano, he immigrated to the United States at the age of ten. The memorable portrayal of a 97-pound weakling being sprayed with sand by a bully which became the centerpiece of his ads, had a basis in real life and, in fact, inspired the creation of his body-building theories. According to Atlas, the incident happened in the following manner:

> One day I went to Coney Island and I had a very pretty girl with me. We were sitting on the sand. A big, husky lifeguard, maybe there were two of them, kicked sand in my face. I couldn't do anything and the girl felt funny. I told her that someday, if I meet this guy, I will lick him.

Atlas added that the girl found herself another date and he started his system of exercises; upon passing by a statue of Atlas at Coney Island shortly thereafter, he decided to adopt the name.

After remolding his body, Atlas—who also had a professional career for some time as an artists' model—entered into the body-building business in 1922. His course was still going out in seven languages to 70,000 people a year at the time of his death in late 1972.

Even in middle age Atlas looked the part, sporting a chest measurement of forty-seven inches unflexed along with seventeen-inch biceps and a thirty-inch waist (on a five-feet ten-inch, 180-pound frame). Ever mindful of the value of public relations coverage, he performed countless feats of strength in public. For example, in 1938 he towed a 145,000-pound railroad car through the sunnyside yards of the Pennsylvania Railroad for 122 feet using a rope.

## BIBLIOGRAPHY

"Eat Well, Grow Strong & Lose Weight," *Mechanics Illustrated*. 69 (January 1973) 46-47ff.

"Atlas Was Right All Along," *Life*. 56 (April 17, 1964) 47-48.

"Charles Atlas, the Body-Builder and Weightlifter, Is Dead at 79," In: *The New York Times Encyclopedia of Sports*. Volume 11: Indoor Sports. New York: Arno, 1979. p. 113.

"Men Who Fascinate Women," *Look*. 19 (October 18, 1955) 134.

"Muscle Business," *Fortune*. 17 (January 1938) 10ff.

"Muscle Makers," *Time*. 29 (February 22, 1937) 75-76.

Taylor, R.L. "I Was Once a 97-Pound Weakling," *New Yorker*. 17 (January 3, 1942) 21-27. Abridged reprint: "Self-Made Man, and Body," *Readers' Digest*. 41 (September 1942) 79-82.

Zolotow, M. "You, Too, Can Be a New Man," *Saturday Evening Post*. 214 (February 7, 1942) 20-21ff.

Obviously, this beefy Adam did not want sand kicked in his face at the beach. So he followed the regimen of Charles Atlas, otherwise known as "America's Most Perfectly Developed Man." Atlas sold his home course of diet and weightlifting through the mail to thousands of weaklings who aspired to become musclemen in the 1920s and 1930s.

# Autographs

In the 19th century there were two types of autograph collectors: (1) the elite collector who received autographs as a family bequest, bought them at auction, or cultivated friendship with a desired correspondent, and (2) the plebian collector who excessively flattered prominent figures for their autographs. The rage for collecting famous signatures came about due to a lingering allegiance to European celebrities and also to the rise of "belles-lettres" in America. For instance, the great scientist Darwin attracted autograph hounds, never mind that his theories were in dispute. To own any piece of paper signed by George Washington or one of the founding fathers highlighted a collection. Likewise coveted were Poe, Hawthorne, Emerson, and Longfellow signatures. Actors, clergymen, soldiers, inventors, whoever achieved a measure of fame was marketable. To have an autograph of an admired figure was like possessing part of that person — much better than a lock of hair or a handkerchief. That is how the fever started.

From 1890 to 1910 a flood of magazine articles defined the "art" of autograph collecting. A series of five papers written by an eminent collector, George Birkbeck Hill, appeared in the *Atlantic Monthly* under the title, "Talk Over Autographs." Hill selected original signed letters from his private collection and explained the circumstances surrounding their writing. A literary man himself, he was able to obtain these priceless letters through regular correspondence. The tone of Hill's talks is one of idolatry, literary posturing, and self-conscious book chat. Hill was very much the first type of collector who would have strongly resented anyone calling his enthusiasm for autograph collecting a fad. Another of his ilk, Richard Henry Stoddard, expressed himself thusly:

> I confess to a liking for the autographs of authors whom I admire; and if I had not checked this liking, it might have

become the passion which animates the collector. . . . The gradual accumulation of treasures like these has been a source of satisfaction to me for more than thirty years.

Not wanting to trivialize the efforts of Hill and Stoddard, the second type of autograph collector was most definitely the faddist. He or she resorted to base flattery to obtain an autograph. It was not so much genuine admiration for the famous person that emboldened this type, but more the spirit of the game — the challenge to break down all defenses. Listen to this confession:

The maniac worthy of the name is not thin-skinned, and does not weep when he is told that he is a bore and a great nuisance. It is an interesting autograph he is after, and once he gets it the world may wag its cruel tongue until it is tired — little he cares!

Now listen to the reply from "one of our foremost novelists":

You are one of those who trouble a busy person unnecessarily. I must say that since there are dealers in autographs in all large cities who can supply specimens of writing at small cost, I believe it is much more considerate, not to say dignified, for collectors to deal with them directly.

Another famous writer replied, ". . . there are only twenty-four hours in a day, and that a man or woman who writes books has the same sordid need of a few of them as a washerwoman or a bricklayer." Such an unsigned reply assumed a prominent place in the collection; and when published without permission in a magazine article inspired other collectors to make nuisances of themselves. The lowest kind of request was for an autograph only. A celebrated poet such as Henry Wadsworth Longfellow received many such entreaties which his kindly nature honored. Other famous writers not so inclined deposited the requests in a wastebasket.

Collecting autographs by the less than serious collector changed somewhat with the advent of radio and motion pictures. Then the faddist went after glittering stars of stage and screen, gaining a more easily gotten reward — a signed, perhaps dedicated, glossy picture. Who cared if the star did not actually sign the picture, or if thousands were mailed out yearly? At least the collector did not have to put up with surly replies from high-and-mighty authors.

## BIBLIOGRAPHY

"Confessions of an Autographomaniac," *Independent*. 56 (May 26, 1904) 1195-1198.

Hill, George Birkbeck. "Talk Over Autographs," *Atlantic Monthly*. 75 (April-May 1895) 445-457, 669-681; 76 (July-August & November 1895) 46-58, 205-217, 605-621.

Joline, A.H. "Collecting of Autographs," *Independent*. 54 (November 20, 1902) 2764-2769.

Stoddard, Richard Henry. "Box of Autographs," *Scribner's Magazine*. 9 (February 1891) 213-227.

"Use for the Autograph Fiend: Ellen Terry's Scheme," *Outlook*. 49 (February 10, 1894) 293.

# Automobiling

When the automobile first became a viable means of conveyance few people considered it utilitarian. The automobile was not meant to drive one to work or to the market, not at all. Its true employment was for touring—to see the countryside, lakes, mountains . . . to see America. In 1902 a writer for *Scientific American* confirmed this purpose:

> Quite naturally touring has become a favorite pastime with those who patronize automobiling not as a fad, but as a healthful, pleasurable sport—a class of automobilists by the way that is constantly increasing, not only abroad but also in this country.

Nonetheless, in the guise of touring, automobiling became a full-blown fad.

It is amusing now to read contemporary accounts (1900-1906) of how primitive roads were "fascinating" obstacles to overcome. With a whole army of antagonists to avoid—sinkholes, chuckholes, and mudholes—early touring was definitely a sport. But before the automobilist could start a journey he or she had to be properly attired and his or her carriage properly equipped. This is where the fad imp danced merrily. All the accoutrement for touring seemed to be more important than the vehicle itself. Leather clothing was a necessity, preferably in kangaroo, "the skin being more pliable, and on account of its rather oily substance it will shed rain a good deal easier than calfskin." An automobile cap with an extra long facemask and goggles worked well in winter. Forget the mackintosh; it interfered with the quick handling of levers. Likewise disdain the Panama hat which invariably blows off the head, and a footbag of furs which overheats the feet.

Touring, of course, required camping out. "When a soldier is able to carry on his back his entire camp outfit in addition to his weapons, the smallest automobile on the market ought to carry everything needed to make its passengers comfortable in camp." Thus the list of camping equipment was formidable indeed:

- canvas tent with a folding center pole
- rubber air mattresses
- air-cushion headrests
- Army blankets
- six-shooter (auto theft protection)
- wicker baskets of food attached to the sides of the vehicle
- aluminum cooking and eating utensils
- rod and gun for obtaining fresh food
- supply of drugs, medicines, plasters arranged in canvas folders
- two portmanteaus of clothing ("The point should be to take along as little as possible and yet be comfortably fitted out.")
- tire chains, tire pump, tire gauge
- efficient jack and wrenches
- towing cable
- oil can, grease gun, and funnel
- chamois skin
- flashlight
- inner tubes
- two-gallon can of gasoline
- two-quart can of gas-engine oil
- can of grease
- can of kerosene
- blowout patches
- leather tire sleeve
- vulcanizing cement
- headlight and taillight bulbs
- spark plugs
- assortment of gaskets
- radiator steam hose and clips
- extra fan belt
- assortment of cotter pins, nuts, lock washers, wood screws, and nails
- 2 two-gallon canvas water bags

- 4 pound-packages of hardtack (bread made with only flour and water)
- 4 half-pound cans of meat or fish
- 2 pounds of sweet chocolate
- 2 cans of fruit

Somehow all these necessities were loaded in the automobile, and there was even a prescribed method for achieving their order. What with poor roads, the cost of a well-appointed vehicle ($2,500 in 1906) and suitable attire, and the large inventory of touring needs, it was a wonder the fad lasted any time at all. But last it did:

> One refreshing fact confronts the friend of automobile development in whatever way his observation may be turned—the serious thought of designers and makers finds utterance in the construction of models first for pleasure and afterwards for commercial uses.

Well-off Americans took a fancy to automobiling at whatever the cost because it was conspicuous consumption at its best. The fad did, though, force some observers to resort to sarcasm:

> With heavier mechanisms and higher speeds, approaching the weight and power of high grade locomotives, automobiles encountering pedestrians or pleasure vehicles on the highways will seldom inflict those injuries which leave the victim in a condition to make unseemly plaint. The 'accident' will be merely a painless out and out killing, so neatly completed that the most sensitively organized ladies and gentlemen of the automobile set can feel little if any shock.

The rich driving helter-skelter as they pleased became more democratic when American engineer Henry Ford introduced reliable, low-cost motor vehicles for the masses. Ford's efficient assembly line made it possible for the average family to own a "gasoline buggy," which then found its true use for utilitarian purposes.

# BIBLIOGRAPHY

"Automobile Manners," *Independent.* 55 (May 28, 1903) 1281-1282.

Bruce, R. "Promise of the Automobile in Recreative Life," *Outing.* 36 (April 1900) 81-85.

*This Fabulous Century. Volume I: 1900-1910.* Alexandria, Va: Time-Life Books, 1969.

Wisby, H. "Practical Automobile Touring Outfit," *Scientific American.* 86 (March 1, 1902) 134-135.

# Bagatelle

Once the Great Depression had become a sad reality (1933), fewer Americans could afford to buy a baseball or hockey ticket. Their plight alerted entrepreneurs who immediately recognized the need for cheaper forms of recreation. Bagatelle had already proven itself a moneymaker in the penny arcades several decades before. It began as entertainment for children but quickly developed into a game for adults. Players cued a ball across an oblong table to hit a mark or fall in a hole, scoring points. It was a one-shot try using several balls, so a game ended quickly. Bagatelle did not require the keen eye and steady arm of the billiards player, nor the patience to devise strategy. It was a poor man's billiards minus the finesse, but with some inventive twists and enough garish packaging to beckon players from across the arcade.

What made bagatelle more of a gold mine the second time around was its affordable nickel-a-game, the variety it offered, and several new features. At five cents for ten shots, playing for the possibility of winning prizes like cameras, fountain pens, clocks, etc., bagatelle was an enticement hard to resist. Somehow, someway, the most down-and-out person found a nickel to drop in the slot. In 1933 there were 62 variations of bagatelle gobbling up nickels with new challenges appearing weekly. Using colorful artists' designs most every sport was converted into one of these cue and ball table games. But what really hooked fans on bagatelle was an innovation whereby pins studded the table "to control the wanderings of the ball." This enlivened the sporting aspect and converted a dull pastime into ten minutes' worth of excitement. The industry noted the change in player response, forgot the old name, and began calling bagatelle "pin games."

Also discarded was the notion of bagatelle as family recreation. The latest establishments were christened "Sportlands" — signifying more serious interest in the table game and gambling. Ernest

Chester of the Chester-Pollard Amusement Co., New York, held the rights to the name. For a businessman to call his place "Sportland" he had to purchase a license and equipment from Chester-Pollard. Actually, twenty years earlier Adolph Caille of Caille Brothers Co., Detroit, constructed the first pin game machine. Strictly a toy, Caille's handheld pinboard was slightly inclined for propelled marbles to roll up an alley to the top, then to roll down hopefully into scoring positions. A simple toy, it sold well. The first pin game machine for adults was the Whoopee Game manufactured in 1930 by the In & Outdoor Games Co., Chicago. It measured 24″ wide by 48″ long and had adjustable legs. If adding pins was a masterstroke for bagatelle, then what a North Carolina inventor named Savage came up with was a stroke of high genius. His crowning feature was a plunger connected to a coin-operated device that completely replaced the old bagatelle cue, and brought in more nickels because it greatly accelerated play.

In the mid-1930s, 250,000 pin machines were sold annually by approximately 200 manufacturers. To the chagrin of Chester-Pollard they did not remain the sole property of Sportland. Soon pin machines materialized in drug stores, cigar stores, and other retail operations to bank loose nickels. The fad spread so rapidly, abetted gambling, and stole so much time from proper endeavors that city councils considered banning pin machines altogether. On June 19, 1939 the Atlanta council passed an ordinance prohibiting the operation of pin machines in the city. Any person convicted of violating the ordinance faced a maximum fine of $20 and a sentence of thirty days assigned to public works.

## BIBLIOGRAPHY

Pinchot, R. "Holey-Bogey Is My Game," *Arts and Decoration*. 38 (December 1932) 40-41.
"Sport in the Nickel Age," *Business Week*. (March 29, 1933) 14.
"Trip'em: Home Pin-Ball Game for Two Players," *Popular Mechanics*. 67 (February 1937) 278-280.

# Balloon Jumping

Talk about fun, for this 1920s' sport the "jumping balloonist" wore a harness fitted around the body and legs. Ropes ten to fifteen feet long radiated up from the harness and attached to a small balloon eighteen feet in diameter. Three thousand cubic feet of hydrogen gas filled the balloon. Thus attired, the balloonist ran for a short distance then leaped into the air, catapulting 40 feet high while covering a distance of 100 yards. As soon as he or she touched ground, another little run and a kangaroo spring propelled the balloonist up and away again. A poetic fan described the experience:

> In balloon jumping the coming back to solid ground is like a gull lighting on water, like a leaf drifting down softly on a still day in October. The wind is your slave and the genii of the balloon take you up and put you down as deliciously as Aladdin's did the Princess, asleep in her royal bed.

If the human kangaroo wanted to go higher he or she tossed off ballast from a belt to surpass the normal 40 feet. In the event a sudden wind threatened, the balloonist pulled an emergency valve releasing gas to lower the balloon. For the first-time jumper ground attendants held a rope attached to the body harness to pull the person back to safety.

Right from the start balloonists explored all the possibilities of cross-country jumping. They happily surmounted automobiles, barns, trees, houses, anything under 40 feet high. Leaping over a whole series of obstacles was the true sport within the sport. To keep going the balloonist pushed off the top of an object or jerked upward to go higher.

A few steps down the field a barn looms ahead. This time the jumper takes off a little farther away and, with a strong spring, upborne by the wind, he and the balloon rise majestically to the rooftop and there, for a moment, he poises on one foot. The lightest of shoves and he floats off and upwards, to sail serenely a hundred feet or so before alighting again upon the turf.

Transforming this delightful diversion into a full-fledged competitive sport seemed just around the corner. Competitors could race between towns, leaping over planned obstacles by carefully calculating where to touch ground to make the next clearance. Other than as a sport, fans praised balloon jumping as health-giving and liberating. Overweight people could cavort in the air, losing their sense of ponderousness. Elderly people could feel like kids again and enjoy a sport that did not require too much physical strength. And kids could jump rooftops in the neighborhood to visit their friends and easily make it back home in time for dinner.

The fad of balloon jumping was short-lived for these reasons: lack of wind meant a dead day; accidents happened regularly, especially around communication lines; and having to carry or tow the empty balloon back home was tedious. All things taken into consideration, this is one fad that would be amusing to revive.

## BIBLIOGRAPHY

Hoppin, Frederick S. "Over the Hills and Far Away: Balloon Jumping as a Popular Sport," *The Forum*. 78 (July 1927) 173-180.
"Small Balloons Provide New Sport," *Scientific American*. 137 (July 1927) 39.

This straddle-legged competitor hurdles an automobile in a cross-country jumping event (1927). After sprinting a few yards, the balloonist leaps into the air, letting the gas-filled balloon take him aloft. Balanced just right—body weight to lift—the balloonist re-lands and sprints again for another takeoff.

# Barking Off Squirrels

Begun in the backwoods of Kentucky and immortalized by none other than Daniel Boone — frontiersman extraordinary — this sport required a keen eye and a steady hand. Boone and his fellow riflemen bet on perfect shot execution to "fall" the most critters. The naturalist John James Audubon witnessed such a contest, leaving us this description of what happened:

> Judge to my surprise, when I perceived that the ball had hit the piece of the bark immediately beneath the squirrel, and shivered it into splinters, the concussion produced by which had killed the animal, and sent it whirling through the air, as if it had been blown up by explosion of a powder magazine.

Boone barked off many a squirrel in the late 1700s and early 1800s (he died in 1820). Because of his fame as a marksman others tried to copy his skill with a rifle and the fad was born. In virgin America the woods were full of furry squirrels. They "were seen gamboling on every tree around us," wrote Audubon who encountered the "delightful" sport elsewhere during his journeys.

Normal shoot-'em-in-the-head squirrel hunts received regular coverage in the newspapers. For May 1796 the *Kentucky Gazette* reported that a party of hunters killed 7,941 squirrels in one day. Tails were taken as trophies which made quite a display back home. Teams competed to waylay the animals like so many clay pipes in a shooting gallery. With such an abundance of squirrels in the woods the real sport was not in hitting the mark, but in seeing who could reload his rifle the fastest. Squirrel hunting has never ceased to amuse rural youth to this day, and is still very much a rite of passage in Southern states. But two hundred years ago only the best shots in the country could revel in the fad of barking off squirrels.

# BIBLIOGRAPHY

Audubon, John James. *Delineations of American Scenery and Character*. New York: Arno & The New York Times, 1970 (reprint edition). pp. 59-62.

Dulles, Foster Rhea. *A History of Recreation: Americans Learn to Play*. New York: Appleton-Century-Crofts, 1965. pp. 70-71.

# The Rise of Baseball

While the legend that a young West Point cadet, Abner Double-day, invented baseball in 1839 at Cooperstown, New York (the conclusion of a committee commissioned by the major league owners of 1905 to determine the origins of the sport) has permeated American thinking for most of this century, ample evidence indicates that it underwent a long period of development considerably earlier than that date. Despite the revisionist efforts of the committee, led by sporting-goods tycoon Al Spalding—a product of the rampant nationalist fervor of the late nineteenth century—it appears that baseball's ancestors consisted of various stick-and-ball games played by generations of Englishmen and American colonists; e.g., "old cat" games, rounders, town ball. Printed references to "base ball" appeared as early as 1700 in America. Robin Carver, in his *Book of Sports* (1827), noted that Americans called their form of rounders "base Ball" because they used bases instead of stakes as in cricket.

David Voigt offers the following insight into baseball's early developmental period:

> That grown men played baseball in rural villages of New York as early as the 1820s was vouchsafed by the grandfather of historian Samuel Hopkins Adams, who played the game as a boy "in Mumford's Pasture Lot."
> 
> What grandfather Adams played was a crude version of the modern game. In his day informal versions competed until a survival-of-the-fittest process narrowed contending versions of baseball to two rivals. One version, the 'Massachusetts game,' employed a rectangular field of play, with the three bases located asymmetrically from each other and with home base located behind the batter's position. Fielders called

'scouts' could put a batter out by hitting him with a thrown ball or catching a hit ball on the first bounce as well as in the air.

The sprightly Massachusetts game lasted until the 1840s, when the rival 'New York game' won the struggle for existence. This triumph owed much to a human catalyst, the urbane New Yorker Alexander Jay Cartwright, whose claim to fathering baseball as we know it is mostly forgotten. In 1845 Cartwright persuaded his young friends to try a symmetrical version of the game that he devised. In quick time his plan of using a diamond-shaped infield, with bases set ninety feet apart, was accepted . . .

Baseball clubs now sprang up in abundance throughout the urban centers of New York and nearby states such as New Jersey, Pennsylvania, Maryland, and the District of Columbia—many based upon Cartwright's rules as employed by his Knickerbocker Base Ball Club. Its westward spread spurred William T. Porter to dub it "The national game" by the 1850s; he helped popularize it by printing the first rules, the first box score, and the first picture of a game in progress in the *Spirit of the Times*. The game's appeal, according to Mark Twain, resided in the fact that it "is the very symbol, the outward and visible expression of the drive and push and rush and struggle of the raging, tearing, booming nineteenth century."

While the Civil War caused a lull in the baseball boom, Appomattox kindled a new surge of nationalism, with baseball chosen as the athletic expression of this unifying force. Growing professionalization proved to be the prime force behind this new growth phase, beginning with the barnstorming success of the Cincinnati Red Stockings in 1869, and culminating with the founding of the National League in 1876. The league entered a "Golden Age" in the 1890s which assured its permanent institutional status as well as baseball's continued recognition as "the national game"—an appellation which remained unchallenged until the rise of professional football during the Super Bowl era.

## BIBLIOGRAPHY

Bartlett, Arthur. *Baseball and Mr. Spalding*. New York: Farrar, Straus and Young, 1951.

Dickey, Glenn. *The History of National League Baseball: Since 1876*. New York: Stein & Day, 1982.

Levine, Peter. *A.G. Spalding & the Rise of Baseball: The Promise of American Sport*. New York: Oxford University Press, 1985.

Seymour, Harold. *Baseball: The Early Years*. New York: Oxford University Press, 1960.

Voigt, David Quentin. *American Baseball: From Gentleman's Sport to the Commissioner System*. Norman: University of Oklahoma, 1966; reprinted in 1983.

Voigt, David Quentin. *Baseball, an Illustrated History*. University, Pa: Pennsylvania State University, 1987.

# Baseball Card Collecting

Interest in baseball card collecting has exploded in the United States since the late 1970s. According to David Seideman,

> Not only are treasured cards of the past fueling a growing re-sale market but new and fancy product lines are popping up like Texas League singles — all at increasingly over-the-fence prices. Powered by nostalgia and the consumer purchasing clout of the mid-'80s, the colorful collectibles are enjoying the kind of popularity normally reserved for the national pastime itself.

Hobbyists, investors, and speculators — not to mention the core buyers, six- to twelve-year-old youngsters — bought an estimated five billion new and old cards in 1988. Total sales for that year approached $150 million. The market included:

- approximately 10,000 dealers, including 3,500 retail shops;
- at least one hundred weekly swap meets;
- countless trade papers, magazines, and fanzines which plotted the fortunes of card assets by means of elaborate graphs and charts.

Baseball card collecting has been around for over a century; they were first issued during the 1880s by U.S. cigarette manufacturers as premiums. Few of these early issues are of interest to collectors today, due to poor quality photography and physical deterioration hastened by the use of cheap cardboard.

Raw material shortages brought on by World War I hastened the demise of promotional cards. After the war, candy and gum companies took over the leadership of the production of baseball cards; these were superior in quality to earlier ones and issued in far greater numbers, typically tens of millions annually.

The so-called second era of card collecting faded during World War II as a result of paper and rubber shortages which sharply curtailed card and gum production. Bowman Gum Co. resumed business in 1948, with Topps (Brooklyn) following in 1951. With its 1956 acquisition of Bowman, Topps had a virtual monopoly on the industry. When, in 1980, a U.S. district court ruled that Topps and the major leagues could not prevent other gum companies from issuing cards, a host of competitors entered into the field. Fleer (Philadelphia) and Donruss (Memphis) initiated serious challenges to Topps' hegemony beginning in 1981. Sportflics (Stamford, Connecticut), which utilized a polarized image process with three sequential action shots on each card, followed in 1986, and Score started up in 1988 (both owned by Major League Marketing). All have reported notable gains during the decade.

In addition to the staple package — today a wrapped group of fifteen to seventeen cards, along with inclusions such as puzzles, team logo stickers, trivia cards, and the traditional bubble gum, retailing for forty to seventy-five cents — all companies have attempted to reach the better-heeled and older baseball fans as well. Topps has developed more than a dozen specialty issues (e.g., bronze and silver replicas, "Tiffany" sets on heavily coated glossy paper stock in serially numbered boxes) while Fleer featured a Commemorative Collectors Edition in a gold-lacquered tin.

The most spectacular growth within the industry, however, has been in the market for old and rare cards, which by 1887 had risen to an estimated $45 million annually. The rapid increase in card values has attracted many new collectors whose love of the game appears to be subject to question. Undoubtedly they have been attracted by documentation such as that provided by David S. Krause, an assistant professor of finance at Marquette University, who argued that baseball cards have been unrivalled with respect to investment returns during the 1980s (see Table I).

The mass media have helped fuel the craze, recounting with relish stories of shylockian youth and public outbursts at various trading shows. However, given the pitfalls of baseball card collecting — Ray Brady termed it "as complicated for investing as Wall Street is" — especially attempting to make sense of the myriad factors affecting value (e.g., age, the fortunes of the player on the card,

TABLE I

| Investment | Compound Annual Return |
|---|---|
| Rookie baseball cards | 42.5% |
| Corporate bonds | 14% |
| Common stocks | 12.7% |
| Treasury bills | 7.2% |
| U.S. coins | 3.5% |
| Diamonds | 3.4% |
| Stamps | 2.9% |
| Chinese ceramics | 1.5% |
| Gold | -2.6% |
| Silver | -8.2% |

The 42.5% figure represents holdings between 1980-1987 of an "emerging stars portfolio" (e.g., George Brett, Rod Carew).

whether it is a rookie card, condition, popularity of that year's complete set, whether there is a manufacturer's mistake), the phenomenon is likely to remain largely in the hands of the true fans; that is, those attracted to it out of a love for the game.

## BIBLIOGRAPHY

"Baseball's Wild Cards," *Time*. 124 (October 15, 1984) 90.

Brady, Ray. "It's Your Money," *Nation's Business*. 74 (June 1986) 80.

Carreri, J. "Baseball Hall of Fame Now Features Baseball Card Collection Dating Back to 1887," *Hobbies*. 91 (September 1986) 69-71.

Goldstein, G. "Hot Cards and Crowded Table," *Sport* (New York, N.Y.). 79 (July 1988) 77. Coverage of the National Sports Collectors Convention held in Atlantic City.

Krause, David S. "Baseball Cards Bat .425," *Money*. 17 (June 1988) 140-147.

"Newly-Discovered Baseball Card Rarity Sells For $10,000," *Antiques Collectibles Hobbies*. 92 (July 1987) 25. Covers the 1909 T206 Joe Doyle baseball card.

Seideman, David. "Buy Pete Rose, Trade Johnny Bench," *Time*. 129 (June 1, 1987) 53.

Slocum, Frank. *Topps Baseball Cards: The Complete Collection, a 35 Year History, 1951-1985*. Warner, 1985.

# The "Battle of the Sexes":
# Billie Jean King vs. Bobby Riggs

The "Battle of the Sexes," which transformed a mere exhibition match into the type of multimedia extravaganza typifying championship contests in the major sports, could only have happened in an era of social ferment; more specifically, in a nation reacting to the massed feminist movement in a highly ambivalent manner. Bobby Riggs, who had risen to one notch below champions such as Don Budge and Bill Tilden in his playing prime, continued to carve out a solid income from tennis in his later years as something of a media huckster. In the early 1970s he captured the public's attention by accusing the women's tennis world of pawning a distinctly inferior product off on sports fans, offering to take on the best female players to prove his point.

While his assertion was hardly a deeply kept secret — later in the decade, Chris Evert would admit to being defeated by her younger brother on a fairly frequent basis — Riggs' taunting manner proved to be hard for some female stars to ignore. The fact that, even as a fifty-five-year-old man, Riggs represented a reasonably stiff challenge to a female pro with everything to lose did not deter two women from agreeing to settle matters via open competition. The first, Margaret Court, became unraveled by Riggs' antics, losing to him 6-2, 6-1 in May 1973, thereafter known as the "Mother's Day Massacre."

The Court defeat rendered it imperative that the reigning queen of tennis, Billie Jean King, recover the lost honor of women athletes in general. A match between the two was set for late September 1973 in the Houston Astrodome. In addition to a paid attendance of 30,472, the television audience was estimated at fifty-nine million. Anticipation was heightened by countless PR ploys on the part of both contestants. Riggs kept up a steady stream of insults aimed at King in particular and in general:

- Women's tennis is so far beneath men's tennis.
- I don't need a game plan for Billie Jean. I'll let her start something and I'll finish it.
- I have so many tennis weapons that I can handle anything she throws at me.
- She won't admit it, but I can see her coming apart at the seams already.
- After Billie Jean it'll be hot and cold running women . . . The best woman player of the year will have to play me. I'll be the Super Bowl or Rose Bowl of tennis. I might even crash the Virginia Slims tour.

King, for her part, cheerfully played along with Riggs in public. While posing for pictures, she felt his arm muscles and, on other occasions, she held the tennis net down so he could get over it. Privately, however, she resented his slights of female athletes and worked hard to prepare for the match.

On game day King entered the dome like Cleopatra, perched on a gold litter and carried by six muscular men. Riggs was carried in, too—by beautiful girls. The preliminary exchange of gifts, which had rattled Court so much in the Mother's Day match, seemed to set the tone for what would follow as King had the satisfaction of presenting Riggs with a baby pig. The match itself proved to be a war of attrition as the difference of twenty-six years in the respective ages of the contestants worked to King's advantage. Unable to rattle his opponent early in the contest, Riggs found it necessary to take an "injury break" midway into the third set for hand cramp. The opportunity to catch his breath and swallow pills and water did not change the general tenor of the match as King went on to win in straight sets, 6-4, 6-3, 6-3.

Riggs proved far more gracious in defeat than previously he had been as a winner. He stated, "I have a lot of crow to eat. It's Billie Jean's night." In addition to garnering a trophy and $100,000 in the winner-take-all match, King's performance appears to have had a number of long-term results. More girls are now attracted to sports competition. Women athletes also garner a substantially greater amount of prize money and draw larger crowds relative to men than was the case prior to the King-Riggs match.

# BIBLIOGRAPHY

Alexander, Shana. "Tennis as Bread and Circus; King-Ring Match," *Newsweek*. 82 (October 1, 1973) 41.

Axthelm, Pete. "Battle of the Sexes; Riggs vs. King," *Newsweek*. 82 (September 24, 1973) 82-85.

Axthelm, Pete. "Hustler Outhustled," *Newsweek*. 82 (October 1, 1973) 63-64.

Baker, Jim. *Billie Jean King*. New York: Thistle/Grosset & Dunlap, 1974.

Flamini, R., and P. Witteman. "How Bobby Runs and Talks, Talks, Talks; Billie Jean King: I'll Kill Him!," *Time*. 102 (September 10, 1973) 54-56ff.

"How King Rained on Riggs' Parade," *Time*. 102 (October 1, 1973) 110-111.

Murray, M. "Billy and Bobby," *Commonweal*. 99 (October 19, 1973) 63-64.

"Riggs vs. Ms. King," *National Review*. 25 (September 14, 1973) 984.

# Bicycling

The rise of bicycling in America represented more than a mere craze; it has been alleged that nothing in sport made a greater cultural or technical contribution. An official of the 1900 Census noted "that few articles ever used by man have created so great a revolution in social conditions as the bicycle."

Invented by a Prussian forester, Freiherr Karl Drais von Sauerbronn, the bicyle received little attention in the United States prior to the exhibition of some technically more advanced English models at the Philadelphia Centennial in 1876. As noted by Green,

> The early celeripedes of the 1830s — two wheels connected by a bar — had no pedaling or braking mechanism and were dangerous, if exciting for the thrill seeker. Crank-driven velocipedes were introduced in the 1860s, but like "celeripedes," they were expensive and exhausting. More people — men especially — took up the bicycle with the introduction of the "ordinary" in the 1870s. With its large front wheel and small back wheel, riding an ordinary was popular sport for those who could master it. But it too had no brakes; its large front wheel — sometimes as much as five feet in diameter — make it difficult to control, and a spill was a nasty experience. Few if any women rode them. The "safety" bicycle, with both wheels the same size, was designed and produced in great numbers by the 1890s. With the addition of pneumatic tires, mass-produced for the first time in 1889, the bicycle assumed its present form.

As the fad reached full stride in the late 1880s, the impact upon the social order could be ascertained from countless perspectives. Doctors advocated its use as an instrument of good health. Women found it to be a source of emancipation from inactive indoor life. *Scribner's* noted that "A few years ago no woman would dare venture on the street with a skirt that stopped above her ankles, and leggings that obviously reached to her knees . . . [the bicycle] has given to all American womankind the liberty of dress for which reformers have been sighing for generations." The League of American Wheelmen, instituted in 1880 and possessing a million members at its peak, campaigned for better roads, and by 1900 half the states had passed legislation calling for such improvements. A host of specialty publications arose devoted to the fad, beginning with the *Wheelman*, founded by Albert Pope, the leading bicycle manufacturer; by 1897, ten percent of all national newspaper and magazine advertising related to bicycling.

With respect to technology, the bicycle was responsible for the ball bearing, wire wheels, hub-braking, the pneumatic tire, and the variable speed transmission. In addition, bicycle manufacturers sparked developments in metallurgy (Pope's metallurgical laboratory, which developed tubular nickel steel, represented the first outside the steel industry), mass production method, special purpose machinery, and interchangeable parts. The bicycle was instrumental in the development of the motorboat, motorcycle, and automobile. Boyle notes that "early cars were little more than covered bicycles with an engine. From the bicycle manufacturers came car after car: the Lozier, the Rambler, Peerless, Columbia and Pierce-Arrow." The accompanying automobile craze eclipsed that of the bicycle by the turn of the century.

The bicycle would have occasional revivals in popularity, most notably the early 1970s vogue and mountain bike craze in the late 1980s, both of which were tied in with a growing health consciousness boom. None of these revivals, however, have approached the magnitude of popularity the bicycle enjoyed during the latter portion of the nineteenth century.

## BIBLIOGRAPHY

Boyle, Robert H. "The Rise of Sport: The Bumps on Uncle Sam's Head," In: *Sport—Mirror of American Life*. Boston: Little, Brown, 1963. pp. 3-57.

Calif, Ruth. *The World of Wheels: An Illustrated History of the Bicycle & Its Relations*. Assoc. Univ. Prs., 1981.

Geist, Roland C. *Bicycle People: The Nostalgia Pictorial Album of the Bicycle Through Art & Prose, Song & Poetry*. Acropolis, 1978.

Green, Hervey. "Living the Strenuous Life," In: *Fit For America: Fitness, Sport and American Society*. Baltimore: The Johns Hopkins University Press, 1988, c1986. pp. 219-258.
Gutkind, Lee. *Bike Fever*. Avon, 1974.
Leonard, Irving A. *When Bikehood Was In Flower*. Seven Palms, 1983.
Murphy, Jim. *Two Hundred Years of Bicycles*. Lipp Jr. Books, 1983.
Renert, Jack. *One Hundred Years of Bicycle Posters*. Darien House, 1977.

The First National Meet of American Bicyclists was not a speedy affair. The high-wheelers were built more for show than acceleration. The Gay 90s were in full swing and Americans loved to get out and promenade conspicuously.

# Billiards

Billiards—which dates back to the early fifteenth century, when it was the favorite sport of kings and the nobility—has had its ups and downs over the years. It began to lose favor in the United States roughly after 1900 as pool rooms came to be viewed by the public as hangouts for an unruly, often criminal element. Between 1929 and 1940 the number of billiard centers fell from 42,000 to 8,000. Many state and local governments passed legislation either controlling or abolishing such establishments. The game was illegal in Texas until late 1963. A Long Island town required the operator of a proposed billiard room to provide two parking spaces for every table inside.

Billiards rapidly became the recreation phenomenon of the 1960s following the release of *The Hustler*, a film portraying the dark underbelly of pocket billiards. Governmental licensing offices and equipment manufacturers were almost immediately besieged by applications and orders.

Two primary growth areas emerged out of this boom—billiard parlor chain outlets and the home market. By mid-1963 an estimated 10,000 billiard centers (including combination bowling and billiard establishments) were operating in the United States. In that same year, ex-world pocket billiards champion Willie Mosconi established Willie Mosconi Enterprises. His Philadelphia-based firm opened about 100 centers during its first year and a half of operation.

The success of Superior Industries Corporation, the largest producer of folding home tables, typified that portion of the industry. Its sales increased more than 1,000 percent between 1955 and 1963, going from $329,091 to over $4,000,000. The company's president, Melvin Zimmers, estimated that more than 500,000 homes had various-size pocket billiard tables by mid-1963, over twice the number from five years previous to that time.

Perhaps most indicative of the sport's widespread acceptance was the fact that many schools, churches, clubs, and other institutions possessed them. More than 500 colleges and universities owned tables by mid-1963. Over 200 institutions had entrees in the June 1963 intercollegiate billiard championships. In addition, sports programs began including increased amounts of pro billiards matches. By the 1970s, the earlier aura of shadiness associated with the sport had been completely eradicated; billiards had come a long way since Robert Preston's diatribe about "trouble right here in River City" in *The Music Man*. Indeed, it continues to prosper up to the present day.

## BIBLIOGRAPHY

Belden, L.C. "Billiards in America Before 1830," *Antiques*. 87 (January 1965) 99-101.

"Business Clicking in Billiard Sets," In: *The New York Times Encyclopedia of Sports*, edited by Gene Brown. Volume 11. New York: Arno, 1979. p. 63.

Craven, Robert R., comp. *Billiards, Bowling, Table Tennis, Pinball & Video Games: A Bibliographic Guide*. Greenwood, 1983.

"Dressing Up Pool for the Family Trade," *Business Week*. (March 10, 1962) 59.

Gehman, R. "Billiards: A Game for Hustlers and Gentlemen," *Holiday*. 44 (October 1968) 18ff.

Hammer, Joshua. "Pool Halls for Yuppies: from Boston to Dallas Upscale Billiards are Hot," *Newsweek*. 112 (December 26, 1988) 47.

"Rack 'Em Up," *Newsweek*. 61 (January 7, 1963) 50-51.

"Rack 'Em Up for the Girls!," *Life*. 53 (November 30, 1962) 105- 106ff.

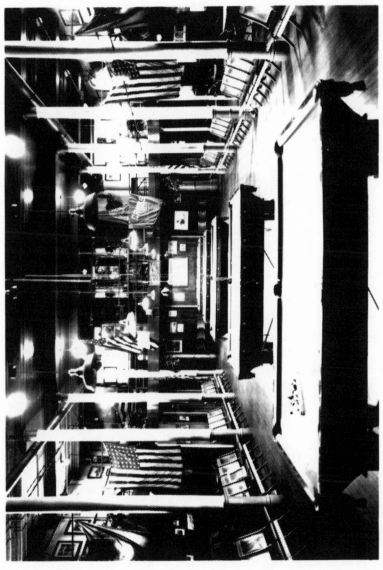

The game of pool has not always been the exclusive domain of barflys and motorcycle gang members. From the 1850s on, pool or billiards have stirred faddish interest among all classes of Americans. Not seen in such glory today, this recreation hall decked-out for a big tournament attests to an earlier high esteem for pocketing balls with a long stick.

*53*

# Bison Shooting

Before white Americans settled the Great Plains bison were free to roam and proliferate. The bearded wild cattle provided American Indians with food, fuel, clothing, shelter, tools, and glue, so that nothing was left to waste. Herds of bison had become so numerous that hunting them was a misnomer, a cross-eyed fool could kill one. By nature bison are gregarious animals which played right into the hands of prodigal hunters. When the Union Pacific and Kansas Pacific railways opened around 1865, bison hunting began in earnest. It was great sport to kill the lumbering beasts from a moving train; or the train might stop to let the curious bison congregate, and then shooting at closer range commenced. By 1900, estimates place the number of bison slaughtered at 50 million, or close to extinction. How and why this slaughter took place is a regrettable chapter of American history.

Traders who explored the Great Plains were fond of "plinking" bison to pass the time. One such trader, Duncan M'Gillivray, who probably spoke for others of his kind, replied, "Hunting is the only amusement which this country affords. . . . I am persuaded that violent exercise is very necessary for the preservation of the constitution." Bison hunting was hardly sport. A horse and rider could run through a herd, the rider sticking his six-shooter next to the bison's brain to squeeze the trigger. A scant bit more sporting, a hunter in a canoe might kill a dozen or more of the animals peacefully drinking water from a river. Like the Indian, white men ate bison meat but, unlike the Indian, usually only the best parts culled from a number of carcasses. Two delicacies were the hump meat and the tongue. Traders profited by creating a culinary fad for pickled bison tongue; civilized city people relished eating the exotic meat. It must have been a vile sight to see twenty to a hundred dead bison untouched except for missing tongues. One redeeming feature of all this carnage was that the dead animals provided sustenance for pumas, wolves, and bears.

Bison smelled heavily of musk, stayed dirty most of the time, and traveled in herds kicking up a lot of dust. Frontier accounts called their appearance around wagon trains, forts, and settlements — swarming. When the bison swarmed they left behind lakes of urine and hills of defecation, all very offensive. Cattlemen despised bison because they ate all the grass. Army parades often had to come to a halt to rid the area of the dumb beasts. These are some of the reasons why the animals were slaughtered. But the two main ones are: delight in destruction and to deprive the Indians of food and goods. Delight in destruction is the most repugnant. As news of bison hunting reached foreign shores, hunting parties sailed for the United States. Incredibly, in 1854 a British sportsman, Sir St. George Gore, headed six wagons and twenty-one carts into the Great Plains. One wagon held only guns; the carts conveyed such necessary items as a brass bed for St. George to sleep on, a linen tent, and carpet to lay on the cold prairie grass. Gore's slaughter (shooting gallery practice) scored him 2,000 bison, 1,600 deer and elk, and 105 bears, most of which was left where it fell. Understandably, the Indians wanted Gore's head mounted and because of him Congress passed the first game protection law. However, unpoliced, the law was impotent. The second main reason for the slaughter — revenge against the Indians — seemed more rational to whites who had suffered the red man's attack. Take away the Indians' free-roaming cattle, beasts that mirrored their own restlessness, and they would have to surrender to life on reservations. Rifles fired gaily behind this kind of thinking. Moreover, our mighty plainsmen loved to scare bison to start a stampede; then shoot them in the knees to watch them fall headlong into the dust. The bison was a plaything. It looked peculiar with its ponderous head, humpback, and scraggly beard. A wounded animal would charge its enemy, offering some sport, but otherwise went down easily. Bison hunting was a fad that vilifies America's past. Engravings for the home pictured the slaughter; the bison's face went stupid when the gallant plainsman killed it. Hanging on the wall of many American homes, depictions of bison hunting enshrined the winning of the West.

Of note, in 1913 the U.S. Mint released the first "buffalo

nickel." Struck with an American bison on one side and an Indian head on the other, the new nickel was an equivocal beauty. Also of note, buffalo are Old World oxlike creatures with long downward curving horns; bison are North American shaggy-maned creatures with short upward curving horns. Forget classification, the public knew it as a buffalo nickel. The artist for the Mint, James Earle Fraser, modeled his bison after "Old Black Diamond," a resident of Central Park Zoo in New York City. Even in captivity safe from plainsmen Old Back Diamond was not allowed to die a natural death. Slaughtered like all of his breed, "Black Diamond Steaks" sold out and the mounted head, if it had been for sale, would have fetched a high price. Flamboyant millionaire Diamond Jim Brady wanted the head so badly he told the owner "name your price." Also at this time bison motifs graced other American currency and stamps. The irony of commemorating by symbol the cruel slaughter of 50 million indigenous wild beasts, followed by New Yorkers feasting on the last of Old Black Diamond, are two unforgettable vignettes of fad history.

## BIBLIOGRAPHY

Barsness, Larry. *Herds, Hides & Horns: The Compleat Buffalo Book.* Fort Worth: Texas Christian University Press, 1985.

KILLING BUFFALO FOR PLEASURE

In the Old West, killing bison for sport instead of for meat and other goods decimated herds to the point of extinction. The white man delighted in murdering thousands of the dumb animals for the sheer thrill of it, and to spite the red man for whom bison were both religion and sustenance.

# Black Power at the XIX Olympiad

Despite the usual quota of pageantry and heroic performances, the 1968 Summer Olympics, held in Mexico City, climaxed a year of threatened boycotts, disruptions, and protests by black militants to become rooted in the American mind as a showcase for black protest against racial injustice.

American sprinter Jim Hines caused the first stir in the aftermath of his world record time (9.9 seconds) victory in the 100-meter dash. Although opposed to a boycott, he told officials that he did not wish to accept his gold medal from Avery Brundage, the conservative president of the International Olympic Committee (I.O.C). Supported by many other blacks in his request, the officials quietly acquiesced.

The award ceremony for the 200-meter dash proved to be a far stronger forum for black protest. Americans Tommie Smith and John Carlos, first and third finishers, respectively, marched towards the ceremony area with heads high, each with a black leather glove on one hand and a track shoe in the other. Their sweatpants were rolled up to show black socks, and they wore protest buttons on their chests. Smith had also tied his wife's black scarf around his neck, while Carlos had borrowed a black shirt from a friend on the Jamaican team. As the band struck up "The Star Spangled Banner," both runners stood stiffly erect on the victory stands, bowing their heads and thrusting black-gloved fists high.

At a press conference shortly thereafter, the two black athletes explained that the black stockings represented poverty, and the black fists meant black power and black unity. Smith noted,

> We are black and proud to be black. White America will say "an American won," not "a black American won." If it had been something bad, they would have said "a Negro."

Added Carlos,

> White people seem to think we're animals. I want people to
> know we're not animals, not inferior animals, like cats and
> rats. They think we're some sort of show horse. They think we
> can perform and they will throw us some peanuts and say
> "Good boy, good boy."

The incident might have caused only minor waves if the I.O.C. had not chosen to react severely. Unless U.S. officials actually punished Smith and Carlos, the I.O.C. threatened to expel the whole U.S. team from the Olympics. Reluctantly, the United States Olympic Committee (U.S.O.C) called an emergency meeting and, approximately thirty hours following the ceremony, charged Smith and Carlos with "untypical exhibitionism" and kicked them off the team and out of the Olympic Village.

Distressed by the perceived severity of the punishment, other U.S athletes — both black and white — rallied to the defense of Smith and Carlos. The U.S.O.C. move put tremendous pressure on 400-meter-runner Lee Evans, who had planned a similar gesture if he ended up on the award stand. Evans talked to the other U.S. 400-meter competitors, Larry James and Ron Freeman, and they decided on a unified course of action. Following a 1-2-3 finish, with Evans setting a world record of 43.8 seconds, the three appeared on the award stands wearing identical black berets and held fists up to the cheering crowd. They took off their berets and stood at attention, however, during the playing of the national anthem. After the long jump competition, Ralph Boston and Bob Beamon joined in the protest; Boston by accepting his award barefoot and Beamon by rolling up his sweatpants to show his black socks.

The Olympic Village itself was caught up in the furor, with a crowd of black athletes demonstrating their support for Smith and Carlos and incidents such as the unfurling of a large banner from the seventh floor of the U.S. dormitory which read "Down with Brundage." In the United States, these developments seemed to pale alongside the disruptiveness of the recently held Democratic National Convention in Chicago as well as the hoopla surrounding the upcoming Presidential election scheduled for the first week of November. The political ramifications of the Olympic demonstrations were largely forgotten amidst the strife of real-life conditions in the U.S. following the conclusion of the XIX Olympiad.

## BIBLIOGRAPHY

"Angry Black Athlete; Olympic Protest Movement," *Newsweek*. 72 (July 15, 1968) 56-60.

Larner, J., and D. Wulf. "Amid Gold Medals, Raised Black Fists," *Life*. 65 (November 1, 1968) 64C-64D.

"Negro Olympic Boycott: Fair Play or Fumble? Pro & Con Discussion," *Senoir Scholastic*. 92 (February 15, 1968) 10-11.

"Olympic Jolt: Hell No, Don't Go! Negro Boycott," *Life*. 64 (March 15, 1968) 20-29.

"The Olympics," *Time*. 92 (October 25, 1968) 62-63.

"The Olympics' Extra Heat," *Newsweek*. (October 28, 1968) 74-80.

"Olympics in Retrospect," *Ebony*. 24 (December 1968) 160-161.

Scott, J., and H. Edwards. "After the Olympics: Buying Off Protest," *Ramparts Magazine*. 8 (November 1969) 16-21.

# The "Black Sox Scandal"

The 1919 "Black Sox Scandal" — in which eight Chicago White Sox players were charged with fixing the World Series — did not represent an isolated occurrence. In the past, conniving owners and gamblers bribing players had formed a portion of the major league baseball landscape. In 1918, Reds infielder Hal Chase had been accused of tampering with games and the Athletics defiantly signed a pitcher who belonged to the Braves. However, it was the public relations dilemma facing organized baseball (these allegations blended with charges that more game fixing was going on in 1920) which forced newly appointed High Commissioner Kenesaw Mountain Landis to take drastic measures regarding the Black Sox case.

The White Sox had been heavily favored to defeat their opponent in the series, the Cincinnati Reds, in a best-of-nine format. Nevertheless, the Reds won four of the first five games; then, after losing a couple, they trounced the Sox in the deciding match, 10-5. While the Reds appeared to have scored an uninspired triumph, rumors persisted of the shady dealings behind the scenes.

Shortly thereafter, sportswriter Hugh Fullerton — with the assistance of Christy Mathewson — compiled a detailed exposé of some questionable plays. This ultimately led to the indictment of seven star players (Eddie Cicotte, pitcher; "Shoeless Joe" Jackson, left fielder; Oscar "Hap" Felsche, center fielder; Charles "Swede" Risberg, shortstop; George "Buck" Weaver, third baseman; Claude Williams, pitcher; Fred McMullen, utility man) and one former team member (Arnold Gandil, first baseman) of the Sox by a Cook County Grand Jury.

Many of the details surrounding the case were derived from open confessions by Cicotte and Jackson, who caused a sensation when they admitted receiving $10,000 and $5,000, respectively. Cicotte's story proved to be especially heart rendering:

> Risberg and Gandil and McMullen were at me for a week before the world's series started. They wanted me to go crooked.

I didn't know—I needed the money. I had the wife and the kids. The wife and kids don't know this. I don't know what they'll think.

Many revisionist baseball historians have placed the indirect blame for the scandal on White Sox owner Charles Comiskey, whose pernicious ways undoubtedly weakened the resolve of his players when faced with offers from gamblers. In 1920, however, Comiskey came across smelling like a rose. Following the grand jury proceedings of September 28, 1920, he stated,

> The consideration which the Grand Jury gave to this case should be greatly appreciated by the general public . . . Thank God it did happen. Forty-four years of baseball endeavor have convinced me more than ever that it is a wonderful game and a game worth keeping clean.
>
> I would rather close my ball park than send nine men on the field with one of them holding a dishonest thought toward clean baseball—the game which John McGraw and I went around the world with to show to the people on the other side.

The confessions of the players led to a 1921 conspiracy trial. Ultimately, all grand jury records were found to be missing, which prompted the defendants to repudiate their earlier confession. As a result, a sympathetic jury determined all eight to be innocent of the charges. Landis, however, arbitrarily banned the players from the game for life, thereby—as the traditional line goes—protecting the integrity of the national pastime.

In 1988, the film *Eight Men Out* revived an interest in the scandal. The work was part of another fad, cinematic portrayals of baseball themes, which flourished in the late 1980s.

## BIBLIOGRAPHY

"Baseball Scandal," *Nation*. 111 (October 13, 1920) 395-396.

"Eight White Sox Players are Indicted on Charge of Fixing 1919 World Series; Cicotte Got $10,000 and Jackson $5,000," In: *The New York Times Encyclopedia of Sports*, edited by Gene Brown. Volume 2: Baseball. New York: Arno, 1979. pp. 25-27.

"Flow in the Diamond," *Literary Digest*. 67 (October 9, 1920) 12-13.

"For Honest Baseball," *Outlook*. 126 (October 6, 1920) 219-220.

Fullerton, H.S. "Baseball on Trial," *New Republic*. 24 (October 20, 1920) 183-184.

"Making the Black Sox White Again," *Literary Digest*. 70 (August 20, 1921) 13-14.

Voigt, David Quentin. *Baseball, an Illustrated History*. University, Pa: Pennsylvania State University, 1987.

# Blacks in Sports Management Positions

Los Angeles Dodgers General Manager Al Campanis took the "Nightline" audience by surprise in spring 1987 when he stated that blacks lack the "necessities" to manage a major league baseball team. The incredulous host, Ted Koppel, provided Campanis with ample opportunities to retract this point, but he declined to substantially modify it. Here was an administrator outwardly expressing a notion many presumed to have disappeared, if not with slavery, then sometime following the civil rights gains of the 1960s and the ensuing affirmative action programs established across the nation. The realization that many prominent sports personalities — as well as individuals in many walks of life — harbored racial bias of one form or another was dramatically reinforced when oddsmaker and television sports analyst Jimmy "the Greek" Snyder was quoted passing along racial slurs in a public restaurant.

While both men were forced to resign their positions, critics such as University of California sociologist Harry Edwards considered the issue worthy of far deeper action. He addressed the Campanis incident as follows during a *Newsweek* interview:

> The problem is in baseball. The problem isn't Campanis. Al Campanis is merely an all-but-irrelevent symptom of the problem. To allow him to be turning out there in the wind makes him a scapegoat and ultimately impedes any progress in dealing with the issues in a constructive way.

Organized baseball, which had long prided itself in its leading role in breaking down social barriers for blacks via the introduction of Jackie Robinson to the major leagues in 1947, was forced to take a hard look at the realities of the situation. While blacks — and other minorities (e.g., Hispanics) — comprised a substantial portion of the

active players, few held any administrative posts of any conse-
quence. Commissioner Peter Ueberroth appointed Edwards as a
special consultant shortly thereafter, with the expressed goal of
opening the doors for minorities to key administrative positions.

Within a couple of years notable progress had been made; the
major leagues had two black field generals (Frank Robinson, who
garnered the manager of the year award for 1989 for his role in
leading the 1988 cellar-dwelling Baltimore Orioles to a second
place finish in the American League's Eastern Division, and Cito
Gaston of the Toronto Blue Jays) as well as a black president of the
National League, Bill White. White noted, in his inauguration address, that true progress will have been achieved when one's racial
background ceases to be an issue in any job appointment.

Other professional sports indicated a similar resolve to rectify
past injustices. On October 3, 1989, Art Shell was named the first
black head coach (of the Oakland Raiders) in the National Football
League in sixty-four years; in addition, black quarterbacks — once a
rarity — were by then starting for a number of teams. The National
Basketball Association, which already had several black head
coaches and general managers, facilitated the sale of the Denver
franchise to two black lawyers in October 1989, making the Nug-
gets the first minority-owned and -operated team in a major professional sport in the United States. While most observers would agree
that further progress needed to be made, as the decade drew to a
close it appeared that minorities were in fact capable of achieving
virtually any position within America's professional sports infra-
structure.


## BIBLIOGRAPHY

Berry, Bill. "They Shot Down the 'Dumb Jock' Label: Athletes Prove They Have
    Both Brains and Brawn," *Ebony*. 36 (May 1981) 82-86.
"A Boom in Black Coaches," *Ebony*. 41 (April 1985) 59-62.
Burwell, Bryan. "Scoring in the Front Office," *Black Enterprise*. 15 (July 1985)
    43-47. Notes the fact that there a few black executives in pro sports.
Cohen, Neil. "And Where are the Black Head Coaches?," *Sport*. 78 (August
    1987) 6.

"Jimmy the Greek's Bizarre Excursion into Racial History Costs Him His Job at CBS," *People Weekly*. 29 (February 1, 1988) 35.

Lieber, Jill. "Dreams Do Come True," *Sports Illustrated*. 71:17 (October 23, 1989) 74-78.

Wulf, Steve. "Opportunity Knocks," *Sports Illustrated*. 67 (November 16, 1987) 15. Column notes that the NCAA will work for the recruiting of black coaches.

Wyss, Dennis. "Fighting From the Inside," *Time*. (March 6, 1989) 62-63. Interview with black educator — and former collegiate athlete — Harry Edwards.

# Boom Cars

The "boom car" reached its apex of popularity in the late 1980s as thousands of young, mostly male, drivers across the U.S. were ripping out their backseats and dashboards to make room for stereo equipment as advanced as audiophiles possess in the home. Danny Moore of East Orange, New Jersey, noted in early 1989, "Girls all want to go out with the guy with the loudest car."

The phenomena was made possible by spectacular strides in the hi-fi equipment field over the last couple of decades. Buffs utilized the latest digital technology to achieve quality as well as quantity in their sound. Steve Seidl, an outfitter of boom cars at Speaker Warehouse in Hollywood, Florida, observed that,

> It is an art form to manage a car interior sonically. We use a spectrum analyzer to measure the "pink noise" in the car or to focus the sound on the driver.

Manufacturers, including mega-giant Japanese electronics corporations (e.g., Sony, Nakamichi) and specialized U.S. firms, promoted their products at crank-it-up contests in which contestants would pit their sonically souped-up cars against one another for cash, trophies, and recognition. The winner of a Laredo, Texas contest, Tom Fichter of Houston, established the world's record when his $27,000 stereo system reached 154.7 decibels during a playback of Irene Cara's "Flashdance . . . What A Feeling," a sound more than twice as loud as that of a jet departing a runway.

Boom cars have received mixed reviews. Doctors have warned that even exposure of short duration to noise levels of more than 115 decibels may result in permanent hearing damage. In addition, ambulances have been involved in accidents with boom car drivers that did not yield the right of way (evidently the sirens could not be heard over the din created by such systems).

# BIBLIOGRAPHY

Girdler, A. "Rare Bach . . . and Let 'Em Have It," *Road & Track*. 40 (October 1988) 20-21.

Gorman, Christine, with Scott Brown and Joseph J. Kane. "Shake, Rattle and Roar," *Time*. (March 16, 1989) 52.

—Competitions

Hodges, R. "Crank 'Em Ups," *Stereo Review*. 52 (May 1987) 132.

Vizard, F. "Thunder Road: The Sound and the Fury at the First Car Audio Nationals," *Rolling Stone*. (November 19, 1987) 123-124.

# Bowling

The 1950s witnessed a spectacular rise in the popularity of bowling in America. During the 1953-1954 season, some 20,000,000 persons rolled balls on 85,000 alleys in 12,250 bowling establishments in the United States. Frank Blunk noted,

> That represented an increase of 3,000,000 bowlers over the previous twelve months. The sport has been growing like that since the start of the last World War. Bowling palaces costing $1,500,000 to $2,000,000 each have sprung up in suburban areas throughout the nation to meet the demand.

By 1958 most Americans were considered at least occasional bowlers. Bowling had become a $350,000,000 industry. There were about 67,000 bowling alleys approved by the American Bowling Congress, the sport's governing body, in the U.S.; new ones were being built at the rate of 4,000 annually. Unlike the old six- and eight-alley establishments located in the business districts of cities, the new bowling centers — generally centered in suburban areas — were ultra-modern in design and featured fifty or more lanes equipped with automatic pinsetters. The new establishments provided ample parking (a serious drawback with respect to the older urban lanes) and enough room to accommodate the vast number of bowlers organized into leagues of all classes.

Bowling's popularity was attributed largely to the fact that it could be played by both sexes and all age groups; it was truly a family sport. The heavy representation of pro bowling matches on television — programming which was cheap and easy to produce — also contributed to the interest in the sport.

Bowling began losing ground during the 1960s in the face of increased competition from outdoor sports such as tennis, jogging, and bicycling. The general demographic shift to Sunbelt states partially explains this change in allegiance. However, bowling's lingering blue collar image — at a time when more and more Americans were going to college and entering the professional job market — also played a role in this downturn.

## BIBLIOGRAPHY

Arena, Joseph M. "A Strike for Bowling," *Newsweek*. 99 (June 28, 1982) 14-15.

Black, J.P. "Big Boom in Bowling," *Rotarian*. 96 (March 1960) 32-33ff. Abridged version in: *Reader's Digest*. 76 (March 1960) 225-226.

Blunk, Frank M. "Merrily They Roll Along Nation's 85,000 Alleys," In: *The New York Times Encyclopedia of Sports*, edited by Gene Brown. Volume 11: Indoor Sports. New York: Arno, 1979. p. 69.

Brailsford, Karen, Patricia King and Bill Barol. "A Clean, Well-Lighted Alley; Bowling Pursues Yuppies and Loses Its Soul," *Newsweek*. 109 (March 2, 1987) 63.

Costello, John. "When Strikes Count," *Nation's Business*. 68 (September 1980) 85-87.

Dunn, K.T. "Why the Ladies Love to Bowl," *Today's Health*. 39 (March 1961) 36-39.

Furlong, W.B. "Big Strike From Alley to Supermarket," *New York Times Magazine*. (November 29, 1959) 42ff.

Gabriel, Alice, and Mark Seliger. "Hot Fun: Following the President's Lead, Americans are Playing Kinder, Wimpier and Dumber Sports," *Rolling Stone*. (May 18, 1989) 92-95.

Isaacs, Stan. "The Bowling Tour is Rolling Down the Right Alley," *Sports Illustrated*. 52 (April 14, 1980) 52. Report on television coverage of the sport.

Pluckhahn, Bruce. "Is Bowling Getting Its Just 'Deserts'?," *Editor & Publisher*. 122 (August 26, 1989) 56-57. Column addressing bowling's coverage on the sports pages.

Skrycki, Cindy. "Finding Big Bucks in the Alleys," *U.S. News & World Report*. 102 (February 16, 1987) 48-49. Bowling centers target yuppies.

Stoffel, Jennifer. "A Search for New Players as Leagues Shrink," *The New York Times*. (September 3, 1989) section 3, F11.

Walley, Wayne. "Bowling Strikes It Big in TV Despite Gutter Image," *Advertising Age*. 57 (September 1, 1986) S14-16.

# Bridge

The card game bridge developed from whist, an offspring of an early 16th-century English game called triumph. Not quite liberated from its antecedent, bridge whist was the most popular card game of its type from 1896 to 1908. In this form the dealer could name trump or pass the privilege on to his or her partner. Bridge whist also introduced a system of doubling and the use of a dummy hand during play. Auction bridge came next and reigned for about 20 years, before giving way to contract bridge in the early 1930s. Harold S. Vanderbilt, American yachtsman and card enthusiast, added the factor of vulnerability to the game and high bonuses for bidding and making slam contracts. These two refinements and others by Ely Culbertson and Charles Goren made contract bridge much more challenging and suspenseful. During the formative years, bridge play continued to build in popularity. Fashionable New York and London clubs offered plush surroundings in which to exhibit skill at the game. Middle-class Americans embraced bridge as heartily as the well-to-do, particularly after several guides to the game were published. During World War I, magazine articles chastized bridge players for wasting time at cards when Europe was at the brink of destruction. Later articles suggested that bridge blighted America's social and intellectual life, causing feuds and bitter resentment among family and friends, and that Vanderbilt, Culbertson, and Goren were pied pipers of anarchy.

By the 1930s, playing cards were selling at the rate of fifty million decks per year. More than 1,000 newspapers carried syndicated articles on bridge play. Two million avid fans listened to the radio as experts explained the game. Bridge instruction for beginning and intermediate players became an industry serving an estimated twenty million. In March of 1934, *Culbertson's Own Summary of*

*Bids and Responses* topped Hervey Allen's *Anthony Adverse* on the best-seller lists. Then even crazier things began to happen. A well-known celebrity of the day painted her fingernails with the different card suits (a diamond for the engagement finger). Two couples in Superior, Wisconsin started and finished a million-point bridge game played over a ten-year span. An extended argument over whether to call the fourth-ranking card in a suit a knave or a jack consumed reams of newsprint. A favorite vacation was to board a slow boat to anywhere and play bridge for hours on end. Expert player Charles Goren personified the mania. Fifty-seven years old, he had never married, citing bridge as the main reason. For Goren there was no such thing as a non-bridge joy.

Furthermore, in the 1930s, bridge jargon permeated written and spoken language. A politician said about his party that "We bid for a grand slam and we were vulnerable and we only took six states and they haven't quit figuring up the penalties on us yet." Short stories, novels, plays, and movies capitalized on bridge mania. Whole fictional scenes revolved around studying the personalities at a bridge table. Parodies in magazines brought smiles with lines such as these in "The Rubaiyat of Bridge":

A book of Bridge rules underneath the bough,
A score card, two new packs of cards, and thou
With two good players sitting opposite,
Oh, wilderness were paradise enow!

Play-aiding devices flooded the market. Machines to keep track of what cards had been played and to keep an accurate score were the favorites. But when the Hammond Clock Co. of Chicago announced its "Electric Bridge Table that Shuffles and Deals," the ultimate convenience had been invented. Today, bridge is still popular but has long since passed the mania stage. Observers of the 1930s phenomenon believe the depression, unemployment, and loss of wealth created a decided need for bridge. People under duress sought an outlet for their problems, and the game gave them a chance to forget momentarily that life had already played them a grand slam.

# BIBLIOGRAPHY

Courtenay, F.D. "Debunking the Game of Bridge," *American Mercury*. 40 (January 1937) 46-51.

Crowninshield, F.W. "Bridge Blight," *Good Housekeeping*. 49 (September 1909) 274-276.

Olsen, Jack. *The Mad World of Bridge*. New York: Holt, Rinehart and Winston, 1960.

Richardson, E.R. "Bridge, Recreation or Racket?," *Outlook*. 158 (August 26, 1931). 524-525.

"Some Thoughts on the Present Propriety of Playing Bridge," *Literary Digest*. 58 (September 14, 1918) 42-44.

# Charades

Most everyone has either seen this form of pantomime played out or has participated in it. During the mid-1800s, American families amused their guests with no less than three types of charades. For a while it was faddish to combine talk with action to get players to guess a word. Here is an example: two men begin walking toward one another. As they pass one man says to the other, "How do, Doctor?" That was the only clue. Dumbfounded, few could figure out the charade was "metaphysician" or "met-a-physician." The two men pass each other a second time, and one says, "How do, again?" This time the answer was "metaphor" or "met-afore."

The second type of charades is more familiar. It was called "charades en action" after the French. No spoken words were allowed, only action. But that action included using whatever props were at hand. An actor might manufacture a Richard Coeur de Lion by going into the kitchen to retrieve tinware. He quickly attached metal pie pans and plates to his body and wore a pot on his head to look the very part of a gallant leader of men. Another player might bring forth a baby's crib and a tea kettle full of boiling water to imitate a steam fire engine. Without props, and for the benefit of children who wanted to play, there were certain words that were always acted out in a conventional way. For instance, the word "bedlam" when divided became "bed" and "lamb" which could be conveyed easily by resting one's head on praying hands, then by bouncing around on all fours. The word "yellow" or "yell" and "low" was presented by opening the mouth as wide as possible while shaking one's head, then by placing one's hand about an inch above the floor.

The third type of charades, foreign to us, required some advance preparation. It was in play form with acts not always connected to tell one story in the usual manner. One such vignette entitled "Pet" went like this: a husband enters a room to find his wife pouting. By gestures he promises to buy her a new shawl and dress; he waves his arms around to suggest how grand they will be. Then he sits down at a bare table and begins to move his limp hands up and down in the air—a second promise to buy her a piano. Then he crouches down and tosses his hair while prancing about—a third promise to buy her a riding horse. Still, his wife pouts. So the husband leaps around and pulls his hair, then seizes an imaginary hat and rams it on his head before exiting. This entire charade was done with pantomime, the only prop being the table and chair. For the riding horse, neighing was permissible.

Some of these charades continued as conventions to be re-acted over and over again such as the popular "Pet" one. But other charades were conceived on the spot to highlight current events or to amuse guests who had seen all the standard charades. In the mid-1800s, people delighted in fully entertaining their guests after dinner and that meant offering them an evening full of fun.

## BIBLIOGRAPHY

Bellew, Frank. *The Art of Amusing*. New York: Arno Press, 1974. (Originally published in 1866.)

# Classic Baseball Shirt Reproductions

Baseball memorabilia in general proved to be a lucrative business during the 1980s, gaining its highest visibility via traveling conventions. While serious collectors have tended to be attracted to original artifacts (e.g., a home run ball hit by Babe Ruth, a glove worn by Brooks Robinson), the market for reproductions — particularly articles comprising major league uniforms — also expanded significantly during this period. The chief outlets for baseball apparel were the big league clubs — who frequently hawked their respective lines on the radio and television stations broadcasting their games — and mail order and chain store retailers offering specially licensed merchandise (in effect, the same products offered by the teams themselves).

In this era of corporate dominance, one entrepreneur gained nationwide attention for his own line of products. Peter Capolino, owner of Mitchell & Ness Sporting Goods in Philadelphia, had long specialized in contemporary pro uniform shirts and historic baseball caps. Then, during a 1985 visit to nearby Maple Manufacturing, he noticed piles of long-discarded wool flannels. The material had been used to make local amateur uniforms in the days before double knits. The switch to the cooler synthetics was initiated by the major leagues in the late 1950s.

Capolino immediately recognized a viable commercial proposition; given the success of his caps and the fact that collectors were paying $2,000 to $25,000 to obtain authentic uniforms, why not put out a line of classic jersey reproductions. He exhaustively researched old sports journals in anticipation of the exacting requirements of his customers. His male patrons were generally mid-life, white collar professionals on a nostalgia trip. Capolino noted,

I have a friend, a stockbroker, who never mentioned baseball until he came in one day and saw a '51 Ted Williams. He turned red and began to shake. He put on the shirt and said, "I've got to have this. When I was nine, I got Ted Williams' autograph. I've had it in my wallet ever since." To borrow that Notre Dame phrase, these shirts are waking up the echoes.

What Capolino had not anticipated was the fact that women found the baggy flannels stylish. He observed,

In the punk world old Japanese baseball shirts were big last year. The Antique Boutique in New York City brought in 15,000 of them. American women are riding that wave. . .

Capolino's wave continued for the time being as well, seemingly threatened less by the likelihood of a sudden downswing in demand than by his limited supply of vintage baseball flannels.

## BIBLIOGRAPHY

Butwin, David. "Baseball Flannels are Hot," *Sports Illustrated*. 67 (July 6, 1987) 105.

# Cooperative Sports and Games

The most vocal proponent of cooperative sports and games is Terry Orlick, a professor and researcher in the psychology of sport and physical activity at the University of Ottawa. By way of definition he makes this contrast between cooperative and competitive sports and games:

> The main difference is that in cooperative games everybody cooperates . . . everybody wins . . . and nobody loses. Children play with one another rather than against one another. These games eliminate the fear of failure and the feeling of failure. They also reaffirm a child's confidence in himself or herself as an acceptable and worthy person. In most games (new or old) this reaffirmation is left to chance or awarded to just one winner. In cooperative games it is designed into the games themselves.

Many of Orlick's cooperative designs are for children and probably work best at that level. For example, "Hug Tag" is like old-fashioned tag except for a player to remain safe he or she must be hugging another player or players to avoid being tagged. "Watermelon Split" calls for children in pairs to pass a whole watermelon from one pair to the next through a zig-zag course, until reaching a table where the melon is divided and enjoyed by all. For a finale, the watermeloners, somewhat in unison, spit seeds into a container. These two games excite children and bring them together for noncompetitive fun. However, at the adult level, non-competitive sports and games tend to be boring. Examples are coed slow-pitch softball in which each team pitches an unlimited number of times to its own players until everyone gets a hit; and cooperative volleyball which allows the players to carry the ball, touch the net, hit the ball twice in a row, whatever it takes to get the ball over the net every time. In both games any number of people can play and there are no set teams since sharing players occurs at random.

No doubt Orlick's cooperative program is a noble one built around the idea that children should not be taught aggression. Moreover, sports and games ought to be enjoyed by everyone and not just by the few who are gifted or ruthless participants. The familiar game King of the Mountain is antithetical to Orlick's plan. The thinking goes, if practiced worldwide, cooperative sports and games will eradicate war and the need for war. Inspirational as this sounds, it is the stuff of faddism. Individual differences among children cannot be disregarded. Some children will always run faster and farther than others; some will always be stronger, brighter, and physically more robust. Why hold them back for the sake of equality? To remove all competitiveness from sports and games robs them of meaning. The epitome of competition is to win an Olympic gold medal signifying that the winner is the best in the world; having the whole world share the medal would be absurd. By their very nature, sports and games thrive on competition and thus build character. American life revolves around competition, not only on the playing field but for our economic well-being. To raise a generation of children unused to the struggle to win would be placing their lives in jeopardy in a world that demands hard-nosed competition daily.

Orlick has had some effect on modern education. "Challenge without competition" is a timely message that has galvanized his followers to try his ideas. Research has shown that mildly mentally retarded children seem to benefit the most from non-competitive sports and games. Normal children respond by overcoming shyness. But adults might find non-competition lackluster and devoid of what makes sports and games rewarding — the exercise of physical and mental acuity to beat a worthy opponent.

## BIBLIOGRAPHY

Acton, Heather M., and Lynne Zarbatany. "Interaction and Performance within Cooperative Groups: Effects on Nonhandicapped Students' Attitudes Toward Their Mildly Mentally Retarded Peers," *American Journal of Mental Retardation*. 93, no. 1 (July 1988) 16-23.
Foster, Wayne K. "Cooperation in the Game and Sport Structure of Children:

One Dimension of Psychosocial Development," *Education*. 105, no. 2 (Winter 1984) 201-205.

Hatcher, Barbara, et al. "Group Games for Global Awareness," *Childhood Education*. 65, no. 1 (Fall 1988) 8-13.

Orlick, Terry. *The Cooperative Sports & Games Book: Challenge Without Competition*. New York: Pantheon Books, 1978.

Orlick, Terry. *The Second Cooperative Sports & Games Book*. New York: Pantheon, 1982.

Rogers, Martin, et al. "Cooperative Games as an Intervention to Promote Cross-Racial Acceptance," *American Educational Research Journal*. 18, no. 4 (Winter 1981) 513-516.

# Crossword Puzzles

Arthur Winn composed the first American crossword puzzle which appeared in the Sunday New York *World*, December 21, 1913. He admitted having gotten the idea after seeing a similar puzzle in the London *Graphic* several years before. Diamond-shaped, Winn's puzzle was all blanks, not yet showing the characteristic pattern of black and white squares. But while designing other puzzles and varying their shapes, he soon hit upon using black and white graphology to produce more interesting and challenging word games. Even if he did borrow the original idea, his innovations in construction still single him out as the father of the American crossword.

A few years later, World War I intervened and bloody headlines took precedence over the amusement page. As spirits picked up after the war other newspapers began to feature crossword puzzles and the craze began. The Baltimore and Ohio Railroad announced it was placing dictionaries in all through trains on its main line. A librarian riding the train from New York to Boston noticed that 60 percent of the passengers were hard at work on crossword puzzles. Throughout the train, newspapers littered the seats mostly undisturbed except for the amusement page. In the dining car, which had not opened yet, the steward and five waiters were trying to think of a five-letter word meaning "serving to inspire fear." By late 1924, with the publication of several crossword puzzle books, a new kind of best-seller was born, which is quite a story in itself. On January 1, 1924, two young men, Richard L. Simon and Max Lincoln Schuster began a publishing company on West Fifty-Seventh Street in New York City. At best, they vaguely knew what they wanted to publish. That very New Year's Day, Simon visited his aunt whose daughter could hardly wait for Sunday to come around so she could work the crossword puzzle in the New York *World*. Hearing that the family guest was a publisher (not even one day yet), she asked him if there were any books of crosswords. Having to languish for six days just to have fun for less than an hour on the seventh was punishment. Not able to answer her, Simon discovered the next day that no such book existed. On January 3rd he and Schuster met with the puzzle editors of the New York *World*. After doubts expressed on both sides, they decided to publish a small edition (3,600 copies) of what was to be the first crossword puzzle book. It was available for public consumption in April.

One year later three book collections of crossword puzzles had sold three-quarters of a million copies. Already, a fad within the fad had arisen. There were Bible, celebrity, Yiddish, and punning crosswords, among others. People dropped their usual reading material to concentrate on the black and white squares. Crossword puzzle fan clubs wrote letters of appreciation to the puzzle editors. The craze tickled a Columbia University professor:

> The frantic search, and the loss of dignity on the part of fans who bother an entire office force, and call up a dozen friends to locate a three-letter word; the outstanding prominence of such animals as the gnu; the laughable definitions of certain words; the inability of people with reputations of wisdom to locate a word; the seriousness with which the search for words is made by busy people; the abandonment of all other activity; the failure to keep appointments until the correct word is found, and the curious places where people are found doing puzzles are all sources of amusement.

The gnu reference became a focal point for satire by another commentator on the craze. He lampooned those who insisted that working crosswords was a great vocabulary builder.

> There is really only one river in this new cosmos. It is the Po. . . . Egypt made her place in history secure by developing a bird named ibis and a goddess named Isis. Gutenberg's real contribution to civilization was the em and the pi. . . . China has done her bit with lao and tael. Japan almost dominates with yen and her immortal broad sash, the obi. There is only one world language worth speaking of. It is Erse. Natural selection operating in the zoological realm favors immensely the

survival of the three-lettered animal. The lion and the elephant are dethroned and in their place rule the emu, the gnu and the eel. If Coleridge's Mariner were living in this cross-world of ours, he would not be carrying an albatross around his neck. He would be proudly sporting an auk.

## BIBLIOGRAPHY

Buranelli, P., and M. Petherbridge. "How the Crossword Craze Started," *Collier's*. 75 (January 31, 1925) 12.

Harding, Allan. "Why We Have Gone Mad Over Cross-Word Puzzles," *American Magazine*. 99 (March 1925) 28-29 + .

Hornaday, W.T. "Behold the Cross Word Puzzle Zoo," *Collier's*. 75 (February 14, 1925) 18-19.

Lynd, R. "Cross Words," *Living Age*. 324 (January 24, 1925) 216-219.

"Origin of the Cross-Word Puzzle," *Current Opinion*. 78 (January 1925) 77-78.

# The Dallas Cowboy Cheerleaders

Just when it became obvious that professional football had supplanted Major League Baseball as the most popular spectator sport in America, the NFL found itself being upstaged by one of its sideshow attractions. Bruce Newman addressed the rise of pro football cheerleaders in an article appearing in *Sports Illustrated:*

> Goodness knows, the only thing anybody talks about anymore is S-E-X and the Dallas Cowboy cheerleaders. Just last week, Ann Landers had to contend with an enraged reader complaining about the trend toward "older, sexier, and more naked cheerleaders" in the NFL. "Talented baton twirlers and really good dancing . . . don't mean a thing," the infuriated correspondent said, asking Ann how she felt about such an "appalling commentary on American taste." How Ann felt was that such preferences were the "last gasps of a dying civilization."
>
> Right. Certainly, whatever Dallas cheerleaders started six years ago, with their plunging necklines winking belly buttons, has spread through the rest of the NFL like a social disease.

The evidence that the Dallas cheerleaders started something big when Cowboys General Manager Tex Schramm professionalized his squad by hiring eight girls from the dance studio of choreographer Texie Waterman in 1972 was everywhere by mid-1978. On April 24, CBS' "National Collegiate Cheerleading Championships" went head-to-head with ABC's "Monday Night Baseball" and won 37% to 22%. Also during April, 1,500 young women applied for twenty-eight spots on the Chicago Honey Bears; in Los Angeles, twenty-four Ram Sundancers were selected from more than eight hundred candidates. Atlanta Falcons Assistant GM Curt Mosher exclaimed, "Everyone is trying to out-Dallas Dallas."

Television, while not responsible for creating the Dallas Cowboy cheerleaders, played a major role in the growth of the phenomenon. Telecasts of pro games—which usually featured countless camera angle shots of the cheerleaders on the sidelines (the exceptions being the Pittsburgh Steelers, the Cleveland Browns, and the Green Bay Packers, each of whom resisted the trend toward sponsoring a cheerleading squad)—drove the number of applicants for the thirty-seven Dallas cheerleader spots up from 250 in 1976 to 1,053 in 1978.

While it was easy to surmise why television viewers (the large majority were reputed to be of the male variety) found them appealing, it was hard to see what was in it for the cheerleaders, who received fifteen dollars per game and were required to clean their own uniforms, attend innumerable practices, and be at the stadium two hours before each home game.

Sensitive to this and other criticisms of the phenomenon, the Cowboys attempted to portray their girls as not only beautiful but bright; e.g., their numbers included a nuclear-medicine technologist and a 4.0 student at S.M.U. who had danced solo with the Bolshoi Ballet. Fundamentalist Christians—particularly strong in the Dallas region—remained strangely silent on this issue, perhaps because sex and violence on the gridiron have been elevated to the level of God, Mom, and apple pie in Texas.

Most critics, however, tended to take a tongue-in-cheek approach when addressing the phenomenon. Bill Allen—director of Miami's long-standing Dolphin Dolls, who were eclipsed by an older, sexier group—noted that "Cheerleading is becoming nothing more than a battle of belly buttons, busts and backsides." John Madden, then head coach of the Oakland Raiders, observed,

> I can see what this game is coming to. Choreographers instead of coaches. It will be a contest to judge which set of girls gets more TV time. After the gun sounds, the losing choreographer will tell the press, "We lost our momentum. We couldn't maintain intensity . . . The losing side will complain about the judges' decisions and the case will go to the commissioner, who will appoint a seventh judge. And after the girls have competed, the football players will come out at halftime for

their exhibition, but the press won't notice because they'll be too busy watching replays of the cheerleaders.

While Madden's prognostication has not yet come to pass, the Dallas Cowboy cheerleaders, the Derrick Dolls, the Ben-Gals, the Pony Express, the Redskinettes, the Embraceable Ewes and others of their ilk remain highly visible. The Dallas contingent have even been fictionalized in a Hollywood film starring Jane Seymour and "Love Boat" alumnus Lauren Tewes.

## BIBLIOGRAPHY

Newman, Bruce. "Gimme an 'S', Gimme an 'E', Gimme . . . ; Cheerleaders for Pro Football Teams," *Sports Illustrated*. 48 (May 22, 1978) 18-19.
"What Hath the Cowgirls Wrought?," *People*. 10 (October 16, 1978) 123-125.

# Dance Marathons

The dance marathon was not so much a dance event as a social phenomenon. It required minimal talent or technique; rather, it placed a premium upon stamina and determination. Although bereft of aesthetic considerations, the typical marathon did incorporate snatches of the tango, fox trot, trucking, Charleston, waltz, and other dances of the depression. Above all, however, it tended to be simply movement, milked by the enterprising promoter to last as long as 100 or more days.

Entrants for marathons of that period were generally given an application form which asked a brief number of questions while containing a lengthy listing of rules. The questions usually focused on (1) demographic information, (2) whether one had venereal disease/body lice/insanity/artificial appendages, (3) membership in the American Legion, and (4) the willingness to participate in a motion picture production of the contest. Rules and regulations typically included,

- Showers are compulsory.
- Contestants must behave as ladies and gents at all times.
- Contestants must get an excuse from a judge for hygienic purposes. Two minutes is the time limit. Only one contestant of either sex at a time.
- No spitting.
- Minor medical requirements, such as extraction of teeth, etc., will be done by competent physicans on the dance floor while contestants are in motion.
- No gum chewing except late hours.

Harold Stern has provided the following account of the events comprising a typical marathon:

During the first week or two, while the contestants were relatively fresh, they were asked and expected to perform so-called specialties. These could range from vocalizing, to reading from the works of Ernest Thayer, to spritely tap dance routines. The mere fact that some participants engaged in such frivolities seemed enough to assuage the omnivorous appetites of the crowd and all too often, the worst performances were the greatest crowd pleasers.

As for the "talent" itself, many of the entrants sought to use the marathon as a showcase and would eagerly perform their specialties for the celebrities who sometimes attended. Though there were never as many celebrities in attendance as suggested by the promotion, stars, directors, producers and even a talent scout or two did occasionally show up for their pound of flesh, particularly on the West Coast.

Sprints and strenuous athletic events were imposed during the latter stages of the marathon in order to weed out contestants and all too often results were determined dishonestly to get rid of unpopular couples and insure the continuation of the favorites.

Although born in the midst of the Roaring Twenties, the dance marathon found a new lease on life during the depression as participating couples competed for big money and illusory security. It represented a last-ditch glimmer of hope for the contestants, while providing a spectacle for anyone able to afford the quarters and half-dollars required to "come in and stay as long as you like for a simple admission."

## BIBLIOGRAPHY

Alder, D. "They Danced 'Til They Dropped, Making of *They Shoot Horses, Don't They?," Life.* 67 (7-25-1969) 58-61.

"Dance Marathoners," *Survey.* 70 (February 1934) 53.

Havoc, June. *Marathon '33* (play).

*They Shoot Horses, Don't They?* Film, 1969, starring Jane Fonda, Bonnie Bedelia, Red Buttons, Susannah York, Michael Sarrazin, Gig Young, and Al Lewis.

Stern, Harold. "Dance Marathons . . . Look Back in Horror," *Dance Magazine.* 44 (February 1970) 68-71.

Hardly Fred Astaire and Ginger Rogers, these participants in a dance marathon hang onto each other for dear life. As the hours wore on, dreams of a feather bed and cool sheets became an obsession. 1920s.

# Joe DiMaggio's Consecutive Game Hitting Streak

Joe DiMaggio's consecutive game hitting streak of fifty-six—considered by many to be the greatest feat in American sports history—began on May 15, 1941. As the string reached the twenties, and then higher, he became the central figure of the baseball world. Interest spread to those who ordinarily do not follow the game as DiMaggio reached two notable milestones in midsummer. On June 29, in a doubleheader with the Senators in Washington, he tied, then surpassed the American League and modern record of forty-one set by George Sisler of the St. Louis Browns in 1922. Then, on July 1, he tied the all-time major league high of forty-four set by Baltimore Orioles infielder Willie Keeler in 1897, eclipsing it the next day.

The streak finally came to an end on July 17, in Cleveland before 67,468 fans, the largest crowd ever to see a game of night baseball in the major leagues. DiMaggio faced veteran left-hander Al Smith three times. Twice he smashed the ball down the third base line, but each time third baseman Ken Keitner collared the ball and hurled it across the diamond for a put-out at first. In between these two attempts, Joltin' Joe drew a walk. Then, in the top of the eighth inning, amid a deafening uproar, DiMaggio came up to the plate with the bases loaded and one out for what appeared to be his last opportunity to extend the streak. Though the Yanks had already routed Smith with a flurry of four hits and two runs in the inning, reliever Jim Bagby succeeded in getting the Yankee Clipper to hit a grounder to the shortstop for an inning-ending double play.

Those still holding out for the chance that DiMaggio would get yet another chance at extending his string, were uplifted by an Indians rally in the bottom of the ninth which threatened to send the game into extra innings. However, atrocious baserunning by the Tribe cut short the rally, resulting in a 4-3 victory for the Yankees.

The fifty-six-game streak unfolded in the following manner:

| Date | Opponent | a.b. | r. | h. | 2b. | 3b. | h.r. |
|------|----------|------|----|----|-----|-----|------|
| May 15 | White Sox | 4 | 0 | 1 | 0 | 0 | 0 |
| May 16 | White Sox | 4 | 2 | 2 | 0 | 1 | 1 |
| May 17 | White Sox | 3 | 1 | 1 | 0 | 0 | 0 |
| May 18 | Browns | 3 | 3 | 3 | 1 | 0 | 0 |
| May 19 | Browns | 3 | 0 | 1 | 1 | 0 | 0 |
| May 20 | Browns | 5 | 1 | 1 | 0 | 0 | 0 |
| May 21 | Tigers | 5 | 0 | 2 | 0 | 0 | 0 |
| May 22 | Tigers | 4 | 0 | 1 | 0 | 0 | 0 |
| May 23 | Red Sox | 5 | 0 | 1 | 0 | 0 | 0 |
| May 24 | Red Sox | 4 | 2 | 1 | 0 | 0 | 0 |
| May 25 | Red Sox | 4 | 0 | 1 | 0 | 0 | 0 |
| May 27 | Senators | 5 | 3 | 4 | 0 | 0 | 1 |
| May 28 | Senators | 4 | 1 | 1 | 0 | 1 | 0 |
| May 29 | Senators | 3 | 1 | 1 | 0 | 0 | 0 |
| May 30 | Red Sox | 2 | 1 | 1 | 0 | 0 | 0 |
| May 30 | Red Sox | 3 | 0 | 1 | 1 | 0 | 0 |
| June 1 | Indians | 4 | 1 | 1 | 0 | 0 | 0 |
| June 1 | Indians | 4 | 0 | 1 | 0 | 0 | 0 |
| June 2 | Indians | 4 | 2 | 2 | 1 | 0 | 0 |
| June 3 | Tigers | 4 | 1 | 1 | 0 | 0 | 1 |
| June 5 | Tigers | 5 | 1 | 1 | 0 | 1 | 0 |
| June 7 | Browns | 5 | 2 | 3 | 0 | 0 | 0 |
| June 8 | Browns | 4 | 3 | 2 | 0 | 0 | 2 |
| June 8 | Browns | 4 | 1 | 2 | 1 | 0 | 1 |
| June 10 | White Sox | 5 | 1 | 1 | 0 | 0 | 0 |
| June 12 | White Sox | 4 | 1 | 2 | 0 | 0 | 1 |
| June 14 | Indians | 2 | 0 | 1 | 1 | 0 | 0 |
| June 15 | Indians | 3 | 1 | 1 | 0 | 0 | 1 |
| June 16 | Indians | 5 | 0 | 1 | 1 | 0 | 0 |
| June 17 | White Sox | 4 | 1 | 1 | 0 | 0 | 0 |
| June 18 | White Sox | 3 | 0 | 1 | 0 | 0 | 0 |
| June 19 | White Sox | 3 | 2 | 3 | 0 | 0 | 1 |
| June 20 | Tigers | 5 | 3 | 4 | 1 | 0 | 0 |
| June 21 | Tigers | 4 | 0 | 1 | 0 | 0 | 0 |
| June 22 | Tigers | 5 | 1 | 2 | 1 | 0 | 1 |
| June 24 | Browns | 4 | 1 | 1 | 0 | 0 | 0 |
| June 25 | Browns | 4 | 1 | 1 | 0 | 0 | 1 |
| June 26 | Browns | 4 | 0 | 1 | 1 | 0 | 0 |
| June 27 | Athletics | 3 | 1 | 2 | 0 | 0 | 1 |
| June 28 | Athletics | 5 | 1 | 2 | 1 | 0 | 0 |
| June 29 | Senators | 4 | 1 | 1 | 1 | 0 | 0 |
| June 29 | Senators | 5 | 1 | 1 | 0 | 0 | 0 |

| July | 1 | Red Sox | 4 | 0 | 2 | 0 | 0 | 0 |
|------|---|---------|---|---|---|---|---|---|
| July | 1 | Red Sox | 3 | 1 | 1 | 0 | 0 | 0 |
| July | 2 | Red Sox | 5 | 1 | 1 | 0 | 0 | 1 |
| July | 5 | Athletics | 4 | 2 | 1 | 0 | 0 | 1 |
| July | 6 | Athletics | 5 | 2 | 4 | 1 | 0 | 0 |
| July | 6 | Athletics | 4 | 0 | 2 | 0 | 1 | 0 |
| July | 10 | Browns | 2 | 0 | 1 | 0 | 0 | 0 |
| July | 11 | Browns | 5 | 1 | 4 | 0 | 0 | 1 |
| July | 12 | Browns | 5 | 1 | 2 | 1 | 0 | 0 |
| July | 13 | White Sox | 4 | 2 | 3 | 0 | 0 | 0 |
| July | 13 | White Sox | 4 | 0 | 1 | 0 | 0 | 0 |
| July | 14 | White Sox | 3 | 0 | 1 | 0 | 0 | 0 |
| July | 15 | White Sox | 4 | 1 | 2 | 1 | 0 | 0 |
| July | 16 | Indians | 4 | 3 | 3 | 1 | 0 | 0 |

Actually, DiMaggio hit in fifty-seven consecutive games in that he connected safely in the All-Star game on July 8; however, that contest did not count in the official league records.

## BIBLIOGRAPHY

"Big Joe," *Time*. 38 (July 14, 1941) 44.

Brebinger, John. "DiMaggio's Streak Ended At 56 Games," In: *The New York Times Encyclopedia of Sports*, edited by Gene Brown. Volume 2: Baseball. New York: Arno, 1979. p. 71.

"Joe DiMaggio," In: *Current Biography 1951*, edited by Anna Rothe. 12th ed. New York: Wilson, 1952. pp. 162-164. Includes bibliography.

"Joe DiMaggio; Edward Laning Paints Him Tying Record for Hits as Baseball's Great Moment," *Life*. 11 (September 29, 1941) 64-67.

Owen, R. "DiMaggio, the Unruffled," *New York Times Magazine*. (July 13, 1941) 9ff.

# Drive-In Restaurants

Intended for serving food and drink with a smile to customers seated in their cars, these flashy eateries quickly evolved into something else. They became recreation—the new meeting places of the 1950s and 1960s. Appearing directly after World War II along with other drive-in businesses, the restaurants, or more properly called, sandwich shops, proliferated in chains across the country. At first, families frequented them for a night out of hamburgers, french fries, and milk shakes. But that changed as restless teenagers drove from one drive-in to the next, often covering a hundred miles or more. They looked for friends, pick-ups, or trouble and usually found all three. Soon, police cars patrolled the drive-ins giving chase to rubber-burning disturbers of the peace. When motorcycle gangs drove in even the brash teenagers reverted to their best behavior. With families forced out and rowdies in command—who spent very little to keep the drive-ins going—the end was near.

The main attraction of the old-style drive-in restaurant, that you could park your car and be served, distinguishes it from today's popular fast-food restaurant. Now the object is head-spinning turnover, but back then things were much different. The kids drove modified cars, hot rods, old jalopies, anything to make the scene. It was very much part of the ambiance of drive-ins to have a constant influx of cars sporting new paint jobs and radios blaring. Food was secondary to hanging out. The whole object was to see and be seen. Eating a hamburger might come later, after a night of cruising. Also missing today are the motley hostesses ranging from pretty to over-ripe in their tight pants or short skirts, the distinctive drive-in smell, and the appeal of claiming turf by parking in the same spot each time.

Simple drive-in operation worked the best: a few carhops, decent food, and managerial tolerance of youth in transition. But then there was the Motormat in Los Angeles (1949) which resembled a factory assembly line and because it was unique (faddish) customers loved it. This is how it worked: a carload of hungry people drove up to a metal track and within seconds a bin holding glasses of water, menus, and a pencil and pad rumbled out. The driver wrote down orders, pushed a button on the end of the track, and the bin rumbled back to the kitchen. A minute later the bin returned with the total bill. Payment made, the bin made one more round trip and returned with the order and change. At top speed, the Motormat bins traveled at 120 ft. per minute. K. C. Purdy, the inventor of this mechanical octopus, expected to fill California and Nevada with Motormats, but alas cold metal tracks and bins could not replace warm, bouncy carhops.

Another innovation on the way to fast-food paradise involved the walkie-talkie (1951). Carhops radioed in orders to the kitchen so the customer could expect to eat right away. Business analysts figured 30 percent more customers were served in this manner. However, the ultimate in fast-food service came in 1966 when electrical engineer Norman Alpert demonstrated his new invention, Orbis. An operator seated at an electronic computer console took customer orders from cars and tables relaying the desired items to the automatic hamburger machine and five other producing units. The units cooked and wrapped exactly what was ordered and indicated whether the food was to be eaten on the premises or taken out. Orbis handled some 30 different food and drink items, produced a bill with the customer's station number on it, and kept inventory of stock. The final step, a carhop did pick up the tray to add a human touch.

# BIBLIOGRAPHY

"Car-Hop Orders Speeded by Walkie-Talkie," *Popular Mechanics*. 96 (November 1951) 227.

"Eating Goes on Assemby Line at California Drive-In," *Business Week*. (July 23, 1949) 22-23.

"Everything Is Automated But the Carhop," *Science Digest*. 60 (November 1966) 32.

Thruelsen, Richard. "Eat and Run," *Saturday Evening Post*. 218 (June 22, 1946) 26-27 + .

# Drive-In Theaters

Variously called "ozoners," "airers," and "passion pits with pix," the phenomenon of watching a movie outdoors while seated in the comfort of your own car began in 1932. Richard M. Hollingshead, an inventor and manufacturer of chemicals, created the first prototype of the drive-in in his own Camden, New Jersey driveway. He placed a 16-mm projector on a stand, attached a screen to supports, turned on the projector, and got in his car to see the results. Hollingshead was not disappointed — the picture looked fine as long as there was nothing in front of him to obstruct the view, such as another car. As the story goes, he sweated through multiple experiments before devising the fan-shaped parking lot, terraced rows, and inclined ramps. He got a patent on the ramp — a metal incline that allowed the driver to park at enough of a tilt to see over the top of the forward cars.

On June 7, 1933, in Camden, Hollingshead and his cousin, W. Warren Smith, opened the world's first drive-in theater. It accommodated 400 cars on eight rows with a thirty-by-forty-foot screen as the object of attention. Successful from the start, the partners began selling blueprints to other builders and issued franchises for a flat fee of $1,000 plus 5 percent royalties on gross receipts. Hollingshead and Smith were to go through several patent battles over the next few years, the most contested with Loew's Drive-In Theaters, Inc. In high court, the decision was that neither the fan-shaped parking lot, terracing, nor the inclined ramp were patentable, even though the U.S. Patent Office held patent No. 1,909,537 for the ramp. Millions of dollars lost, the partners still got rich and Hollingshead lived to see his invention sweep the nation.

Before World War II there were only 100-odd drive-in theaters. After the war, construction accelerated so that by 1950, 2,200 drive-ins were in operation. People loved being able to get out of their homes without troubling themselves too much. Their cars became an extension of their living rooms. They did not have to get fixed up and dress fancy. They did not even have to comb their hair or bathe. All they had to do was pile in their cars and pay a small admission price to see several movies and much more. The movies they watched were usually third-rate — by contract the indoor theaters got to show the top first-run films. Since families comprised the bulk of the drive-in audience, their needs were catered to. At some ozoners there were picnic areas, merry-go-rounds, dance floors, shuffleboard courts, on-duty mechanics to start stalled cars, and bottle-warming, car-washing, and laundry services. At others there were elaborate children's play areas, pony rides, swimming pools, miniature railroads, monkey villages, miniature golf, driving ranges, and, of course, concession stands. The concession stands did particularly well. Consumer studies showed people got hungry faster outdoors than indoors and as a result bought mounds of food and buckets of drinks. The ozoners opened early to provide all this pre-movie fun and service, so that a family could stay all evening, making everyone happy.

Patron demographics broke down like this: (1) moderate-income families who could not afford anything else and saved on babysitting, (2) the aged and physically handicapped, (3) blue-collar workers who wanted to relax without having to go to town, and (4) young neckers. For a while, concern over the last group prompted drive-in owners to make spot checks of cars. They concluded that what happened in their establishments was no worse than what took place in the balcony of indoor theaters.

The fad continued apace, problem solving as it went along. At first, sound quality was not good; speakers sat atop poles forcing the listener to lean out of the car window to hear the soundtrack. An individual speaker attached to the car door remedied that. Change of weather reduced the outdoor season to just thirty weeks (except in the West and Southwest) until the drive-ins supplied portable electric heaters, glycerine sprays on windshields to turn a downpour of rain into transparent sheets, and DDT foggings to kill mosquitoes. There was no limit to what an owner would do to insure a full parking lot. Motorized bingo was perhaps the height of faddish enticement; the jackpot went to the car with the winning speedometer mileage.

Drive-ins lasted for another thirty-five years, though after the mid-1960s settled into moderate operations without all the frills and gimmicks. Speaking of which, the "Oasis" in Bensenville, Illinois attracted customers with a desert motif. A turbaned Arab directed traffic under a neo-Taj Mahal archway in front of waving palms and gurgling waterfalls. In Brattleboro, Vermont, the Theatre Motel offered a 100-foot screen for viewing movies in your car at 75¢ per person, or for $16.00 and up per couple a private room with bath, air conditioning, television, and venetian blinds to open—if you really wanted to watch the movie. When drive-ins began to die out, it was a pitiful sight, their faded screens on rusty rigging, their lots whipped by whirling dust. But who could forget 1958 when there were 4,063 screens in the land, many of which did show a first-run film—Charlton Heston as Moses in *The Ten Commandments*. When Heston-Moses parted the Red Sea, water splashed the stars. The few drive-ins that remain today do minimal business and appear antiquated. Place the blame on rising real estate cost, television and cable television, movie companies' disinterest, and greater teenage independence for consigning drive-ins to oblivion. In 1950 the prestigious journal *Architectural Record* ran an article—complete with drawings and photographs—on designing drive-ins to provide the utmost comfort and utility. Then the future did indeed look progressive.

## BIBLIOGRAPHY

"Dark Clouds Over the Drive-Ins," *Time*. 122 (August 8, 1983) 64.
"The Drive-In Lie-In," *Newsweek*. 62 (July 8, 1963) 78.
"Drive-Ins: Theaters," *Architectural Record*. 108 (August 1950) 140-145.
Durant, John. "The Movies Take to the Pastures," *Saturday Evening Post*. 223 (October 14, 1950) 24-25 + .
"Ozoners," *Time*. 51 (April 26, 1948) 96.
"Twice As Many Drive-In Theaters?" *Business Week*. (January 1, 1949) 44-45.

# Dungeons and Dragons

Dungeons and Dragons, a complex role-playing game manufactured by Tactical Studies Rules (TSR) of Lake Geneva, Wisconsin, has grossed millions of dollars since its creation in 1974. It was estimated to be the favorite pastime of more than 3,000,000 people at the peak of its popularity in the early 1980s. It became best known to rank-and-file Americans, however, due to the criticism it has received from various authority figures, particularly evangelicals. News coverage accorded the game included the following items:

- one group forced it out of the summer recreational program of a Sacramento suburb
- a minister in Hutchinson, Kansas, expressed a wish to collect enough money to buy up and burn every copy of Dungeons and Dragons he could uncover

Its inventor, Gary Gygax, started out as an indifferent insurance underwriter with a passion for writing war games for toy soldiers (termed "Miniature Rules" in the trade) as H. G. Wells had once done. Gygax ultimately developed a sort of war game not confined to historical reality, drawing upon his extensive reading of fantasy fiction. His idea was turned down by all of the leading game companies, including Avalon Hill — the leading producer of wargames — for being too complicated and open-ended.

Gygax's resolve might have dissipated at this point had he not lost his insurance job. Jolted into questioning his motivation in life, he decided upon starting a game company, TSR, utilizing a $1,000 investment. Some of TSR's early successes — geared primarily to college students — included Top Secret (espionage), Gamma World (science fiction) and Boot Hill (the Wild West). In the meantime, Gygax continued to refine Dungeons and Dragons; its appeal steadily increased throughout the latter portion of the 1970s. By 1978,

*109*

the median age of new buyers had dropped from college age to the ten-fourteen bracket, thereby drawing the attention of parents and other authority figures.

In its fully realized form, Dungeons and Dragons might best be defined as a combination fantasy trip, war game exercise, drama workshop, and psychological act-out session. Its overall look is not like typical "age twelve-to-adult" games. Rather than the usual game contents of board, player pieces, printed cards, etc., a basic Dungeons and Dragons set consists of two booklets, which are barely sufficient to get a player started. To play at a genuinely competent level, however, at least four more books are required: *Player's Handbook*, *Dungeon Master's Guide*, *Monster Manual*, and *Dieties and Demigods*. It does not play like most games, either, being open-ended and lasting indefinitely, unless a player is retired or destroyed. One player, appointed Dungeon Master, controls play by making up maps that include traps, treasure, monsters, and magical devices. Other players assume characters such as druids, thieves, clerics, magic users, or elves, each possessing special abilities. The object of the game is for players to band together to fight through a monster-laden maze of tunnels and dungeons in order to grab as much treasure as they can.

The opponents of Dungeons and Dragons made the following points:

1. It encourages sex and violence. Physician and Dungeons and Dragons player John Holmes noted in *Psychology Today:* "The level of violence in this make-believe world runs high. There is hardly a game in which the players do not indulge in murder, arson, torture, rape, or highway robbery."
2. The bizarre cast of characters—which includes demons, dragons, witches, zombies, harpies, gnomes, and creatures who cast spells and exercise supernatural power—disturbs some, evangelicals in particular. They say the game dabbles with demonic spirits and promotes the influence of the occult.
3. Its role playing can become an obsessive retreat from the real world.
4. It is expensive to play. Besides manuals and basic instruction sets, players can invest up to $900 in hand-painted miniatures

in medieval costumes with ratten replicas of ancient weap-
onry, twenty different modules that map out adventures,
"hex" pods for recording the journey, or even a subscription
to the $2 monthly, *Dragon*, published by Gygax.
5. The guidebooks themselves are disconcerting as well.
   a. From *Deities and Demigods*:
      No fantasy world is complete without the gods, mighty
      deities who influence the fates of men and move mortals
      about like chess-pieces in their obscure games of power.
      Such figures can be the perfect embodiment of the Dun-
      geon Master's control of the game.
      Serving a deity is a significant part of D & D, and all
      player characters should have a patron god. Alignment
      assumes its full importance when tied to the worship of a
      deity. (A rich assortment of deities or demigods are avail-
      able for selection as patrons.)
   b. From *Player's Handbook:*
      It is so interesting, so challenging, so mind-unleashing
      that it comes near reality.

TSR Hobbies spokesman, Bryon Pritzer, called such criticisms
absurd, noting that Dungeons and Dragons is merely a game and
that critics do not understand it. He added that it "can be absurd —
like any other game," but, in actuality, it has more benefits than
dangers (e.g., it can be used by educators, psychiatrists, and even
ministers to help youth, via role playing, to assist clients in sorting
out real-life problems). In the meantime, the game continues to
attract converts, although garnering less media-hyped hysteria. To
hard-core fantasy game enthusiasts, however, it has long since lost
its primacy to a wave of newer titles.

## BIBLIOGRAPHY

Adler, Jerry. "Kids: the Deadliest Game?," *Newsweek*. 106 (September 9, 1985)
   93.
Alsop, Stewart, II. "TSR Hobbies Mixes Fact and Fantasy," *Inc.* 4 (February
   1982) 68-71.
Elshof, Phyllis Ten. "Dungeons and Dragons: Fantasy Fad or Dabbling in the
   Demonic?," *Christianity Today*. 25 (September 4, 1981) 56.

"The Gameslayers," *Newsweek.* 98 (October 26, 1981) 66.

Gygax, Gary. "Role Playing Games Lead to More Active Entertainment," *Playthings.* 79 (June 1981) 124.

Holmes, John Eric. "Confessions of a Dungeon Master," *Psychology Today.* 14 (November 1980) 84-88.

MacRae, Paul. "The Most Popular Fantasy of All," *Maclean's.* 93 (April 21, 1980) 48.

Mills, Barbara Kleban. "If Students' Tails are Dragon and Their Minds in the Dungeon Lately, Blame Gamesman Gary Gygax," *People Weekly.* 13 (January 14, 1980) 64-65.

Shuster, William G. "Critics Link Fantasy Games to 29 Deaths," *Christianity Today.* 29 (May 17, 1985) 64-65.

Smith, Geoffrey. "Dungeons and Dollars," *Forbes.* 126 (September 15, 1980) 137-142.

# The Endless Summer

Bruce Brown produced, directed, wrote, edited, photographed, and narrated this quintessential film about surfing. At the time of its release in 1966, *Variety* announced: "Independently made documentary on surfing around the world has enough action and wit to make a dent in market with proper promotion." Little did anyone know *The Endless Summer* would make new converts to the sport everywhere, reinvigorate seasoned surfers, and charm thousands of moviegoers who previously had no interest in surfing. A surfer himself, Brown spent two years trekking 35,000 miles in search of the perfect wave. His quest served to build the plot to an exciting climax as he filmed surf action in Hawaii, Senegal, Ghana, South Africa, Australia, Tahiti, and other exotic spots. The stars of the film were two young Californians, Mike Hynson and Robert August. Both were slender dynamos of energy, perfectly tanned with glossy hair. They did not say much since Brown did all the talking, which worked well because it was their job to master the waves. Hynson and August performed sleek maneuvers in some treacherous surf. They always seemed to be having the time of their life and never tired of paddling out for one more wave. Halfway through the documentary their charisma was evident. They made surfing look like such a "blast" and seeing them framed time and again by soft morning light or brilliant setting sun romanticized their trip even more.

Another of the film's charms was the musical background provided by the Sandals. The group's incessant guitar beat perfectly mimicked row after row of curling, crashing waves. It was as if their guitars were at the heart of nature synchronizing sun, sand and surf. Movie audiences got so caught up in the feverish blend that they did not want the musical sequences to end. But there were other vicarious thrills. By following the summer sun around the world, the film gave its audiences the illusion of an endless good time, endless youth and vigor and provided breathtaking shots of a sport that photographs well. These thrills were too contagious to leave behind in the movie theater. Young and old surfers-to-be flocked to the beaches—which was not easy if the novice lived in Topeka. Many of the newly smitten were horribly landlocked and fantasized about one day catching a big wave in California or Hawaii.

John Severson personified the relaxed attitude of *The Endless Summer*. In the mid-1960s he launched *Surfer Magazine* which *Life*, the top magazine in the country, took note of in an article. Severson told the *Life* reporter: "There is no point waiting until I am 65 to have some fun. I don't like to wear a coat and tie. Even for business purposes. In the evening for fun it's OK, but just a sport-coat, never a suit." Severson contented himself with living in San Clemente, California with his wife and two daughters. His endless summer was to publish a picture magazine, surf, and play golf. Becoming rich and famous did not concern him, nor did having an impressive house in the suburbs. *Life* made this very clear in its photo essay which provoked envy nationwide.

Severson had it made lolling on the California coast, but what about the landlocked dreamers of the endless summer? Why, they drove to the best beach in Arizona. By the late 1960s, surfing was alive and prospering in Tempe. At a recreation center called "Big Surf" a machine-made wave rolled across a 2-1/2 acre lagoon every 40 seconds. Phil Dexter, a Phoenix draftsman, invented the wave machine complex which Clairol, Inc. liked well enough to invest two million dollars in. Clairol marketed hair care products that guaranteed the blond and beautiful look. Lightening hair color while darkening the skin sold a lot of lemons and baby oil to those "closest to nature," and prepared products like Clairol to less-hip customers. "Big Surf" hired Hawaii's premiere surfing champion Fred Hemmings, Jr. as head instructor to underscore that the center was no play pond for inner tubes. Surfing on perfect waves cranked out by a tireless Neptune in the middle of the desert left fad-watchers incredulous. Often as many as thirty riders crowded onto one wave, all of whom chased an endless summer.

The surfing craze took root all along the East and Gulf coasts, where wave production was meager. It took a hurricane to generate a decent wall of water there, unlike the steady sets of waves common off California and Hawaii. No matter, those wanting to surf hit the beaches at sunrise, and more often than not were sorely disappointed. They got revenge by repeating to latecomers a faddish phrase from *The Endless Summer*, "You should've been here an hour ago." Surfing gave birth to a whole subculture of beach life replete with faddish language, dress, and outlook. For some devotees it was the fast-action sport depicted in Brown's documentary; for others an evasive shift from conformity.

## BIBLIOGRAPHY

"The Endless Summer," *Variety*. 243 (May-August 1966) 20.
"Making Waves," *Time*. 94 (October 10, 1969) 97.
Phinizy, Coles, "Instant Ocean: It Just Keeps Rolling Along," *Sports Illustrated*. 31 (November 10, 1969) 7478.
"Riding the Crest of Surfing's Wave," *Life*. 61 (September 9, 1966) 37-38.
"Surf's Up; The Wet-Set Revolution," *Newsweek*. 70 (August 14, 1967) 52-56.

# Exercise Videos

Name recognition is everything in this game. A whole library of exercise videos exists from the "ultimate" fitness package to concentration on just one body part. The videos that sell the best feature a celebrity instructor. Movie star and political activist Jane Fonda is at the top of the pyramid. "Jane Fonda's Workout" started the fad in 1982; other videos have followed and all have been best-sellers, e.g., "Jane Fonda's Prime Time Workout," "Jane Fonda's Challenge," "Jane Fonda's Pregnancy, Birth, Recovery," and "Jane Fonda's Low Impact Aerobic Workout." Over time, she has improved her videos in accordance with new knowledge gained from sports medicine. Her warm-up and warm-down periods are much longer and she avoids "ballistic-type movements" (bouncing). One of the biggest worries of exercise video makers has been how to monitor the participant who huffs and puffs at home alone. If the participant gets hurt, then word-of-mouth will stymie the sale of videos or prompt a change to another program. Heaven forbid anyone having a major health problem while trying to keep up with the relentless instructor. Such anxiety has resulted in slowing down the videos and giving verbal cues that the next exercise is not for beginners.

Women's magazines rate video fitness programs, mainly because most every tape is directed at women. As with fashion, cosmetics, and other consumer items too attractive to resist, the target is the woman's purse, and secondarily her waistline. Beefy ex-Los Angeles Raider Lyle Alzado shows men how to use household items as objects of resistance, but he is an exception to the rule of resculpting women. And the late, prunish ex-dictator Ferdinand Marcos even made an exercise video, but he is an exception to any rule of credible living.

Other celebrities decked out in tights are Raquel Welch, Debbie Reynolds, Mary Lou Retton, and Irlene Mandrell. Three women who achieved celebrity status through physical excellence have also joined the group: Jacki Sorensen (with Fonda first on tape in 1982), Kathy Smith, and Marine Jahan (she performed the strenuous dance numbers in *Flashdance*). These celebrity instructors dominate the field which grows each year as other famous faces exhibit the rest of themselves for our benefit. An ancillary fad is the latest service for stars in Hollywood—a personal fitness trainer. The well-muscled trainer makes a mansion-call to explain nutrition and exercise selection, and then barks encouragement to beat away fat. The current symbol of prestige on Rodeo Drive is to have a "body by Jake." Surely, none of our exercise video queens—all epitomes of discipline—would dare employ these "hunks" to tighten them up? That would be backsliding, renegadism, sacrilege.

Of the group, Jane Fonda is the most charismatic. In her early 50s, she looks great: slim, bright-eyed, and elegant. She does not act the part of love-goddess like Linda Evans and Joan Collins, two other aging actresses. Fonda combines a young girl's charm with a graceful maturity that enchants viewers of her exercise videos. Her lean, shapely body is proof positive of what she sells. She tells women her age: "I'm stronger—physically and mentally—than I was at twenty; my body has better definition because I work at that. I have a few more wrinkles, a few more gray hairs, and that's okay." She also advises women to "go for the burn," that is, work the muscle until it tires. "The risks of starting to exercise in midlife have been exaggerated," she points out, "The real danger comes from not exercising." Fonda's exercise empire is worth many millions of dollars and also includes self-help books, notably *Women Coming of Age* written with Mignon McCarthy. Because of her dedication to lifelong exercise, Fonda joins the ranks of Charles Atlas and Jack Lalanne. If she meets the challenge of subduing flab into her golden years, she will become an icon of American exercise like the two men, and to her credit, be the first woman.

One fad that should not disappear, exercise videos are a boon for people who cannot or will not go to a gym or dance studio. However, it is a well-known fact that people need constant encouragement to keep exercising day after day. People also need a physical fitness environment, a support group, someone to answer their questions, and witnesses to their effort. One's living room does not qualify as a no-nonsense environment; family pets do not count as a support group; no exercise video can answer personal questions; and no one else is there to see that every exercise is completed. Producers pull their hair fretting whether their videos bear repeat viewing. The same smiling faces, tights, and music might get old after awhile. Will the consumer buy another video for variety, or just quit altogether?

Some sports medicine experts criticize the videos for not including enough aerobic exercise, and for not driving home the fact that all the exercise in the world will not readjust fat — only cutting calories will. Another frustration factor is that few, if any, women will ever step into the light of day resembling Jane Fonda. Naturally, it is disheartening if, after a year of "Prime Time Workout," one still looks like Jane Doe.

## BIBLIOGRAPHY

Kaplan, Janice. "Fonda on: Fit After Forty," *Vogue*. 175 (February 1985) 374 + .

Leepson, Marc. "Running in Place — Your Own Place," *Nation's Business*. 75 (February 1987) 64.

Spain, Tom. "New Exercise Line from Esquire and Kartes Targeted at Female Consumers," *Publishers Weekly*. 229 (April 25, 1986) 44 + .

Wilmore, Jack H. "Video Fitness: What's Hot, What's Not," *Vogue*. 175 (October 1985) 499 + .

# Fantasy Baseball

While isolated instances of fantasy baseball can be found going back a generation or more (e.g., Joe Morgan of Middletown, Ohio has operated a league since 1964 called Wheelin' 'n' Dealin' With Your Own Baseball Franchise, and wrote a book about it in 1975), it did not enter the national consciousness until after a group of New York baseball fans, with strong connections in the media, gathered for lunch at an East Side restaurant called La Rotisserie Francaise in January 1980. They all shared the perception that they could run a major-league club better than those actually doing it.

One of the group's prime movers, Dan Okrent, provided the germ of the idea adapted from a system practiced by a professor at the University of Michigan, Bob Sklar, several years before. The "rotisserie" concept included the following features:

- Team owners each have a pot of $260 to bid on players in assembling twenty-three-man rosters from the National League.
- Each roster has nine pitchers, five outfielders, two catchers, and seven infielders.
- Their statistics are computed in four hitting categories (batting average, home runs, runs batted in, and stolen bases) and four pitching categories (wins, earned-run average, saves, and ratio, i.e., hits plus walks per innings pitched).
- There can be trading, waivers and juggling of playing through the disabled list.
- The team with the best overall stats wins the pennant.

The first Rotisserie League utilized *The Sporting News* for stats; later, *USA Today* became the publication of choice for box scores.

The league gained visibility through word of mouth and writings by group members. The concept emerged as a full-blown fad shortly after the publication of *Rotisserie League Baseball (The Greatest Game for Baseball Fans Since Baseball)* (1984), by Glen

Waggoner and Okrent. The 211-page handbook, list priced at $5.95, sold approximately 50,000 copies. Leagues modeled after the New York example began springing up across the nation. While the original rotisserie concept remains the most popular version, many variations can be found in the different leagues regarding the size of rosters, scoring categories, player moves, etc.

Observers of the phenomenon have frequently noted its addictive nature, resulting in absence from family events, the changing of travel plans, etc. Psychologist Jonathan Spivak has offered a number of theories regarding the fanaticism of fantasy baseball buffs:

> The length of the season has a lot to do with it. Baseball is played daily, and you get a jolt of excitement every morning when you read the box scores . . . it sets up a competitive type of thing, where you feel almost like you're down on the field competing against other owners in the league.

The craze is also notable for the impact it has had upon the organized sport scene itself. A growing number of cottage industries have sprung up to serve fantasy players including stat services. One entrepreneur, Jerry Heath of Virginia Beach, Virginia, has expanded from three client leagues in 1985 to 126 in 1988. Established baseball publications have thrived as well in recent years due to fantasy league activities. *Baseball America* doubled its circulation between 1988 and 1989 (19,000 to 38,000), and early in 1989 it increased its frequency from twenty issues to twenty-four a year. For fantasy players, the periodical supplies material on the minor leagues not available elsewhere, and thereby enables them to snap up the best prospects when they hit the majors. *USA Today*, which sells notably more copies on Tuesdays and Wednesdays during the baseball season, when it runs the American League and National League stats, respectively, is considering "some sort of statistical breakout related to fantasy ball." The electronic media have also been affected, with both ESPN and CNN showing fantasy-related stats regularly. Even the major league teams themselves have gotten involved, providing information via phone (as long as it does not interfere with regular business) as well as marketing gimmicks designed to attract this group (e.g., the Houston Astros hosted a "mixer" for local fantasy players on August 15, 1988).

As the 1980s came to a close, the phenomenon has shown no sign of slowing down. With time, it may well achieve permanent institutional status within American sports fandom alongside gambling on games and NFL Sunday Football on the tube.

## BIBLIOGRAPHY

Friedman, Jack. "The Most Peppery Game Since the Hot Stove League? It's Rotisserie Baseball," *People Weekly*. 21 (April 23, 1984) 40-42.

Hiodt, P. "A Draft Day Survival Guide," *Sport* (New York, NY). 79 (May 1988) 71.

Hiodt, P. "Star Search: How to Draft a Dream Team," *Sport*. 78 (May 1987) 83ff.

Morris, Scott and Phil Wiswell. "Games," *Omni*. 7 (December 1984) 172-176. Evaluation of Rotisserie League Baseball (game).

Murphy, Cullen. "A Whole Different Ball Game," *Atlantic*. 255 (June 1985) 30-34.

Walsh, M. "In New York: Major League Fantasies," *Time*. 129 (May 4, 1987) 10-11.

Welch, Wayne M. *The Fantasy Baseball Abstract 1989*. New York: Perigee/ Putnam, 1989.

Wulf, Steve. "For the Champion in the Rotisserie League, Joy is a Yoo-Hoo Shampoo," *Sports Illustrated*. 60 (May 14, 1984) 8-14.

Wulf, Steve. "Rotisserie Revisited; a Founder of Fantasy Baseball Has Second Thoughts," *Sports Illustrated*. 71 (August 7, 1989) 78.

# Mark "Bird" Fidrych

Mark Fidrych enjoyed only one successful season in the big leagues, but oh what a season! In 1976, as a rookie pitcher for the Detroit Tigers, he recorded the following accomplishments:

- He went 19-9 on a next-to-last-place team while leading all major league starters in Earned Run Average (2.34).
- He became the second rookie in history to start in an All-Star game.
- He was voted Man of the Year by the National Association of Professional Baseball Leagues.
- He singlehandedly boosted Tiger attendance by more than 400,000 over the previous years.
- He became the centerpiece of Bird T-shirts, buttons, and records.
- He was greeted by helicopters circling Tiger Stadium.
- At least one man named his baby after him.
- A resolution was introduced in the Michigan state legislature demanding that the Tigers raise his pay, then at the major league minimum of $16,500.
- One competing team, the California Angels, were afraid to disappoint a packed house when he missed a start, so they placed him in a cage in the stadium concourse to sign autographs.
- He was courted by the William Morris Agency, which assisted him in earning $125,000 in endorsements, speaking engagements, and a book.
- He was forced to move into another apartment equipped with a twenty-four-hour security patrol in order to escape his fans.

His appeal to fans went beyond his quality pitching performances. His antics became legendary. As noted by Peter Bonventre:

> Before each inning, Fidrych drops to his knees and uses his hands to rearrange the dirt on the mound. Before each pitch, he talks out loud to himself — and even to the ball. After each out, he struts in a circle around the mound, applauding the teammates — or consoling them for a misplay.

His behavior was natural and spontaneous rather than calculated in nature. Jim Campbell, then president of the Tigers, observed,

> Never in my 37 years of baseball have I seen a player like him, and never will I again . . . He was what he was. All natural. So hyper, so uninhibited.

Teammate Rusty Staub added, at the time, "Mark brings out the exuberance and youth in everybody." All of this was topped by Fidrych's slender, slightly gawky, physical build, crowned by a headful of blonde curls. Although Fidrych claimed that he received his nickname from his first minor league manager for no apparent reason, the Tiger players insisted that he resembled Big Bird of television's "Sesame Street" in both appearance and actions.

The beginning of the end came in March 1977 when Fidrych tore cartilage in his left knee while shagging flies in the team's spring training headquarters at Lakeland, Florida. Then, ten days after returning from the disabled list, his right shoulder popped. He spent all of the 1977 season plagued by arm pain (due, many felt, to his overeagerness to return to form). Most of the next six years were spent in the minors trying to regain his lost form. He tried every possible cure-all: doctors, osteopaths, chiropractors, hypnotists, psychologists, rest, aspirin, anti-inflammation pills, linaments, and even considered various miracle cures touted by fans (e.g., sticking his arm in a swarm of bees, packing it in red Florida clay). Finally, in June 1983, with a 2-5 record and 9.68 ERA with the Norfolk, Virginia minor league club, he was let go.

He tried an assortment of ill-fitting jobs, including promotional work for an auto-parts company, color commentary for the Tigers' cable television network, and a non-speaking role in the film, *The Slugger's Wife*. In the mid-1980s, he settled on a 121-acre farm near his hometown of Northboro, Massachusetts, just to have something to do. Amidst the relative calm of these surroundings, he mused,

> You know, I still get fan mail. I wait a week before I answer it, so it builds up. It sounds crazy but it makes me feel important.

## BIBLIOGRAPHY

Bonventre, Peter. "Sweet Bird of Youth," *Newsweek*. 88 (July 12, 1976) 63.

Clark, Tom. "Mark Fidrych (poem)," In: *The Fireside Book of Baseball*.

Furlong, W.B. "Will Success Spoil the Bird?," *The New York Times Magazine*. (August 22, 1976) 12-13ff.

Green, J. "Cuckoo Over A Rara Avis," *Sports Illustrated*. 45 (July 12, 1976) 39-40.

Smith, Gary. "The Bird Fell to Earth," *Sports Illustrated*. 64 (April 7, 1986) 44-66.

# Bobby Fischer and the Chess Craze

In 1956, Bobby Fischer, then age thirteen, predicted, "I'm gonna win the [chess] world championship, hold it a couple of years, then take up something else and make a lot of money." He would prove correct on all counts; he made good on the first part of his promise by defeating Russian Boris Spassky, 12-1/2 to 8-1/2, at Reykjavik, Iceland in August/September 1972.

Until the emergence of Fischer, Americans had generally dismissed chess as a game for eggheads. However, Fischer's flair for showmanship combined with the pride felt by U.S. citizens in identifying with the success of their Cold War surrogate warrior, resulted in a national mania for the game. Evidence of this newfound popularity for a pastime roughly as old as civilization itself could be found on a wide variety of fronts:

- Chess clubs throughout the country reported their memberships to be swelling.
- Employees in a variety of companies and agencies began organizing their own tournaments.
- Chess became front-page news in many American newspapers.
- Television chess commentators garnered large audiences, most notably George Koltanowski, a retired international master serving as an analyst for San Francisco's KQED, and chess master Shelby Lyman of New York City's educational channel.
- The Reykjavik match proved to be attractive to bettors; in Las Vegas, oddsmaker Jimmy "the Greek" Snyder installed Fischer as a 6-5 favorite at the outset of the match, then raised the odds to 8-5 following the American's early spurt.
- A dying breed—the chess shark—received a new lease on life.

One Manhattan hustler was viewed cleaning up by betting chess novices that he could checkmate them within ten minutes in a game requiring a move every thirty seconds.

• New chess aficionados were grabbing up all the instruction manuals now flooding bookstores. Bantam rushed out a fifth 50,000-book press run of *Bobby Fischer Teaches Chess*, while works analyzing the Reykjavik match were released in droves (e.g., Yugoslav Grand Master Svetozar Gligoric's *Fischer vs. Spassky*, by Simon and Schuster, *Fischer-Spassky: The New York Times Report on the Chess Match of the Century*, by Bantam).

• Retailers began offering a substantially wider variety of chess sets ranging from the functional sets to the bizarre and ultraexpensive (e.g., a $100,000 gold and silver set designed by Antique Dealer Arthur Corbell, and LRH Enterprises' "The Contemporary Game, Chess '72," which pit Republicans against Democrats and employed well-known politicians — Nixon and McGovern were kings — as the major pieces).

Chess insiders — caught up in the euphoria of it all — dared to envision a prolonged U.S. renaissance. They talked about the institution of a U.S. Chess League consisting of six teams, each headed by a grand master, playing once a week with a fast time limit for cable television, climaxing with a chess world series. It would be just a matter of time before all seven American grand masters became household names and earned huge amounts of money in tournaments, exhibitions, and publishing.

Fischer's behavior after winning the championship played its part in dampening the national craze. His incorrigibility, visible enough at Reykjavik (e.g., his use of "non-chess means" to disturb his opponent; for example, not showing up for the originally scheduled first game — thereby forfeiting it, holding out for a change of venue — to Belgrade — and for more prize money, claiming that the playing area was poisoned, and expressing annoyance over the presence of televison cameras), was no longer overshadowed by his genius, and effectively turned off a public accustomed to heroes more committed to playing the public relations game. Of greater significance in the long run, however, was the essential anti-intellectual core of the nation; chess simply was not a part of its soul. Nevertheless, Fischer's abdication of the championship in 1974 effectively terminated the fad.

## BIBLIOGRAPHY

Andrews, P. "Chess Mob on West 10th," *Saturday Review*. 55 (August 19, 1972) 13-14ff.
"Battle of the Brains: Fischer-Spassky Match," *Time*. 100 (July 31, 1972) 32-36ff.
"Bobby and the Black Bishop's Last Raid," *Life*. 73 (July 21, 1972) 52.
"Bobby Checkmates the Cameraman," *Business Week*. (July 22, 1972) 22.
"Bobby's Onslaught," *Newsweek*. 80 (August 7, 1972) 66.
Busch, N.F. "Bobby Fischer: Prodigy of the Chessboard," *Reader's Digest*. 100 (February 1972) 193-194ff.
Cant, G. "Why They Play; the Psychology of Chess," *Time*. 100 (September 4, 1972) 44-45.
"CDC 6400 R-B4ch; Computerized Chess Tournament in Boston," *Newsweek*. 80 (August 28, 1972) 79.
Edmondson, E.B. "All the World's A Pawn," *Newsweek*. 80 (July 31, 1972) 42-46.
Evans, L. "At Last, King Bobby," *Time*. 100 (September 11, 1972) 57.
Evans, L. "Steamroller Ride to the Summit," *Sports Illustrated*. 37 (September 11, 1972) 34-39.
"Game of Kings, War of Nerves," *Senior Scholastic*. 101 (September 18, 1972) 22-23.
"Hot War in Iceland; Spassky-Fischer Match," *Time*. 100 (July 17, 1972) 58-59.
"Infighting in Reykjavik," *Time*. 100 (August 28, 1972) 47.
"Master Bobby," *Newsweek*. 80 (July 24, 1972) 53-54.
"New Game in Town," *Time*. 100 (August 21, 1972) 46-49.
"Nichevo No Longer; Fischer-Spassky Match," *Time*. 100 (August 7, 1972) 34.
Ponce, N. "Chess Crown Returns to the Americas," *Americas*. 24 (November 1972) 25-29.
Richardson, J. "Reykjavik vs. Miami," *Commentary*. 54 (October 1972) 75-77.
Rinard, S. "Check Out Chess; Christmas Gift Suggestions," *McCalls*. 100 (December 1972) 44.
Rogoff, K. "Beating Russia at Its Own Game?," *Seventeen*. 31 (August 1972) 278.
Schonberg, H.C. "Chess at the Summit," *Harper's*. 245 (July 1972) 20ff.
Schonberg, H.C. "Psychic Murder at the Chessboard," *New York Times Magazine*. (September 3, 1972) 13-16.
"Sputtering Start," *Time*. 100 (July 24, 1972) 84.

Steiner, G. "Sporting Scene," *The New Yorker*. 48 (October 28, 1972) 42-46ff.
Wade, N. "Fischer-Spassky Charges: What Did the Russians Have in Mind?,"
    *Science*. 177 (September 1, 1972) 778.
"Waiting for Bobby," *Time*. 100 (July 10, 1972) 58.
Wason, Peter. "The New Interest in Chess; Are We Suffering From a New Chess
    Fever?," *Current*. 143 (September 1972) 44-48.

# Flagpole Sitting

There are fads that people eagerly participate in and there are those that people only watch in wide-eyed wonder. Sitting atop a flagpole for days on end was definitely an exhibition to be gawked at and not tried. For a brief two years (1929-1930) America followed the zany heroics of Alvin "Shipwreck" Kelly. However, his career began earlier in 1924 in Hollywood. A theater manager hired him to attract crowds by, of all things, sitting on a flagpole. Kelly agreed and climbed up on the small perch (a disc 13" in diameter). The stunt produced exactly what it was supposed to — large numbers of people pointing skyward. A huge success, soon other businessmen bid for Kelly's services.

Five years later Kelly was still sitting on flagpoles, now across the country, up to 145 days a year. But these were all stunts paid for by entrepreneurs. The real sport officially got underway in Atlantic City during the summer of 1930. Kelly broke his own endurance record by over 600 hours; he remained atop a flagpole for an incredible 1,177 hours or almost 50 days. When he again touched ground amidst 20,000 onlookers he wobbled a bit before falling into the arms of his wife and son, Alvin, Jr. Just before his descent, a barbarette was hoisted up to give Kelly a haircut, manicure, and liberal spraying of aromatic scent. Presented with a bill for $4.25, the gallant Kelly gave the barbarette $5.00 and waved off the change. This was not the first time he had charmed a lady "off her feet." Back in his advertising days upon hearing that a young woman had slapped a man for calling him a fool, Kelly invited her up to his perch. Then and there he made a date and shortly afterwards they married — the same woman who shared his glory in Atlantic City.

No doubt Kelly was an original. His nickname "Shipwreck" came from a previous career in boxing. Known then as "Sailor" Kelly he hit the canvas so often that ringside fans began shouting, "The sailor's been shipwrecked again." Kelly mastered flagpole sitting through his ability to take five-minute catnaps when needed; he also drank plenty of liquids to avoid dizziness. Flagpole sitting was perhaps the most fanciful fad of the late 1920s unless one considers that Kelly received warm congratulations from Captain Jack Evans, the man who remained buried alive for one week.

So much for the professional circuit, in Baltimore, Maryland, Avon "Azie" Foreman was making history. Fifteen-year-old Avon stuck an 18-foot hickory sapling in the ground and climbed to the top of it. He perched on an old ironing board above the crowd for 10 days, 10 hours, 10 minutes, and 10 seconds to establish the juvenile pole-sitting record. As with "Shipwreck" Kelly there was a best girl waiting on terra firma named Lena who exclaimed several times, "Oh, ain't he grand!" The press had a field day with the Baltimore fad, pointing out that this most irrational act had happened in the ultra-rational H. L. Mencken's own backyard.

> The older Baltimore could hardly believe its ears when it learned the details of the hullabaloo following Avon's descent. For days before this amazing event crowds had gathered nightly to see him perched on his platform upon which bright searchlights had been trained by his father, who is an electrician.

The stunt stimulated Baltimore Mayor William F. Broening who in a speech lauded Avon for demonstrating "that the old pioneer spirit of early America is being kept alive by the youth of today." For his misplaced zeal, the press unmercifully lampooned the Mayor. Avon's instant celebrity inspired other Baltimore teens to take to perching. During one week in 1929 seventeen boys and three girls sat atop poles in an effort to beat Avon. The ever-witty press nicknamed them "stylites" after the early Christian ascetics who lived unsheltered on top of high pillars. Some of the young stylites were not as fortunate as Avon; two of them broke their legs, one an arm, and one girl was ill for days from the experience. But still they climbed atop poles and Mayor Broening continued making speeches about the display of "grit and stamina so essential to success in the great struggle of life."

Frederick Nelson, a writer for *The New Republic*, put the craze in perspective, though he could not explain what had caused the Baltimore outbreak.

> When a boy, through the simple expedient of installing himself in a coop at the end of a pole, can bring the Mayor to call on him, cause a minister of the Gospel to hold services with sermon at the foot of the pole, and be the central occasion for a brass band, scores of popcorn vendors, offers of free dentistry for a year, and a 'write-up' in the newspapers, parental authority . . . avails very little.

All in all, "Shipwreck" Kelly set the standard; the stylites were mere pretenders.

## BIBLIOGRAPHY

"Kelly Quits Perch After Fifty Days." *New York Times.* (August 10, 1930) 22:1.

Nelson, Frederic. "The Child Stylites of Baltimore," *The New Republic.* 60 (August 28, 1929) 37-38.

"Teaching the Young Idea to Sit on Flagpoles," *Literary Digest.* 102 (August 31, 1929) 34-38.

Fifteen-year-old Avon Foreman of Baltimore sits atop an 18-foot hickory sapling in imitation of his hero "Shipwreck" Kelly. "Shipwreck" had already stormed the country once, perching precariously on flagpoles for days on end. Avon set such a fine example of derring-do that within a week after his ascent, 20 + amateur polesitters roosted all over Baltimore. 1929.

# Fletcherizing:
# A Dietary Route to Fitness

Originated by Horace Fletcher, "fletcherizing" advocated chewing food so thoroughly that all flavor was extracted and the remains involuntarily swallowed; therefore, people would eat less, digest their food more easily, and more efficiently use the food they ate. However quixotic his doctrine may have seemed, Fletcher cited his own life as a testament to its value. In the early 1890s, in his late forties, Fletcher's weight had ballooned to 205 pounds on a five-foot, five-and-one-half-inch frame. Denied a life insurance policy due to his weight, Fletcher used his program over a four-month period to pare down to 169 pounds, a weight he remained at or below for the last twenty years of his life. He noted the broader ramifications of his feat in a letter to his lawyer in 1898:

> I have been experimenting with about a dozen people . . . and [have] prove[n] my discovery to be applicable to any condition. It has not only cured obesity and leanness . . . but I have entirely cured indigestion, bleeding piles, catarrh, pimpled skin and a variety of other ailments.

While the popularity of fletcherizing owed something to the boisterous charm and assertive demeanor of its originator, Fletcher's feats of physical strength and endurance proved to be his major asset. The June 1903 issue of *Popular Science Monthly* made a notable impact upon the mass consciousness, recounting tests of Fletcher's prowess in a series of exercises utilized by the Yale rowing team. One of the testers, William G. Anderson, director of the Yale Gymnasium, professed to be most impressed by the fact that Fletcher's condition seemed to result solely from diet, and an unusual one at that (i.e., eating as much as and whatever one wanted), "with no systematic physical training." Anderson felt that fletcherism was "not only practical but agreeable" based upon Fletcher's fitness and evidence that total mastication left "little or no excess material to be disposed of by bacterial agency," which "might account for the absence of toxic products in the circulation."

Fletcher's success also owed something to his ability to align his beliefs with other populist movements; e.g., the back-to-nature vogue. As noted by Harvey Green,

> . . . Fletcher implicitly criticised a civilization he thought had somehow diverted men and women from the purity that was part of life in 'primal times.' He joined Kellogg and other dietary reformers by criticizing 'sav'ry stew,' or highly seasoned dishes, and he blamed cookery for people's digestive troubles. Like many enthusiasts of the arts-and-crafts movement and the colonial revival, he wished to go back in time, to allegedly purer days, when "instincts reigned supreme." This primitivism also harmonized with many aspects of Roosevelt's 'strenuous life' idea; it was also the sentiment that provoked advocates of such contact sports as football to appreciate 'healthy barbarism' in young men.

Fletcherizing declined for a number of reasons:

1. the absence of disciples possessed of Fletcher's flair for the dramatic;
2. Fletcher's lack of interest in physical training troubled many would-be followers; and
3. Fletcher's ideas lost credence in the face of more scientific approaches to the nutrition field.

Despite the virtual disappearance of Fletcher's teachings shortly after his death, mothers continue to admonish their children to "chew their food carefully."

## BIBLIOGRAPHY

Bjorkman, F.M. "Horace Fletcher and Fletcherism," *Independent*. 64 (March 19, 1908) 623-626.

Bjorkman, F.M. "Philosophy of Fletcherism," *Good Housekeeping*. 48 (April 1909) 504-506.

Bjorkman, F.M. "Practical Experiment in Fletcherism," *World's Work*. 15 (February 1908) 9877-9880.

Bjorkman, F.M. "What Fletcherism Really Is," *Ladies' Home Journal*. 25 (November 1908) 38.

Cady, C.M. "Way to Health," *World's Work*. 20 (October 1910) 13564-13568.

"Dietary Righteousness," *Ladies' Home Journal*. 27 (March 1910) 15.

Fisher, H.W. "Eating For Pleasure," *World's Work*. 22 (July 1911) 14600-14605.

Fisher, I. "Instinct to Eat," *Independent*. 63 (August 1, 1907) 267-269.

Fletcher, Horace. "Fletcherizing; the New Diet System," *Harpers' Monthly Magazine*.

Fletcher, Horace. "How I Feel at Sixty-Five," *Ladies' Home Journal*. 31 (May 1914) 25.

Fletcher, Horace. "How I Made Myself Young at Sixty," *Ladies' Home Journal*. 26 (September 1909) 9-10.

Fletcher, Horace. "What I Am Asked About Fletcherism," *Ladies' Home Journal*. 26 (October 1909) 20.

Green, Harvey. "Dietetic Righteousness," In: *Fit For America: Health, Fitness, Sport and American Society*. Baltimore: The Johns Hopkins University Press, 1988, c1986. pp. 283-317.

Hendrick, B.J. "First Man to Stimulate Wide Popular Interest in Nutrition," *McClure's Magazine*. 34 (April 1910) 656-658.

"How a Fletcherite Can Live," *Putnam's*. 5 (March 1909) 762-765.

Hubbard, E. "Gentle Art of Fletcherizing," *Cosmopolitan*. 46 (December 1908) 48-53.

Kahn, R.L. "Wise Eating and Good Health," *Craftsman*. 26 (June 1914) 337-339.

Marcosson, I.F. "Growth of Fletcherism," *World's Work*. 11 (March 1906) 7324-7328.

"Shall We Fletcherize?," *Literary Digest*. 47 (July 26, 1913) 130.

Van Someren, I.F. "Raising Children by Fletcherism," *Ladies' Home Journal*. 26 (October 1909) 55.

Wardell, E. "What One Woman Got Out of Fletcherism," *Ladies' Home Journal*. 30 (March 1913) 69.

Williams, M. "Horace Fletcher's Philosophy," *Sunset*. 24 (March 1910) 284-290.

"Yale's Experiments With Fletcherism," *American Monthly Review of Reviews*. 36 (November 1907) 609-610.

# The Flying Wedge

Walter Camp, the American authority on the game of football during its formative period, described the flying wedge thusly:

> . . . a half dozen good, solid fellows get in motion and concentrate their force and weight, running at full speed against one, two, or three men who are able to get under but partial headway, and who are obliged also to look for the man with the ball coming behind this mass, the shock is pretty severe, and repeatedly practiced, will use up even the stoutest and pluckiest.

A cushioning helmet and body pads were not in use yet, so the flying wedge stopped hearts on and off the football field. All the opposing team saw was a gang of piston-legged granite blocks coming at them with no intention of giving way. Later, protective gear made it much easier for the defense to infiltrate six "solid fellows." But for the moment, fan response to the flying wedge was overwhelmingly positive. Bludgeoning opponents with a triangle of fast-moving muscle brought roars of approval. It was 1894 and those were the days of rough and tumble football which more closely resembled a brawl than an orderly display of sport. In addition to the flying wedge, players indulged in other aggression, manifesting their fierce competitiveness with fists, elbows, and knees. One such incident that became a cause celebre was the Hinkey affair. Captain Hinkey of the Yale eleven was charged with intentionally kneeing Wrightington of Harvard. The blow from whatever source was crippling enough to sideline Wrightington for the rest of the game. Anti-football factions viewed the incident as pure malice and nothing else; to their collective mind Hinkey intentionally wanted to maim Wrightington — if the flying wedge did not get him first. An investigation eventually cleared Hinkey but did little to placate the anti-footballers.

Pro-footballers merely turned their heads and left well enough alone. The flying wedge was a crowd pleaser and besides:

> Brutality in football, as in any other game in which animal strength is a potent factor, depends upon the personality of the player and his proneness to lose his temper or ability to control it. The elimination of brutality rests wholly with the individual.

Anti-footballer response to this casual outlook was to get rid of the brutal individual, or better yet, the sport that encouraged such behavior. Walter Camp and company continued making rules to de-brutalize football. For example, a player receiving a kick downfield should not have his legs cut out from under him as he looks skyward at the ball; nor should he then be driven into the ground like a spike from piling on. Camp's solution was to implement a fair catch rule. On going improvements failed to impress President Eliot of Harvard who wrote in his annual report:

> It should be distinctly understood, however, that the players themselves have little real responsibility for the evils of the game. They are swayed by a tyrannical public opinion—partly ignorant and partly barbarous—to the formation of which graduates and undergraduates, fathers, mothers, and sisters, leaders of society, and the veriest gamblers and rowdies all contribute.

Fans adored the flying wedge. American football was not supposed to be lawn tennis. It was sheer excitement either way: if the wedge worked and the runner scored—fantastic; if the defense pulled off the impossible and tackled the runner—fantastic. Dr. Eliot went on to compare football to cockfighting, bullfighting, and Roman gladitorial combat. He also pointed his finger at the profit motive: "Extravagant expenditure for teams throughout the season and by the spectators at the principal games continues to disgust the advocates of simple and rational manly sports." After the national press reported several deaths from football injuries caused by the flying wedge and other punishing play, Camp's new rules brought about a saner game. Still, it took a few generations to quiet ardent fans who remembered with pleasure the bone-crushing, eye-popping flying wedge.

## BIBLIOGRAPHY

"Did Not 'Knee' Wrightington: Investigation of Charges Against ex-Capt. Hinkey in Springfield Game," *New York Times*. December 17-6-1, 1894.

"Football Come to Stay: Brutality an Incident Not a Necessary Accompaniment of the Game," *New York Times*. December 16-12-5, 1894.

"Football Unfit for College Use: President Eliot Talks of Athletics in His Report on Harvard for Last Year," *New York Times*. January 31-6-4, 1895.

"Less Brutal Football," *New York Times*. December 17-6-1, 1894.

"Rugby Football Brutalized: An English Criticism of Flying Wedge and Mass Plays," *New York Times*. January 8-8-2, 1894.

"Walter Camp on Football Rules," *New York Times*. January 8-8-2, 1894.

Before football became a safer sport, every maiming tactic inflamed fans. Smashing a forearm against glass teeth, kicking an opponent in the groin, piling on to break bones, and the fearsome flying wedge increased attendance dramatically. Due to public outcry, teams tempered their violence and football survived this faddish stage in its development.

# Franchise Shifting
# in Major League Baseball

The fifties saw the onset of transfer fever in major league base-ball following many decades of franchise stability with respect to geographic affiliation. Prior to that time, the majors had been con-fined to the northeast quadrant of the United States; i.e., with St. Louis as both its westernmost and southernmost city. This configu-ration reflected the origins of the game as well as the nation's popu-lation distribution up until the middle of the twentieth century. A complex set of factors set into motion following World War II, however, would render the spread of the majors an inevitability. These included:

1. the cultural intermingling of American G.I.s during the war broadened baseball's appeal and increased the demand for more balanced geographical representation in the big leagues;
2. an increase in the leisure time and disposable income of Amer-icans;
3. the rise of new media to cover the game, particularly televi-sion; and
4. the beginning of a realignment of the U.S. populace first in a more westerly, then southerly, direction.

The situation was exacerbated by the fact that many existing big league cities were represented by two or more teams. Accordingly, those clubs finding themselves hopelessly behind their intra-city ri-vals in the hearts — and pocketbooks — of the local citizens began to cast about for greener pastures. The Boston Braves became the first franchise to relocate, shifting to Milwaukee in 1953. In rapid suc-cession the St. Louis Browns became the Baltimore Orioles in 1954 and the storied Athletics of Connie Mack moved from Philadelphia to Kansas City in 1955. Other franchise owners were quick to note that all teams became successful financially, particularly the Braves, who set National League attendance records and went on to win the pennant in both 1957 and 1958 (and the World Series as well in the former year).

Up until this point, the departing teams were not missed to any great extent by the fans of the original cities in which they had resided. Boston still had its Red Sox; St. Louis, the Cardinals; and Philadelphia, the Phillies. The events of 1957 gave many National League fans and officials second thoughts about the transfer mania then in vogue. On August 19, 1957, the board of directors of the National Exhibition Company, the corporation operating the New York Giants, voted heavily in favor of moving that franchise to San Francisco beginning in 1958. The team president, Horace C. Stoneham, cited declining attendance, an attractive incentives package offered by San Francisco officials, and the inevitability of westward expansion by the major leagues as key factors in making the decision.

If the loss of a club which had been a city institution for seventy-four years — winning seventeen pennants and five world's championships — had shocked New Yorkers, then the October 8, 1957 announcement by Brooklyn Dodgers officials that that franchise would be playing in Los Angeles the following season must have been positively heart wrenching. The Dodgers had represented the borough in the National League since 1890. The team had gained international renown, first due to their zany, erratic mode of play, and later, because of their highly successful post-World War II campaigns. The Dodgers' shift appeared to be highly questionable in that the team — unlike the Giants, who had lost money in six of the last eight years — had been consistently making more money in recent years than any other National League club. The league president, Warren Giles, attempted to diffuse the situation by issuing the following statement:

> The National League has again demonstrated it is a professional organization. The transfer of the Giants and the Dodgers means that two more great municipalities are to have major league baseball without depriving another city of that privilege . . .

Developments in the sixties, however, indicate that the major leagues became committed to a more prudent course of action following the twin bombshells of 1958. Henceforth, franchise expansion was employed more frequently than city-to-city shifting as a means of obtaining representation for baseball in new markets. With respect to cities victimized by the shift mania, New York was awarded a new team shortly thereafter — the Mets — and later moves by the Washington Senators (to Minneapolis), Kansas City Athletics (to Oakland), and Milwaukee Braves (to Atlanta) would be okayed only with the provision that the cities losing clubs be granted new franchises.

## BIBLIOGRAPHY

Angell, Roger. "Farewell, My Giants!," *Holiday*. 23 (May 1958) 82-85ff.

Becker, Bill. "Giants Will Shift to San Francisco For 1958 Season," In: *The New York Times Encyclopedia of Sports*, edited by Gene Brown. Volume 2: Baseball. New York: Arno, 1979. pp. 119-120.

"Gold Rush West; New York Giants," *Newsweek*. 50 (September 2, 1957) 84.

"Home of the Bums and a Migrant Bum," *Newsweek*. 51 (April 28, 1958) 86.

"Left Field in L.A.," *Newsweek*. 51 (February 3, 1958) 85.

Perlmutter, Emanuel. "Dodgers Accept Los Angeles Bid to Move to Coast," In: *The New York Times Encyclopedia of Sports*, edited by Gene Brown. Volume 2: Baseball. New York: Arno, 1979. pp. 120-121.

"Ten-Year Winners? Westward the Course," *Newsweek*. 50 (October 21, 1957) 100.

"Walter in Wonderland," *Time*. 71 (April 28, 1958) 58-60ff.

# Frisbee

After a generation of slow, albeit steady, growth, the Frisbee ascended to superstar status in the 1970s. Perhaps best described as a plastic discus or flying saucer-like object with its outer edge curled under, the Frisbee's ancestry can be traced back with some surety to the late Victorian era, when Yale college students found that tossing the pie tins of an area bakery — the Frisbie Pie Company of Bridgeport, Connecticut, founded in 1871 — offered a modicum of recreational enjoyment. Then, in 1947, two Californians, Fred Morrison and Warren Francioni, constructed a flying disk from plastic. The name — already in use among some aficionados from the start — was eventually copyrighted by the Wham-O Manufacturing Company of San Gabriel, California (misspelling and all; other companies have had to provide their disks with other names).

The Frisbee's spurt in popularity began in earnest when creative enthusiasts began devising various games which offered an alternative to the monotony of simple throwing and catching sessions. One of the earliest breakthrough games was Ultimate Frisbee. A zany mixture of razzle-dazzle football, playground basketball, and soccer, it was invented in a parking lot at Columbia High School in Maplewood, New Jersey in 1969. Its originators were interested in finding a simple, inexpensive, low-key sport geared to the nonathlete. The sport quickly spread to colleges, first in the East and then westward.

The official version (sanctioned by intercollegiate groups, as opposed to sandlot variants) requires an open field measuring sixty yards by forty-five yards, two teams of seven players, a clock to time the two twenty-four-minute halves, and, of course, a Frisbee. Goals are scored by catching the Frisbee in the end zone. The plastic disk can be moved only in the air, and whoever catches it is allowed only three momentum steps before passing it on; when passes are blocked, intercepted, dropped or go out of bounds, possession reverts to the other team.

Ultimate Frisbee has been instrumental in the development and perfection of a special repertory of hard-to-stop releases because the traditional mode of throwing — i.e., holding the plastic disk parallel to the ground and flipping it forward with a backhand motion — proved to be too easily blocked. These have included the thumb throw, the finger throw, and the wrist flip.

Other games include Guts Frisbee (one to five players per team with the teams facing each other along parallel goal lines fourteen meters apart; the obect being to make a toss so fast and accurate that no one of the other team can clearly field it), Circle Frisbee, and Dog-Bee. Variants of existing games include Basebee, Frisbee Football and Folf, or Frisbee Golf. The latter has achieved fad-like status on its own. Developed in California by Wham-O executives, the sport had its first national championship in 1974 at the Rochester (New York) Frisbee Club. At least twenty-five "golf courses" were built in parks around the country between 1975-1977. In 1977, the four courses in Los Angeles were drawing 10,000 players a week, and a tournament in Cragmere, New Jersey was offering a $5,000 purse.

Most Frisbee golf courses have an eighteen-hole layout, with holes rated par three or four. The disk is thrown from a prearranged "tee," usually a cement platform. From its resting place, it is then rethrown over or around various hazards such as trees or statues to reach the "disk-pole hole" — a wire basket on a stick. According to a winner of the Women's Over-All World Frisbee Championship, Monika Lou, its appeal is that "it is cheap, you can play it anywhere, get a lot of exercise, and women can compete too — it is not determined by strength."

The popularity of Frisbee-related activities has slackened off somewhat in the 1980s, probably due in no small part to the seriousness with which the Yuppie generation has pursued fitness. However, it appears likely that wherever self-deprecating humor and off-the-wall creativity are held in high regard, the Frisbee will not be far away.

# BIBLIOGRAPHY

"And Now, Frisbee Golf," *Newsweek*. 90 (September 8, 1977) 48.

Averill, B. "How-To For Frisbee Players," *Mechanics Illustrated*. 74 (December 1978) 24.

Flagg, M.J. "Aerodynamics: Secret of the Frisbee Toss; Skimming a Disk — It's a Living," *Science Digest*. 83 (June 1978) 73-75.

"Frisbee For Fanatics," *Esquire*. 86 (October 1976) 88-89.

Grehen, S. "St. Andrews of Frisbee Golf; Oak Grove County Park in Pasadena," *Parks & Recreation*. 11 (October 1976) 22-23.

"How Serious Can You Be About a Plastic Flying Disc?," *Sunset*. 161 (August 1978) 40-41.

"How to Play and Set Up Your Own Frisbee Golf Course," *Glamour*. 76 (April 1978) 52.

Johnson, Stancil E.D. "A Slightly Slanted Pitch on Frisbees," *Smithsonian*. 6 (September 1976) 179-180.

Johnson, Stancil E.D. "Frisbee Imperiled," *New York Times Magazine*. (July 18, 1976) 47.

O'Rourke, P.J. "Play It Where It Lays; Frisbee Golf in Central Park," *New York Times Magazine*. (June 12, 1977) 24-25.

Park, E. "Around the Mall and Beyond," *Smithsonian*. 8 (January 1978) 14-16.

Reed, J.D. "They Are My Life and My Wife; J. Kirkland and V. Malafrontw, First Frisbee Professionals," *Sports Illustrated*. 42 (February 24, 1975) 62-65ff.

"Ultimate Frisbee," *Time*. 105 (May 26, 1975) 44-49.

"What Next? Why, Frisbee Golf," *Mechanics Illustrated*. 74 (March 1978) 80.

# Game Improvement Sports Gear

Fueled by higher expectations and promises made by sports equipment manufacturers, free-spending baby boomers began viewing technology as the key to athletic prowess by the late 1980s. According to J. Tom Stitus of the Ben Hogan Company, "Game improvement is becoming the buzzword of the industry."

Following a time-honored tradition that shifted into high gear as early as the late 1950s, when P. F. Flyers was successful selling sneakers it said could help you run faster and jump higher, footwear makers have set the pace in the improvement sweepstakes. Brooks Shoes has unveiled its HydroFlow line, retailing for up to $100, which includes a dual-chambered, silicone-filled heel for cushioning and performance. Nike and Reebok International followed with models which enabled wearers to inflate the ankles of their shoes with built-in air pumps.

Manufacturers in other fields also exploited the trend. Hogan was running shifts seven days a week by mid-1989 to meet demand for its new club, called "The Edge." Priced at $630 for a set of nine irons, the clubs featured a hollowed cavity behind the hitting surface and were constructed of forged rather than cast steel — a combination Hogan claimed would improve accuracy. Karsten Manufacturing Corporation's Ping Eye 2 golf club, created by the ex-designer of the electronic guidance systems for the Atlas missile, was banned by the Professional Golfers Association because its square grooves (as opposed to the normal V-shafted ones) increase spin on the ball, giving its users an unfair advantage.

The Wilson Sporting Goods Company may have been the biggest beneficiary of the game improvement craze. Its $225 wide-body racket, which weighed the same as conventional models despite a notably wider frame, was a smash with consumers.

Sports physiologists remained dubious about the potential for equipment to enhance a player's performance. However, as noted by Todd Barrett,

> [such equipment] may help you *feel* stronger, faster and more accurate — and for the true hacker, that's half the game.

## BIBLIOGRAPHY

Barrett, Todd. "Weekend Hackers, Take Heart," *Newsweek*. (July 17, 1989) 41.
— Baseball Bats
Grover, R. "James Easton: Putting a 'Ping' in Baseball's Swing," *Business Week*. (June 13, 1988) 57.
— Footwear
Aaron, E. "Shoes With Built-In Bounce," *High Technology Business*. 8 (September 1988) 8.
"Fancy Footwork," *Gentlemen's Quarterly*. 58 (July 1988) 186-189.
Lewis, R. "Fancy Footwear Fitter," *Health* (New York). 20 (April 1988) 22. Delineates the computerized gait analysis system.
Serrani, P. "The Right Shoe For the Sport," *Gentlemen's Quarterly*. 58 (August 1988) 246-254.
Sweet, H. "Gym Chic: Sporting the Hot New Shoes," *Vogue*. 178 (November 1988) 294.
— Tennis Rackets
Higdon, D.J. "The High-Tech Racket Simplified," *Sport* (New York). 79 (June 1988) 84. Regarding ceramic composites.
Sikowitz, P. "Is Lighter Better?," *World Tennis*. 35 (September 1987) 98.
Sikowitz, P. "Radical Rackets," *World Tennis*. 35 (October 1987) 43-44. Regarding Dynaspot.
Sparrow, D. "Better By a Wide Margin," *World Tennis*. 36 (November 1988) 48-58.
Sparrow, D. "Putting Vibration to Rest," *World Tennis*. 35 (May 1988) 56-58.

# Games of Deception

Gambling in Las Vegas or Atlantic City is no more than a fad for those who go infrequently, but for the inveterate loser it becomes a nightmare. Intelligent people throw away good money at the casinos in these resort areas when they know full well the odds against winning are high. Their glee in handing over dollars, their faces pained, is paradoxical. Of course, the ultimate paradox of gambling is that the player agrees to participate in games of deception in the belief that he or she will not be deceived. Today's gambling casinos are more or less legitimate because they can rely on volume business to earn millions of dollars. Even slight odds in favor of the house will pile up money quickly when thousands of people gamble each week. Yesteryear's games of deception were not quite as legitimate. Supposedly, in the frontier West, people were more gullible and easily fooled. Con men found their dupes at county fairs, circuses, and the like. And no different from today, parents warned their children, and friends their friends, not to get taken in. Yet the newest dupes had to learn the hard truth for themselves, and some never did.

During the latter half of the 19th century "Wheel of Fortune," "Red and Black Spindle," and "Arrow Spindle" were roulette-like games of deception controlled by a secret brake. The dupe picked a number or color off a fancy mechanical device and was allowed to win at first. Then when temptation overcame good sense the operator applied his brake and won every dollar in sight. The dupe naively thought the mechanical device was impartial and as likely to make him a winner as its owner. Another guaranteed profit maker was flipping coins; the con man enticed the dupe into trying his luck at an "honest" game by inviting a third player — a stranger. Of the three, the one who had the odd head or tail won the other two coins. The dupe flipped and flipped, not knowing the stranger was actually a confederate of the con man. Using weighted coins, each time one of them had a head, the other a tail, so that the dupe could only match one of their coins and never win. Another confederate scam was automobile gambling. No sooner had the 20th century ushered in the horseless carriage than con men got to work. One of them begged a ride with the dupe and suggested a little wager. They would bet on the next license plate number they saw, whether it was odd or even. A fifty-fifty chance of winning was too good to pass up. But the dupe had no idea that the con man sitting next to him had a confederate driving close by to deliver a winning "guess" every time.

Slot machines are not modern inventions. In the 19th century they were prevalent and manufactured with gears that could be set to stop regularly on certain numbers — losing ones. A totally dishonest owner could set the machine to never pay off, but that might have discouraged players. Like today, someone has to win occasionally to heat up the action. Operator control of sundry other games of deception continued to madden law enforcement. Similar to Bingo, Keno was played with a goose-neck receptacle for shaking numbered balls, drawn to mark off on a player's card. A skilled operator could shake out any number at any time giving the game to the house. Deception entered the sports arena when owners rigged cockfights by adjusting the blade of the heavily bet on bird to a lethal position; the losing bird's blade was turned nearly flat. In the Old West, saloons held fake lotteries with frequent drawings; the pots were not large, but they consistently went to the house. The half-stewed customers did not seem to notice they never won. Again, the simple device of the confederate working for the house should have been detected, but was not. Simple contraptions controlled by a brake or electricity, confederates, and a little sleight of hand (the infamous shell game), made con men a comfortable living.

The faddish recreation these games of deception provided and still provide is not easy to explain. A sucker born every minute is not the answer to why people are willing to lose their money. A hundred years ago it might be said rubes were the victims, but what about today? Professor Ernest E. Blanche's opening words in *You Can't Win: Facts and Fallacies About Gambling* (1949) are, "The man who can explain why people gamble rates a place beside King

Solomon.'' Then he lists fourteen points to remember about gambling in general:

1. Every system of betting breaks down and fails sooner or later.
2. So-called skill games are really games of chance that even the most skilled players can't beat.
3. The mathematical probabilities are always against the bettor.
4. Luck has very little to do with most gambling games.
5. Gambling has always been and always will be a crooked business.
6. The odds are inevitably against the dice tosser.
7. The roulette wheel operator is ahead of the game before it even starts.
8. Carnival wheels are invariably fixed.
9. Only the race track operators are sure of their take.
10. The numbers racketeers get from 46% to 55% of the money wagered by the public.
11. The card sharper uses a score of tricks to deceive the amateur.
12. Most of the tickets for the Irish Sweepstakes sold in the United States are counterfeit.
13. Punch boards pay out less than half of what they take in.
14. You have only 1 chance in 2,000 of getting any money back in a chain-letter scheme or in Pyramid Club participation.

Las Vegas and Atlantic City have grown by leaps and bounds catering to people who get the itch to gamble. Con men do not have to travel the countryside anymore, victims come to them. The dupes catch a cheap flight, book into a plush hotel at a reduced rate, eat and drink themselves into delirium, see lavish entertainment, and then proceed to pay through the nose for it. The money they save in room and board to get them there to gamble is also a game of deception. Las Vegas and Atlantic City make their stay so inviting that the sting of losing hundreds of dollars is not so bad after all. Mario Puzo, author of *The Godfather* and other best-sellers, wrote *Inside Las Vegas* (1976) to explain the lure of gambling and his past addiction. By the end of the book he was still of two minds:

Gambling is foolish because you cannot win. The casino or house has that 2 percent to 14 percent edge on the player in every kind of gambling. A gambler is a loser. . . . Here is the terrible truth. I got more pure happiness winning twenty grand at the casino crap table than when I received a check for many times that amount as the result of honest hard work on my book. . . . I no longer really enjoy gambling, but the infantile lust can return.

Psychologists continue to study gambling behavior and their research has produced some interesting, if not controversial, results. They have learned that "recreational gambling" increases worker productivity and gives meaning to the lives of people in retirement; that gamblers are more emotionally stable than non-gamblers; and that gambling arouses and stimulates the individual to achieve peak experiences. That is recreational gambling; pathological gambling is another story. Be that as it may, to reiterate: players who participate in games of deception fully believe they alone will not be deceived. Lady Luck will smile on them, and by God they will beat the house. The truly lucky ones will realize that gambling is a faddish pastime and get out quickly.

## BIBLIOGRAPHY

Blanche, Ernest E. *You Can't Win: Facts and Fallacies About Gambling.* Washington, D.C.: Public Affairs Press, 1949.

Brolanski, Harry. "Games and Schemes of Deception." *Frontier Times* 49 (August-September 1975): 22-24, 48-49.

Comstock, Anthony. *Traps for the Young.* New York: Funk & Wagnalls, 1883.

Levinson, Horace C. *Your Chance to Win: The Laws of Chance and Probability.* New York: Farrar & Rinehart, 1939.

Puzo, Mario. *Inside Las Vegas.* New York: Grosset & Dunlap, 1976.

Quinn, John P. *Gambling and Gambling Devices: Being a Complete Exposition Designed to Instruct the Youth of the World to Avoid All Forms of Gambling.* Canton: O.J. Quinn Co., 1912.

# Gliders

Between world wars, interest in aviation ran high. All forms of flying and types of aircraft fascinated those who kept up with the rapidly changing scene. Smitten Americans dreamed of owning a small airplane one day and maybe even a glider. Lieutenant H. E. Reynolds, writing for *St. Nicholas Magazine* in July 1930, offered encouragement:

> One of the beauties of this glider craze, which is now sweeping over the country, is the fact that these little machines can be constructed very cheaply at home. The writer has built a primary training glider from plans secured from an airplane supply company located in the Middle West. . . . The sport of gliding is here indeed, firmly established as an American institution.

Launching a homemade glider required having at least four to six friends to pull tow lines attached to the aircraft to create lift for takeoff (unless the pilot had access to a dirigible, which was unlikely). A training school for Navy glider pilots in Cape Cod provided just such an imposing mother ship. Lieutenant Ralph S. Barnaby made news by being the first glider pilot to drop from a dirigible, the *Los Angeles*. His German-made glider weighed 200 pounds and severed its tie with the *Los Angeles* at 3,000 feet, landing at Lakehurst, New Jersey after a thirteen-minute flight. The Germans led all other countries in the development of gliders and used glider flying as part of basic training for pilots. Every media glider story stimulated the public. But the real impetus came when the world famous Lindberghs experimented with the emerging sport.

First, Charles Lindbergh flew a glider aloft for thirty minutes reaching an altitude of 500 feet to qualify for a first-class license. Thus, he became only the ninth holder of a motorless flying license in the United States. Next, Mrs. Lindbergh sat in the pilot's seat but stayed aloft for only six minutes and ten seconds, qualifying for a second-class license. Uncooperative updrafts sabotaged her flight, though photographs of her dressed in a man's overalls, looking enveloped but cute, graced many a journalistic page. Not long after America had taken to heart the Lindberghs' love of gliders, another story appeared. In California, Charles found himself piloting a stricken glider. One of its controls had simply fallen off and hit the ground. He was able to maneuver the aircraft close to a landing, but then a wind current sent him soaring out of sight over a hill. Ground observers feared the worst. When they caught sight of him again he had landed the glider safely — if not exactly where he was supposed to. Everyone was relieved. To have lost Charles Lindbergh, America's greatest pilot, in an ignominious glider accident would have been inexcusable. Also in 1930, Captain Frank M. Hawks completed the first flight across the United States in a glider towed by an airplane. His daredevil exploit elicited admiration especially after his telling of what happened:

> Between Syracuse and Buffalo I experienced the toughest tow-flying of the entire flight. Twice I began to fear that I might join the Caterpillar Club, via my parachute. The wind was so strong and gusty that, nose the Eaglet down as I might, at sharper and sharper angles, I could not make it descend until the wind abated.

The Lindbergh and Hawks stories should have dissuaded the public from attempting the hazardous sport. Instead, the harrowing accounts added glamour and romance to the chancy enterprise of motorless flying.

Divided into four classes, the first class of gliders was the hanging or suspension type. The pilot hung by his arms from the wings and shifted his body weight to control the glide of the machine. This prototype has had a recent rebirth in California where fans of the sport (called hang-gliding) jump off cliffs to soar over the Pacific. The second class was much better built and had a full set of standard airplane controls. Its wingspread was thirty-three feet with an open fuselage. The third class added an enclosed cockpit which greatly advanced glider design, reducing wind resistance. The fourth class exhibited a streamlined design and a sixty-foot wingspread, the wingtips tapered to dagger points. In the Navy's hands, gliding was a "safe sport." When the public constructed gliders and flew them without benefit of training, the results were often less than perfect. Americans dearly wanted to join the birds and gliding seemed to grant them that desire. But the cost of owning a glider and the obvious element of danger were drawbacks. Gliding never approached Lieutenant Reynolds' assertion that it was "firmly established as an American institution."

## BIBLIOGRAPHY

Barstow, J. "How I Broke the World's Glider Record," *Popular Mechanics*. 54 (July 1930) 1-3.
"Hawk's Coast-to-Coast Air-Train," *Literary Digest*. 105 (April 19, 1930) 13.
"Making America Glider-Conscious," *Literary Digest*. 104 (February 22, 1930) 39-40.
Reynolds, H.E. "Gliding, Safe Sport," *St. Nicholas*. 57 (July 1930) 680-681.

# Gouging

Before bare-knuckle fighting came into vogue — no picnic itself — brawling backwoodsmen engaged in maiming contests. Boxing by the rules in 18th century America was unheard of, so a fight ended up being a barbarous affair. The disputants could use any physical weapon they had, and by a perverse code of conduct, a sharpened fingernail was their most potent one. Indeed horrible to contemplate two centuries removed, these ignorant early Americans actually tried to dig a fingernail under each other's eyeball to pop it out of its socket. Called gouging, a number of witnesses have left written testimony describing the abhorrent practice. Other types of maiming occurred such as a chewed-up ear and nose, or completely severed ones; hunks of flesh ripped out from every part of the body; and "kicking one another on the Cods, to the Great damage of many a Poor Woman." An Englishman, Isaac Weld, claimed he saw four or five men castrated by kicking, gouging, biting, or a combination of all three.

Because of the hideous aspect of meeting a man with a missing eye — his socket excavated like an apple by a worm — gouging came to stand for the whole event. These rural southerners clashed at the drop of a hat; simple name-calling might start them at one another. To say to a man then, "You buckskin," was like hissing out "poor white trash" today. The bloody battles hinged on very little worth fighting about, and from the accounts of those who watched them, appeared to be merely attention-getting devices. Often a fight would not take place until a crowd had gathered, somewhat dissipating the heat of the moment.

Another Englishman, Thomas Anburey, left this chilling exchange:

"You have come off badly this time, I doubt?" declared an alarmed passerby on seeing the piteous condition of a renowned fighter. "Have I," says he triumphantly, shewing from his pocket at the same time an eye, which he had extracted during the combat, and preserved for a trophy.

Weld and Anburey might not have seen gouging before coming to America, but it was not unheard of in Great Britain. As late as 1838, "Rules of the London Prize Ring" outlawed gouging, which means it must have been a brutal reality for some time prior. American artists depicted the implements of a gouger; in one such rendering the human hands look more like animal claws. Two or three nails on each hand are grown out an inch or more, sharpened, and fired to make them hard. A finger is missing on one hand — bitten off either before or after it had done its gouging. Incidently, teeth were also filed to points all the better to rip and tear. A Harvard-educated Presbyterian minister, Timothy Flint, wrote, "I saw more than one man who wanted an eye, and ascertained that I was now in the region of 'gouging.'" The infernal region Flint entered was the Mississippi Valley on his way to Louisiana. Like attending to any other sign of danger, evidence of gouging sobered one quickly. The clear signal was that men of crazed disposition stalked the earth not far ahead.

Some revisionist historians and folklorists wonder whether gouging was a common practice among backwoodsmen. Elliott J. Gorn, who has written persuasively on the subject, illuminates the controversy:

> Frontier braggarts enjoyed fulfilling visitors' expectations of backwoods depravity, pumping listeners full of gruesome legends. Their narratives projected a satisfying, if grotesque, image of the American rustic as a fearless, barbaric, larger-than-life democrat. But they also gave Englishmen the satisfaction of seeing their former countrymen run wild in the wilderness. Gouging matches offered a perfect metaphor for the Hobbesian war of all against all, of men tearing each other apart once institutional restraints evaporated, of a heart of darkness beating in the New World.

Gorn and others make a good case for gouging as primarily a tall tale with only isolated examples of its practice occurring. But moralistic Englishmen were not the sole observers of gouging; the meaning of the word itself was understood from London to New Orleans; and the artist depictions are all too real to dismiss. History textbooks mention rough-and-tumble fighting on the frontier, though usually fail to describe one man scooping out the eye of another, while that man seeks to bite off his tormentor's testicles. Probably all for the best to believe that gouging dwells in the realm of fable. Yet, should bear-baiting, cockfights, gander pulls (speeding by on horseback to tear the head off a gander), and other blood sports also be consigned to myth? Gouging ceased to interest savage men when pistols and Bowie knives became more prevalent. Then what used to take a whole afternoon to do could be accomplished in less than a minute with cleaner results.

## BIBLIOGRAPHY

Gorn, Elliott J. "'Gouge and Bite. Pull Hair and Scratch': The Social Significance of Fighting in the Southern Backcountry," *The American Historical Review*. 90 (February 1985) 18-43.

Moore, Arthur K. *The Frontier Mind: A Cultural Analysis of the Kentucky Frontiersman*, Lexington: University of Kentucky Press, 1957.

Parramore, Tom. "Gouging in Early North Carolina," *North Carolina Frontier Journal*. 22 (1974) 58 + .

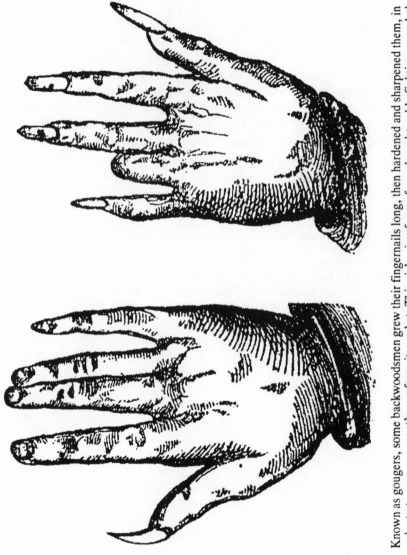

Known as gougers, some backwoodsmen grew their fingernails long, then hardened and sharpened them, in order to tear an opponent's eye from its socket. This sickening form of rough-and-tumble fighting appealed to the rowdy frontier mentality. The missing finger was bitten off during a bloody battle, which of course was better than losing an eye.

# The Herkie Jump

Lawrence Herkimer, known throughout the United States as Mr. Cheerleader, will forever be remembered as the creator of the Herkie jump. While considerably more difficult acrobatic stunts exist, this all-purpose leap best captures the energy and exuberance identified with cheerleading. The maneuver consists of the jumper entering into what appears to be a free-form splay, the right fist punching the air and the left hand resting firmly on the hip, the left leg thrusting forward and the right leg bent at the knee and tucked behind in a modified midair split.

Joe Nick Patoski provided a survey of its origins in an article appearing in *Texas Monthly*:

> Herkimer first developed the Herkie jump at North Dallas High School in the early forties. Being the shortest kid in his class had led the young gymnast to a career on the sidelines, exhorting crowds to show their school spirit. He perfected the move at SMU, where he was head cheerleader during the Doak Walker era. "Actually, the Herkie was the natural way I jumped in college," Herkimer says. "I used to jump real high. When I did, I would swing my right arm up to help me get off the ground, and it would jerk my right leg up behind it. The right arm is the counterweight, the spark for the takeoff. Before I knew it, people started imitating me."

Immediately following college, Herkimer was recruited by Sam Houston State band director Clint Hackney to work with cheerleaders at the latter's drum major and baton twirler camp. Four years later, in 1951, the success of his training program spurred Herkimer to resign from his physical education instructor's post at SMU to found the National Cheerleaders Association.

Under the corporate banner of National Spirit Group, his Dallas-based organization had grown into a fifty-five-million-dollar business by the late 1980s which trained cheerleaders annually across the nation and abroad. Herkimer holds the patent for Pom-poms (a crepe-paper-on-a-stick device) and has created specialized activities such as an aerobic program called Cheerobics. He has also continued to farm out many of his NCA cheerleading, drill team, and dance instructors, as well as the best students culled from clinics, to participate in such events as the Macy's Thanksgiving Day Parade, the Saint Patrick's Day Parade in Dublin, the Cotton Bowl, and NFL halftime exhibitions in Tokyo and London. And all the while his earliest creation, the Herkie, has, due to its elusive quality of timelessness, endured three generations of cheerleading.

## BIBLIOGRAPHY

Patoski, Joe Nick. "The Herkie Jump," *Texas Monthly*. 17:10 (October 1989) 146-147.

# Hoosier Hysteria

Each year between October and March, the entire state of Indiana submits to an affliction known as "Hoosier Hysteria." Case in point #1: *Sports Illustrated* documented the start of the Indiana basketball season at Warren Central High at one second past midnight on Monday, October 8, 1984 — a start calculated to "get a jump on the rest of the state." Case in point #2: In 1984, California — the most populous state and one of the game's hotbeds — drew almost 200,000 to its Division I, II, and III playoffs. Indiana, with eighteen million less people and one-third the number of high schools, had well over one million spectators for its state tournament (which, until recently, was not divided into divisions based on schools' sizes). As noted by Bruce Newman,

> That's Hoosier Hysteria — love and death and lunacy, one of America's goofiest tribal rites. "This isn't a game in Indiana, it's a religion," declares Howard Sharpe, who has coached in the state for 45 years. "There was a year once when nobody was buried in Indiana for a week. Big snowstorm paralyzed everything . . . And there were 250 high school basketball games played in the state that week. They just put the people on snowplows and brought 'em to the gymns."

Although basketball was invented by Dr. James Naismith in Springfield, Massachusetts in 1891, the first game ever played outside of that state was in Indiana — a YMCA match in Crawfordsville in spring of 1893. Dr. Naismith, upon attending the Indiana state high school final in 1925, noted, "The possibilities of basketball as seen there were a revelation to me."

By this time, Indiana's reputation as the basketball capital of America had spread across the nation. Famed sportswriter Grantland Rice paid tribute to its status in the poem, "Back in 1925":

Round my Indiana Homestead
As they sang in days gone by.
Now the basketballs are flying
And they almost hide the sky;
For each gym is full of players
And each town is full of gyms
As a hundred thousand snipers
Shoot their goals with deadly plims.

Jerry Hoover, an assistant coach at Indiana State, recounted,

If you went into the military and said you were from Indiana, they automatically told you to report to the gym. A lot of guys were saved from KP, guard duty and generally getting their asses shot off because they were from Indiana.

While ascertaining just why Indiana's love affair with basketball—particularly the high school version—has exceeded that of other states would be difficult to do, a number of determinants of note include: (1) the long, cold winters; (2) the relative lack of competing activities during the game's formative years; (3) the early date at which basketball put down roots in the state; (4) the fierce rivalries that quickly sprang up; (5) the extremely effective administrative record of the Indiana High School Athletic Association (established in 1903); and (6) the contributions of a number of talented coaches.

Despite the state's continued association with the sport, however, the great days of Indiana basketball—which began shortly after World War I—were over by the mid-1960s. Reasons for the decline included the consolidation of schools (which, although improving the overall quality of public school education, terminated the close allegiance many local citizens had felt for their respective teams), the splitting up of larger high schools, television (which provided an increasing number of entertaining programs—including many basketball games—within the privacy of one's home), increased family income (which led many to eat out more as well as to seek out alternative forms of recreation), and the building of better highways, which brought Indianapolis closer. Still, hoosiers follow the game assiduously to the present day, and talk about it morning, noon, and night.

Basketball has also left its mark on the social fabric of the state to a degree which has affected even those rare souls who are not actual fans of the game. For instance, public school integration appears to have resulted largely because the prospect of all-black schools dominating the state tournament spurred citizens to accept the lesser of two evils. More recently, moviegoers around the nation (and abroad) were applauding *Hoosiers*, a film which adapted the combined history and mythology of Indiana high school basketball (little Milan High, with only 161 students, of whom 73 were boys, won the state championship in 1954 against almost impossible odds) into a morality play about the meaning of life and the American way.

## BIBLIOGRAPHY

Aitken, L. "Milan, Indiana Still Weeps For Joy Over Its 1954 Championship Team That Inspired *Hoosiers*," *People Weekly*. 27 (March 30, 1987) 34-35.

Halberstam, David. "The Basket-Case State," *Esquire*. 103 (June 1985) 137-140ff.

Lang, J.S. "Indiana Goes A-Courtin'," *U.S. News & World Report*. 101 (December 8, 1986) 73-74.

Newman, Bruce. "Back Home in Indiana," *Sports Illustrated*. 62 (February 18, 1985) 38-60.

Nuwer, H. "Hoosiermania," *Saturday Evening Post*. 259 (March 1987) 52-53ff.

Wind, Herbert Warren. "The Heart of Kokomo," *The New Yorker*. 56 (April 14, 1980) 53-100.

# Horseless Carriage Races

In 1896, Charles Duryea won the first significant horseless carriage race in America. Thirty vehicles were entered but only six showed on race day. Of the six, four belonged to the Duryea Motor Company of Springfield, Massachusetts. The remaining two entries were a Booth-Crouch carriage and the Roger Carriage, a French invention. The course for the Cosmopolitan Horseless Carriage Race was from City Hall, New York to Irvington and back, the day was May 30th, Decoration Day, and the purse was a respectable $3,000. The judges agreed to employ the following points system to score the race: top speed maintained by vehicle, 35 points; simplicity of construction and durability of vehicle, 30; ease in operating and safety of vehicle, 25; and cost of vehicle, 10 — for a maximum of 100 points. As the carriages awaited the start of the race a crowd of onlookers grew to such proportions that police reserves stood ready to maintain order. At five minutes to noon, the six fanciful vehicles began their assault on the streets which had not been cleared for the race.

> The ride through the city was very exciting. The carriages dodged back and forth in front of and around cable cars and wagons and demonstrated beyond argument that the horseless carriage is much more capable of control than the ordinary horse and carriage. They passed through the most crowded portions of the city, which was in holiday attire in honor of the day. . . . The only serious accident of the day occurred on the Boulevard, where a wheelman was run into and seriously hurt by one of the horseless carriages. The operator was arrested.

At 7:13 p.m. Duryea crossed the finish line amidst cheers and hurrahs. In the words of the *Scientific American* reporter who was at the scene, "The trial proved beyond question that the American horseless carriage of the day is a success and is well adapted for use in our city, as it appears that it can be turned and stopped more easily than ordinary vehicles." The same reporter had written just a few lines before about the accident-arrest and that on Peabody Hill "several of the carriages met with misfortune." But that was part of the sport. The horseless carriage was revolutionary and here to stay.

> The five horse power Benz motor is actuated by gasoline. The ignition is produced by an electric spark; the cylinder is cooled by a water jacket; the power is transmitted to the rear wheels by means of belts, sprockets, and chains. Two belt shifters permit different speeds, and differential gear allows the back wheels to turn with ease. . . . The race demonstrated that the pneumatic tires were better adapted for the motor carriages than the solid tires.

One month after the New York race, the Rhode Island State Fair Association announced that $5,000 would be given away in prizes in a series of horseless carriage races to be held in September. This time, instead of motoring on the street, the races would take place on a regulation trotting track—the final ironical insult to the horse. The Providence Horseless Carriage Race established these rules: vehicles must be able to show a rate of speed equal to 15 miles per hour to compete; vehicles must carry one person in addition to the driver (weight 165 pounds); only vehicles propelled by other than animal power are allowed to compete; and vehicles are not limited in number, but no one owner can enter more than one carriage and start the race (presumably the anti-Duryea rule). One doubting Thomas, speaking of the rage for horseless carriage races, wrote in another article for *Scientific American:* "Certainly no 'infant industry' was ever so coddled and fostered by the offer of larger rewards; up to the present time the results in this country have not been worth the cost." He was a poor prophet indeed.

At the turn of the century, an event as novel as horseless carriage racing drew fervent crowds. The fad of watching the races greatly accelerated growth of the incipient automobile industry. If Duryea and the other carriage makers had only exhibited their machines in showrooms, public acceptance of the new invention would have taken longer. Races were the perfect contrivance for generating excitement in moving from the stable to the garage.

## BIBLIOGRAPHY

"Cosmopolitan Horseless Carriage Race," *Scientific American*. 74 (April 4, 1896) 377-378.

"New Horseless Carriage Race: Rhode Island State Fair," *Scientific American*. 74 (May 16, 1896) 307.

"Rules of the Providence Horseless Carriage Race," *Scientific American*. 75 (August 1, 1896) 122.

Not immediately thought of as utilitarian, the automobile first gained acceptance as a sporting vehicle. This 1907 race photograph shows a predominately male audience liking, but also not sure what to make of, the new-fangled contraption.

# The Hot Rod Cult

Robert Boyle defined the hot rod cult as the most popular form of "automobilism" (a term denoting a devout interest in cars entirely apart from their use as transportation). Hot rodding developed rapidly from the late 1940s, when there were only 3,000 hot rodders in the United States, to an estimated one and a half million by the early 1960s, the peak period of the craze. Their impact included the spending of more than $250 million per annum on car-related products as well as influencing automotive design; the Chrysler 300 represented but one mass-produced line incorporating hot rod innovations.

While most hot rodders were males between fourteen and forty years old from working-class backgrounds, Boyle ascertained several major hierarchical categories:

> At the bottom of the hierarchy, which feeds upward in baseball farm system fashion, is a high school youngster with a hot rod that might go, show, or show and go. More often than not, the youngster will belong to a car club. If he does, he will exhibit a club plaque in the rear window of his rod and wear the club jacket to school. . . . Most clubs have an aggressive, evocative name: Black Widows, Cam-Twisters, Cannibals, Demons, Igniters, Miss-Fits, Nomads, Satans, Shafters, Undertakers, Vampires, Vandals, Voodoos, Wipers.
>
> Higher in the hierarchy is a more or less independent rodder in his twenties. Many of his contemporaries will have given up hot rodding—half the hot rodders are teen-agers—but he has stayed with it and channeled his passion in a particular direction. If he is interested in the "show route," he will spend hour after hour adding new touches to his car. If he is interested in racing, he will spend an equal amount of time tinkering with his "dragster," nothing more than an engine

on wheels. The dragster is run only on a drag strip, a straight-
away quarter-mile course where rodders stage acceleration
races against one another in pairs, or individually against the
clock. . . .

At the top of the hierarchy is a speedster like Mickey
Thompson, who drives a Streamliner, a car specially built to
perform on the Bonneville Salt Flats in Utah.

The sudden growth of the cult gave rise to an entire culture. Central to this world was the hot rodders' own slang, a melange of bop
talk, beat talk, teen talk, and paragese. Some of the more exotic
terms included:

| | |
|---|---|
| bear, beast | a good car |
| pig | car that's "nothing" |
| Sally Rand | car with "no radio, no heater, no nuthin'—stripped" |
| gook wagon | car with tabooed ornamentation |
| stove | Chevrolet |
| can | Ford |
| deuce | sporty 1932 Ford, probably the most desirable machine a hot rodder could own |
| Cherry | untouched |
| to channel | to lower the body of a car |
| to chop | to lower the top of a car |
| mutha | connotes endearment (e.g., "Look at that mutha go!") |
| let's dance or let's make it | let's do it |
| shuck | talk |
| shams, fuzz, heat | police |

The mass media—which were quick to capitalize upon the phenomenon—played a key role in spreading awareness of hot rodding
to the general public. Toy manufacturers swamped the retail outlets
with hot rod model kits. Hollywood cranked out a series of lame,
technically inaccurate (according to members of the fraternity)
films with titles such as *Drag Strip Girl*, *Hot Rod Gang*, and *Ghost*

*of Drag Strip Hollow*. A slew of paperback hot rod novels also appeared (e.g., *Street Rod*).

The record industry was particularly successful in exploiting the craze. The first genre recording, "Hot Rod Race," released in November 1950, sold 200,000 copies. "Transfusion," by Nervous Norvus (Dot, 1956), infused black humor into the fad and sold about one million copies. The Beach Boys—along with imitators such as Jan & Dean, the Ripchords, Ronnie & the Daytonas, etc.— raised the genre to an art form in the early 1960s with hit records like "Little Deuce Coupe" and "Shut Down." Riverside Records went after the hardcore enthusiast, releasing albums containing only the sounds of the engines themselves.

The craze soon elicited a notable backlash from the public at large. Laws were passed which aimed at penalizing various activities of hot rodders, and some educators went so far as to deplore ownership of any car by a high school student. Sociologists, psychologists, and psychiatrists also tended to explain the phenomenon in negative terms. Dr. Eugene Kaplan, of Long Island, noted the differences between "go" and "show" hot rodders as follows:

> . . . the "customizer" was sicker, saddled with a larger component of peooedipal conflicts, most deficient ego-organization, stronger passive tendencies with consequently greater emphasis on the negative oedipal conflict, more pronounced identity conflict, and more intense ego-superego tension. Whereas the "customizer" had not achieved a stable body-image and sense of identity, and therefore still had to cope with the overwhelming preoedipal mother, the "hot rodder" had achieved all this, and was struggling primarily with oedipal conflicts.

While the hot rod cult has never really disappeared—professional drag racing and customizing spinoffs such as easy riders are flourishing today—its impact on the general public has diminished considerably since the mid-1960s, a casualty of the rash of imported cars, economy-minded engineering, and newer youth-oriented pastimes such as drug taking.

# BIBLIOGRAPHY

Borhek, J.T. "Rods, Choppers, and Restorations: the Modification and Re-creation of Production Motor Vehicles in America," *Journal of Popular Culture*. 22 (1989) 97-107.

Boyle, Robert H. "The Hot Rod Cult," In: *Sport — Mirror of American Life*. Boston: Little, Brown, 1963. pp. 135-179.

Dianna, J. "NHRA Teardown," *Hot Rod*. 22 (June 1969) 72-74.

Herlis, Bob. "Holy Hollywood; the King of the Kustomizers Puts the Cars of the Stars on the Auction Block," *Car and Driver*. 29 (February 1984) 35-39.

Horsley, Fred. *Hot Rod It — And Run For Fun!* New York: Prentice-Hall, 1957.

Lang, B. "Hot Rod Magazine Drags Or, Lights Out!," *Hot Rod*. 21 (June 1968) 44-47.

McFarland J. "Hot Rod Twentieth Anniversary; Scrapbook, 1948-1968," *Hot Rod*. 21 (January 1968) 28-39.

Moses, Sam. "The Man Who Would Be Greyhound," *Sports Illustrated*. 55 (September 23, 1985) 45-49.

Unger, H. "Girls Are Hot Rodders Too!," *Hot Rod*. 14 (May 1961) 90.

# Hot Tubs

Soak away fatigue and care each time you slip into the swirling water; enjoy your family even more in a communal bath; return to romance with your spouse or friend in the intimacy of your own backyard; and do not forget to show off the fine wood tub and tropical setting to your neighbors. These were the allurements of hot tubbing in the last half of the 1970s. For the weekend warrior and home gardener, the hot tub became a place of sanctuary at the end of a long day. Water, bubbles, and splashing, always favorites with children, enticed adults just the same. As for lovers, an invitation to go hot tubbing meant only one thing: champagne, no swimsuits, and little conversation. Though no more than a large half-barrel, the tub was a work of art. Its staves came in redwood, teak, oak, cedar, or some other rot-resistant wood. In California, where hot tubs originated and became a way of life, redwood was the most popular around the San Francisco area; around Los Angeles it was not uncommon to see a mahogany tub. Usually surrounding the tub was a whole hothouse of humidity-loving plants; they provided color and a lush atmosphere for the tubbers to enjoy.

It may or may not be difficult to determine why hot tubs evolved when spas were just as good. The spa looked much different from the tub yet provided the same warm comfort. Made of molded fiberglass with a smooth interior surface of gelcoat or acrylic, spa sales lost ground to the cruder tub. The heating, filtering, and hydromassage action were identical, still the tub predominated. By 1979, 300,000 hot tubs had been sold for installation inside the home or outside in the garden; manufacturers expected to sell another 120,000 before year's end. The cost of one ranged from $1,000 to $6,000. *Sunset*, a California publication, offered plans for building a hot tub; the $3.50 guide explained that the do-it-yourself handyman needed $400 for the wood, base, etc. and $800 for the support system to run the tub. For not too many more dollars an entire swimming pool, ten to twenty times the size of a hot tub, could be constructed by a contractor. But no one thought about things like that in the delirious days of hot tub mania. Kids screamed for them, backache sufferers looked to them for nirvana, and men's magazines promoted them as the ultimate aphrodisiac.

All was well in hot-tub land until notice of the first death from hyperthermia made the news. A couple in Simi valley, California outside Los Angeles were found dead, floating in their hot tub. The Ventura County medical examiner pronounced them victims of heatstroke. The couple had been basking in 114-degree water — ten degrees hotter than recommended by all manufacturers of hot tubs. Most likely, they stayed in the dangerously hot water for more than twenty minutes, also a manufacturers' limit. Their bodies tried to sweat in a vain effort to return to normal body temperature but could not because of their immersion in the hot water. Their hearts pumped faster to supply blood to the skin's capillaries to force out the sweat, which in turn deprived the brain of oxygen, making them light-headed. Alcohol intake, thought to cool the body, actually placed an additional strain on their hearts. They fainted, lapsed into a coma, and died.

Other warnings followed. Researchers discovered that in addition to death, overly hot water and extended immersion caused miscarriages, birth defects, and vaginal infections in women, and skin infections in both men and women. People with heart problems were told to stay out of hot tubs altogether. However, the lethal blow to hot tubbing came in the early 1980s and worried people more than the foregoing, palpable reasons. Acquired Immune Deficiency Syndrome (AIDS) was a new insatiable killer that spread its virus when a clean person came in contact with the seminal/vaginal fluids of an infected person. Reactionaries swore that a hot tub was the perfect incubator for AIDS, considering the type of uninhibited activity associated with it. A fear grew that the virus that causes AIDS lay like scum on the water just waiting for a human host. Hot tubs had already gone public with the expansion of communal clubs. In many hip metropolitan areas these clubs catered to parties of fun lovers who behind closed doors did anything they wanted to in the hot tubs. After AIDS, the less hygienic clubs vanished without a trace.

The fears that slowed the spread of hot tubbing were somewhat irrational. Spas, saunas, and hot communal baths are age-old pleasures enjoyed in Scandinavia and Japan. These people know how to take pleasure without endangering themselves. As fad would have it here, Americans tend to throw themselves into something easily and just as easily retreat from it if it bites.

## BIBLIOGRAPHY

Chester, Mark. "Barrel of Fun," *American Home*. 80 (June 1977) 36 + .

"Cooling It," *Time*. 113 (June 18, 1979) 62.

Flower, Joe. "Hot Tub: A Rub-a-Dub Guide to the Sensuous Sport of Soaking," *Oui*. 8 (April 1979) 76 + .

"The Hot Tub Pros and Cons: Should You Consider Getting Yourself into Hot Water?," *Sunset*. 163 (July 1979) 76-79.

"Of Hot Tubs and Hyperthermia," *Consumers' Research Magazine*. 62 (November 1979) 12.

# Hula Hoops

While small boys have played with hoops for centuries, the entire world became obsessed with them for a six-month period in 1958. The boom began in the spring in Los Angeles when Spud Melin of the Wham-O Manufacturing Company took note of the phenomenal sales of hoops in Australia and made a few prototypes out of a light, stiff polyethylene plastic formed into a circle held together by a wooden plug and staples. After he demonstrated them personally at local parks and schools, kids began buying them by the thousands. The craze quickly spread east. Grown-ups even got into the act. By September 1958, Wham-O's San Gabriel plant was turning out 20,000 hoops daily and was still falling behind on orders. In the meantime, over forty more novelty makers hopped on the hoop wagon, and sales, retailing from one to two dollars, ultimately reached an estimated 120 million units.

The brightly colored rings, three feet in diameter and also called "spin-a-hoops" and "hoop-de-doos," were employed in a variety of ways:

1. most frequently, keeping it moving around the torso—or other parts of the body—without using the hands (instructions accompanying Spin-a-hoop said: "Hug the hoop to the backside . . . Push hard with the right hand . . . Now rock, man, rock! . . . Don't twist . . . Swing it . . . Sway it . . . You got it!")
2. tossing it in the air
3. skipping through it
4. making it climb stairs
5. hoop diving (i.e., into swimming pool)
6. spinning and swimming (normal hoop movements performed in pool)

7. running hoops (i.e., leaping through the ring as it is rolled by)
8. multiple hooping (a *Life* magazine photo showed one eleven-year old who could keep fourteen hoops in operation simultaneously)
9. hooping quarry (i.e., lassoing)
10. alley hooping (i.e., stunts by animals)
11. mass demonstration or mass "hoopla"
12. endurance contests
13. applications aimed at toning, weight reduction, stress reduction, etc.
14. assorted stunts (e.g., *Life* noted that one boy could take his shirt off and put it back on again without dropping his hoop)

A 1967 reincarnation of the fad, called the Shoop-Shoop Hula Hoop (filled with ball bearings to make a swishing sound), briefly sparked interest, but failed to reach anything approaching the proportions of the 1958 explosion.

Then, in 1982, Wham-O introduced a third-generation version, called the Peppermint Hula Hoop, because it had barber pole stripes and was peppermint scented. Noting that the first introduction coincided with the 1958 recession, while the second came during the trauma of the Vietnam War, executive vice president and general manager Barry Shapiro stated during the launching of the new line, "Wham-O has always felt that when the world is in kind of a messy way and people are unhappy, something like the hoop lets them just forget everything while they go crazy for a minute or two spinning around." Despite a substantial promotional push—which included Miss U.S.A. on display whirling it at the 1982 annual toy fair in New York City, prominent exposure in an episode of the television series "The Dukes of Hazzard," and an appearance at an Olympiad of hoop-based sporting events during the spring break for college students at Daytona Beach—the Peppermint Hula Hoop was a spectacular flop. A fourth edition is likely sometime in the future; whether or not Americans are receptive to it is anyone's guess.

## BIBLIOGRAPHY

Gilligan, Eugene. "Classic Toys Sport New Look," *Playthings*. 80 (July 1982) 34-36.

"Grandson of Hula Hoop," *Time*. 119 (March 15, 1982) 63.

"Whole Country Hoops It Up In a New Craze," *Life*. 45 (September 8, 1958) 37-40.

# Ice-Yachting

The essentials for this sport which became newsworthy in the 1920s were a light-weight scooter rigged with a mast and sail, a frozen river or lake, a stiff wind, and two or three daredevil sailors. More specifically this is how the scooter was designed:

> Modern ice-boats are built in the form of a crossed letter t — the perpendicular line of the letter representing the timber from the base of the mast to the stern called the keel, and the horizontal line, the runner plank. These slender but strong spread-timbers give the boat the appearance, as someone has said, of "a huge water spider with a sail on its back." Lightness and strength are obtained by a careful selection of wood, by the use of trusses or composite backbones, hollow spars and a lightly built cockpit.

Powered by the wind, such a technically sleek craft could reach speeds of 80 miles per hour. If the wind were "flukey," lifting the ice-yacht at either end, it could not dip into water like a regular yacht to reestablish equilibrium. Instead it raised four to five feet in the air only to slam back down on the unforgiving ice. This rough treatment shocked both craft and sailors, but was considered an exciting part of the sport. The best month for races was February when 0-degree days and 40-mph winds were frequent.

For fifty years (pre-1920s), headquarters for ice-yachting in America was on the North or South Shrewsbury rivers at Red Bank and Long Branch, New Jersey. Conditions for the sport were ideal there. The Shrewsbury season became so popular with spectators that other locations were sought out in which to enjoy ice-yachting. Dressed like an Eskimo, one fan remarked, "There is no prettier sight than an ice-boat race, seen through a mist of sparkling crystals torn from the ice by the grinding runners." Owing to Shrewsbury, the fad spread to the Great Lakes, the St. Lawrence and Hudson rivers, Minnetonka and White Beach Lake in Minnesota, Winnebago and Pepin Lake in Wisconsin, and Orange and Champlain Lake in New York.

The extreme cold for sailor and spectator alike, the great difficulty in sailing the frail craft, and capricious winds that made sailing a constant adventure limited ice-yachting's growth as a sport. The ice offered no resistance to the craft's runners so that an invisible gale might send it shooting across the frozen water in a sudden burst of electric energy. With a field of ice-yachts bouncing up and down then firing off like torpedoes to the glee of the spectators, it is no wonder the sport spawned faddish interest.

## BIBLIOGRAPHY

"Faster than the Wind," *Mentor*. 15 (February 1927) 22-23.

Hutchins, L.W. "Where the Scooter Scoots," *St. Nicholas*. 55 (March 1928) 383+.

"Ice-Yachts that Outstrip the Winds," *Literary Digest*. 92 (February 12, 1927) 62-64.

# The Ickey Shuffle

Every National Football League season seems to produce one headlines-grabbing player from out of left field; in 1988 it was Cincinnati rookie running back Elbert "Ickey" Woods. Ickey, the nickname he acquired back in infancy because his older brother Rodney mispronounced his given name, became known as the originator of perhaps the hottest dance step (certainly the most imitated) of the post-disco era.

It all started just prior to the September 25 game between Ickey's Bengals and the Browns. With his mom in town on a visit, Woods was "just acting crazy" to Bobby Brown's number one hit, "My Prerogative," and before long he had begun scratching out the now famous steps. Despite the admonishments of his mother, he stated, "When I score tomorrow, I'm going to do this dance in the end zone."

He scored—and he performed his dance. After a moment of disbelief the fans seemed to see the joke. "They said it was unblack, had no rhythm," says Woods. As the regular season wore on—resulting in fifteen touchdowns (the necessary prelude to doing his shuffle) and 1,066 yards gained for Woods—interest in his antics reached a fever pitch. There were a dozen different Ickey Shuffle T-shirts produced as well as four songs. One went, in part, as follows:

> He shakes it to the left
> He sweeps it to the right
> He dances in the end zone
> Like his underwear's too tight.

La Normandie, a Cincinnati restaurant, served an Ickey Shake, which entailed taking ice cream, Midori liqueur and Tuaca liqueur, eating the ice cream, drinking the liqueurs separately, and then shaking. The Bengals' general manager, the venerable eighty-year-old Paul Brown, tried imitating the steps. Even non-fans talked about it. The Arthur Murray dance studios added it to their curriculum. Stars from other sports tried it; e.g., the 1989 Daytona 500 winner and right wing Ron Jones of the Ontario Hockey League's London Knights (after scoring a shorthanded goal against the Kitchener Rangers). Bengal teammate Cris Collinsworth expressed amazement over the phenomenon, noting, "When we go out to a nightclub, we've got guys on the dance floor doing backflips and the most unbelievable disco-John Travolta moves you've ever seen."

The dance itself consisted of the following steps: (1) step left, (2) step right, (3) repeat steps twice, (4) hop three times, (5) spike ball, and (6) gyrate finger while yelling "woo-woo-woo." Dayton (Ohio) *Daily News* sports columnist Gary Nuhn had his paper's dance critic, Terry Morris, provide an analysis of it. She noted,

> His little divertissement is in such obvious good taste . . . and it's classic simplicity itself. He knows his Terpsichorean limitations, and a critic can appreciate that. I say, encourage him. The world needs more dancing big men.

The NFL officials, who proved to be overly tolerant of Ickey's hotdogging throughout 1988 (while, in theory, they should have penalized him, they only did so in Buffalo), made it clear that Woods would have to limit his dance to the sidelines (rather than the playing field) during the 1989 season. Accordingly, Ickey — upon scoring a touchdown in the opening game on September 10 — confined his antics to that allotted space; nevertheless, the spectators (and all of America via the replay) got to see the shuffle yet one more time.

It appeared that as long as Woods could continue to score touchdowns, there would be an audience for Ickey's peculiar brand of two-step. However, the following week Woods sustained serious damage to the ligaments in his right knee; he was immediately operated on and lost for the duration of the 1989 season.

# BIBLIOGRAPHY

Ballard, Sarah. "Riverfront Rag," *Sports Illustrated*. 69 (December 19, 1988) 23.

Neff, Craig, ed. "Scorecard at the Super Bowl," *Sports Illustrated*. 70:4 (January 30, 1989) 9.

Reilly, Rick. "Dash and Flash," *Sports Illustrated*. 70 (January 23, 1989) 51-54.

# Bo Jackson and Two-Sport Athletes

According to Nexis, the computer-accessed information service which was employed to scan the 650 newspapers, magazines, and wire services it carries, Bo Jackson represented the eighth most written about sports topic of the 1980s. Much of this coverage was devoted to Bo's unique status as a genuine star performer in two major professional sports. A television ad by Nike sportswear in heavy rotation during 1989 helped spread awareness of his status; it exhibited Bo engaged in a succession of physical activities, each one punctuated by comments from representative athletes (e.g., Bo playing baseball has Bobby Valentine stating, "Bo knows baseball"; Bo playing football has Howie Long exclaiming, "Bo knows football"; etc.).

Due to considerations such as (1) overlapping seasons, (2) the heightened risk of injury, (3) the differing athletic skills required by different sports, and (4) the demands — and financial opportunities — ensuing from national celebrity, most athletes opt for concentrating on only one sport at the professional level. However, precedents for splitting time between pro sports existed prior to Jackson. Christy Mathewson, Charlie Dressen, Rube Waddell, and Jim Thorpe all played pro football and major league baseball simultaneously. Notable baseball-basketball switchers included Ron Reed, Steve Hamilton, Dick Groat, Dave DeBusschere, and Gene Conley.

Jackson's case was unparalleled in that he was a bona fide superstar in both football and baseball. A winner of college football's Heisman Trophy in 1986, Jackson astounded the experts by signing a contract to play baseball with the Kansas City Royals organization. While his potential was unquestioned, Jackson had played baseball on only a sporadic basis while at Auburn University, accumulating mediocre statistics. After a few months of minor league seasoning, however, Jackson made the parent club, showing occasional flashes of brilliance. When Jackson's fast start out of the gate stalled midway through the 1987 season, he announced his intention to join the NFL's Oakland Raiders following the fulfillment of his baseball obligations. Sportswriters speculated that he was planning to switch to football full-time once his contract with the Royals had expired.

Despite the unfortunate remark made at his inaugural Raiders press conference that he would pursue football as a "hobby," Jackson swiftly rose to the top in both sports. He chalked up a 200-yard rushing performance for Oakland during the 1987 season and was selected to start for the American League in baseball's 1989 All Star Game. Jackson quieted the last of the Doubting Thomases in that game, hitting a home run, stealing a base, and garnering the Most Valuable Player award.

In his wake, other athletes—most notably, Deion Sanders, the Florida State football star who signed first with the New York Yankees, and later with the Atlanta Falcons, in 1989 (becoming, in September 1989, the first athlete to homer in the major leagues and score a TD in the NFL in the same week)— have shown an interest in going the two-sport route. It is likely, however, that most are merely using that option as a trump card to acquire a more favorable financial settlement with the team holding rights to them in their sport of choice; e.g., Tony Mandarich's talk of fighting Mike Tyson while awaiting a more acceptable contract offer from the Green Bay Packers.

## BIBLIOGRAPHY

—Jackson, Bo

Berkow, Ira. "Bo Jackson: A Star For All Seasons," *New York Times*. 138 (July 16, 1989) sec 1, 21(N).

Berry, Jon. "Scott Bedbury: Bo, Beer and Nike's Bottom Line," *ADWEEK Western Advertising News*. 39 (August 21, 1989) 24-25.

"The Brightest Star Belongs to Jackson," *New York Times*. 138 (July 13, 1989) B8.

Brown, Kathy. "Beyond Bo: Nike's New Heroes," *ADWEEK Western Advertising News*. 39 (August 14, 1989) 6.

Brown, Kathy. "Nike and W&K Know Diddley," *ADWEEK Western Advertising News*. 39 (July 10, 1989) 10.

Callahan, Tom. "Bo's Going To Follow His Dream; Two Games Changed by the Small Event of a 'Bama Childhood," *Time*. 128 (September 29, 1986) 62.

Clark, N. Brooks. "Which Way You Gonna Go, Bo?," *Sports Illustrated*. 62 (May 13, 1985) 71-72.

Friedman, Jack. "Running From a Troubled Childhood, Bo Jackson Rushes Toward the Heisman and — Just Maybe — NFL Glory," *People Weekly*. 24 (December 2, 1985) 151-152.

Friedman, Jack. "Turning His Back on a Football Bonanza, Bo Jackson Finds the Early Going Rough in the Diamond," *People Weekly*. 26 (July 21, 1986) 43-44.

Gammons, Peter. "Will Bo Be a Hit or a Miss?," *Sports Illustrated*. 66 (May 4, 1987) 36-38.

Garfield, Bob. "Jackson's Nike Performance Proves He's Simply Irresisti-Bo," *Advertising Age*. 60 (July 17, 1989) 52.

Lippert, Barbara. "For Nike, Bo Brings Natural Talent to Another Hobby," *ADWEEK Western Advertising News*. 30 (July 31, 1989) 19.

Looney, Douglas S. "Bo's Not One To Go With the Flow," *Sports Illustrated*. 65 (July 14, 1986) 36-40.

Lyons, Douglas C. "Bo Jackson's Big-League Double Play; Can Superathlete Succeed in His Dual Pro Baseball-Football Careers?," *Ebony*. 44 (November 1988) 56-58.

Magiera, Marcy. "Bo-daciously Nike; Jackson Touches Many Bases in TV Spot," *Advertising Age*. 60 (July 10, 1989) 1ff.

Martinez, Michael. "Jackson Hits Homer and Steals All-Star Show," *New York Times*. 138 (July 12, 1989) A17.

Neff, Craig. "The Bo Show," *Sports Illustrated*. 71 (July 24, 1989) 11-12.

Neff, Craig. "Say It Ain't So, Bo," *Sports Illustrated*. 71 (August 14, 1989) 18.

Neff, Craig, and Robert Sullivan. "Where's the O, Bo?," *Sports Illustrated*. 64 (March 31, 1986) 11.

Raissman, Robert. "Sponsor Deals Enrich Bo and Boris; Nike Prefers Grid; Coke Inks Becker," *Advertising Age*. 57 (July 14, 1986) 1ff.

Shahoda, Susan. "Nike, Wieden & Kennedy Hit a Home Run with Bo Jackson: Pytka Directed Winning Commercial," *Back Stage*. 30 (July 28, 1989) 6.

Sullivan, Robert. "Bo the Bobber?," *Sports Illustrated*. 68 (March 21, 1988) 18. Report on Jackson's interest in competing as a member of the U.S. bobsled team.

Underwood, John. "Bo's Two-Way Stretch: Can a Super Athlete Conquer Pro Football and Baseball?," *Life*. 10 (October 1987) 36-38.

Whitford, David, and John Scuderi. "The Best Football Player in Alabama . . . Is a Baseball Player," *Sport*. 76 (July 1985) 46-50.

Wiley, Ralph. "Which Way Will You Go, Bo?," *Sports Illustrated*. 67 (December 14, 1987) 24-27.

Wulf, Steve. "Say It Ain't So, Bo," *Sports Illustrated*. 67 ( July 20, 1987) 10.

— Mandarich, Tony

Burke, Dan. "Tackling the NFL: Canadian Tony Mandarich Is a Rising Star," *Maclean's*. 102 (May 8, 1989) 49-50.

Murphy, Austin. "Crime and Punishment," *Sports Illustrated*. 69 (August 22, 1988) 15. Notes the inconsistency in the NCAA's suspension rulings for Pitt's Terry Austin and Tony Mandarich of Michigan State.

Neff, Craig. "Tale of the Tape," *Sports Illustrated*. 70 (May 29, 1989) 14. Column concerned with the proposed fight between Mandarich and heavy-weight boxing champ Mike Tyson.

"No. 2 Pick Lowers His Demand to Green Bay," *New York Times*. 138 (August 10, 1989) B12, D22.

Telander, Rick. "The Big Enchilada," *Sports Illustrated*. 70 (April 24, 1989) 40-46.

— Sanders, Deion

"Fast Start For Sanders," *New York Times*. 138 (September 11, 1989) C9.

Kim, Albert. "A Double Play for Deion?," *Sports Illustrated*. 70 (June 12, 1989) 26.

"Sanders on Roster For Falcon Game," *New York Times*. 138 (September 10, 1989) sec 1, p. 20.

"Sanders View," *New York Times*. 138 (September 11, 1989) C3.

Scheiber, Dave. "Decisions, Decisions, Flashy Deion Sanders is Having a Devil of a Time Choosing Between Baseball's and Football's Millions," *Sports Illustrated*. 71 (July 3, 1989) 30-33.

Schwartz, Jerry. "Sanders Returns to Glory in Atlanta," *New York Times*. 138 (September 14, 1989) B11, D25.

# Lotteries

The name shortened to "Lotto," at the end of 1988, twenty-eight states and the District of Columbia had legalized participation in lotteries. In the same year, Massachusetts residents on average spent $235 for lottery tickets; this marked a high, in Kansas the amount spent was only $27. A research psychologist, Dr. Srully Blotnick, investigated the phenomenon of lotteries and discovered that they are most popular with low-income people who seek celebrity status. A shipping clerk told him: "If I win, I want all that lights, camera, action stuff. I want everyone to see that I didn't become a bum after all." Other findings revealed that 37% of the players felt guilty about buying lottery tickets, and 43% would not play regularly if they had to give their name and social security number. Also part of the need for secrecy, many players did not tell their families about their purchase, and mistakenly believed that silence protected them from the eagle eye of the Internal Revenue Service if they won. The big payoff of many millions of dollars is the driving force although a bigger payoff means less of a chance to win because more tickets are in circulation. This fact fails to register on players; a 1-40 million-dollar payoff is just too tantalizing a prospect not to get involved. To underscore Dr. Blotnick's research, a recent California Lotto winner happened to be an illegal alien who truly realized the American dream overnight, not speaking English well and having been here only a brief time. That certainly made for instant celebrity.

Lotto mania actually began in the early 1930s with the Irish Hospital Sweepstakes, known familiarly as the Irish Sweeps. The Irish Free State legalized the Sweeps in 1930 to benefit hospitals that provided free beds for the poor. Since the Irish have always loved horse racing, they connected the Sweeps to the three most famous English horse races each Year: the Grand National in March, the Derby in June, and the Cambridgeshire in October. Three days before each race Sweeps tickets were drawn, then paired by another draw with the horses in the particular race. The winning horse produced a top prize of 30,000 British pounds, or $150,000; the second place horse, 15,000 British pounds; and the third, 10,000. Prize money for the 1933 Derby totaled almost two million British pounds, divided among 2,404 winners. Nineteen Sweeps players were paired with the winner, Hyperion, for 30,000 pounds apiece. In order, Great Britain had 1,647 winners; the United States, 214; and the Irish Free State, 124. Deducting the 2,404 winning tickets from the total of 6,758,664 sold, made the odds of winning very faint indeed.

Playing the Irish Sweeps in the United States was allowed, even though homegrown lotteries were illegal. American banks handled prize money transfers, yet technically were not supposed to. The IRS took its share of the top prize of $150,000 by asking for $58,300 or 39%. Counterfeit tickets became commonplace in the U.S. and Great Britain, so that a much larger, inestimable number of tickets were sold. The people duped had no idea their tickets were bogus and probably never thought twice about it — they did not expect to win anyway. Sweeps management provided an unusual service in that they upheld confidentiality; a ticket buyer could use a fictitious name which would be honored through the whole process of purchase, drawing, notification, and payment of winnings. These people did not want the whole world to know of their sudden windfall, unlike today's status-seekers. Sweeps management maintained a card file of every ticket buyer (many bought books of tickets), and employed more people than any other firm in Ireland just to keep up with the booming business. The situation got complicated when the U.S. Postmaster General reminded the nation that advertising or mailing lottery information was illegal, under penalty of a one-thousand-dollar fine and two years' imprisonment. But U.S. law enforcement authorities were locked in a losing battle. The Irish Sweeps were too popular and represented a worthy cause. Millions of pounds went to Irish hospitals, as did millions in taxes for the state coffers. The Irish Free State was a poor nation and a sentimental favorite abroad. American newspapers and magazines published the prize announcements and each rags-to-riches story sparked more ticket buying. During the 1930s, the Irish Sweeps were just too good a thing to do away with. The only mark against them was the counterfeiting of tickets.

An editorial writer for the *Christian Century* had something different to say. A 1932 article pronounced lotteries "wrong and stupid" and "thoroughly demoralizing." The United States and Europe were in the grasp of economic depression, so "To dangle glittering prizes before the eyes of men who are clutching at any straw to keep them afloat, is the most cruel kind of financial malpractice." Leaping ahead to our own time, an editorial writer for *Christianity Today* in a 1989 article, fears that gambling will be the drug of the 1990s: "That Gamblers Anonymous and various treatment centers for compulsive gamblers have grown rapidly is further evidence of the nation's emerging addiction." The article also cites a Minnesota decision to set aside $300,000 for the establishment of gambling treatment centers out of a potential revenue of $90 million from legalized Lotto. New Jersey will do the same. The writer concludes, "By and large, the irony of these disproportionate grants is lost in the legislative lust for expanded state revenues."

How far the current Lotto fad will go is anyone's guess. The extremely large payoffs do appear to be sinful, and the original idea to assist needy organizations like hospitals is not evident today.

## BIBLIOGRAPHY

Blotnick, Srully. "The Lure of Lottery," *Forbes*. 137 (January 13, 1986) 302-303.

"Loot for Lotto," *U.S. News & World Report*. 106 (May 22, 1989) 81.

"Lotteries Are Both Wrong and Stupid," *Christian Century*. 49 (October 5, 1932) 1190-1191.

"The Lottery Plague," *Christianity Today*. 33 (September 8, 1989) 15.

McCarthy, John J. "The Irish Sweeps," *Harper's Magazine*. 169 (June 1934) 49-59.

# Joe Louis vs. Max Schmeling
# for the Heavyweight Championship

On June 22, 1938, Joe Louis defended his heavyweight boxing title in Yankee Stadium against Max Schmeling who, two years earlier, had inflicted the only loss up to that point on the record of the "Brown Bomber." This was not, however, merely a grudge match for Louis. James A. Cox outlined the broader implications of the bout in an article for *Smithsonian*:

> The striking change that in the past two years has begun to take place in much of white America's perception of the two contenders has moved the fight off the sports pages and into the social consciousness of the country. In the first meeting between Louis and Schmeling, the polarization of blacks and whites in the United States was dramatically evident: a great many white Americans cheered when the white German won. But now, as a result of the savage threat to decency and peace evident in Nazi Germany, for most Americans the fight, because of Adolf Hitler's special brand of racism, has become a symbolic showdown between us and them, between America and the enemy. Ironically, at a time when blatant racism was a pervasive part of American life, a young black man was being asked to prove the superiority of his country, to become, in fact, a national hero for all Americans.

In their previous bout, Schmeling had exploited an opening which resulted when Louis threw his left hook; after sending Louis to the canvas in the fourth round, the German won on a knockout in the twelfth. The second meeting lasted only 124 seconds with Louis smothering his opponent with lefts and rights, forty punches to Schmeling's two. Cox noted that although Louis' reign as heavyweight champion had just begun — he would retire unbeaten eleven years later — the second Schmeling match remained the most memorable performance of his life.

Louis joined the Army following the outbreak of war, risking his title twice for charity fights in which he donated his purses to Army and Navy relief funds. Following his retirement, the IRS went after him for back taxes he did not realize he owed; Louis returned to boxing and fared badly, and then turned to pro wrestling in order to earn money. Later, he turned to the after-dinner circuit (even teaming with his one-time opponent, Schmeling, with whom he became fast friends) and, ultimately, public relations work for Las Vegas casinos.

At his funeral in Arlington National Cemetery in 1981, a bugle solemnly sounding taps was punctuated by the incongruous clanging of a cowbell. A soldier whispered fiercely to the bell ringer, a young black man, "Time for a low profile, brother." "We been low profile for a long time, brother," the young man replied. "This is the bell of Liberty, rung for Joe Louis."

## BIBLIOGRAPHY

"The Brown Bomber," *Sports Illustrated*. 54 (April 26, 1981) 23.

Cox, James A. "The Day Joe Louis Fired Shots Heard 'Round the World," *Smithsonian*. 19 (November 1988) 170-196.

Graves, Earl G. "Three Examples of Leadership," *Black Enterprise*. 11 (July 1981) 7.

Head, Chris. "Black Hero in a White Land," *Sports Illustrated*. 63 (September 16, 1985) 86ff. Excerpts from recently released biography on Louis.

Head, Chris. "Triumphs and Trials," *Sports Illustrated*. 63 (September 23, 1985) 74ff. Part two of article excerpted from Head's biography.

"Joe Louis' Greatest Fight," *Modern Maturity*. 25 (June-July 1982) 72-74.

"Joe Louis, 1914-1981," *Newsweek*. 97 (April 27, 1981) 161-162. Obituary.

"A Salute to the Champ Joe Louis," *Ebony*. 35 (June 1981) 132- 136.

# The M & M Boys' Race with Ruth

While many sluggers have flirted with breaking Babe Ruth's single season record of sixty home runs set in 1927, 1961 proved to be a benchmark year in that (1) not one, but two, players — members of the same team, the Yankees — mounted a challenge; and (2) the mark was, in fact, finally eclipsed (well, sort of).

Outfielders Mickey Mantle and Roger Maris, known that year to sports headline junkies as the M & M boys, began receiving serious coverage in early June with both running close to — and sometimes ahead of — Ruth's 1927 pace. Skeptics noted that because Ruth hit so many of his home runs late in the season (twenty in his final thirty-two games), any serious challenger would need to enter the homestretch with a cushion. Supporters were quick to note that when Mantle hit his final 37th homer in the Yankees' 92nd game (followed closely by Maris with thirty-six round trippers), giving him a twenty-two-game lead over Ruth, the twosome had exactly that sort of cushion.

While arguments could be made for the inherent advantages of either Ruth or the M & M boys, the latter appeared to have several points in their favor not enjoyed by previous challengers to Ruth's record:

- The recent expansion from eight to ten teams had unquestionably weakened American League pitching. In 1961 there were suddenly twenty-five percent more pitchers than in the previous season, minor leaguers by the old standard (ironically, the hurler who ultimately gave up homer number sixty-one to Maris, was, in fact, a rookie).
- Expansion had also put two new ballparks in the league, Wrigley Field in Chicago and Metropolitan Stadium in Minnesota — both cozy bandboxes with prevailing winds blowing out from home plate to aid hitters.

• After a year in which relations between the two were notice-
ably strained, Mantle and Maris provided an ever-present
stimulus to each other. Reporter Walter Bingham noted that
during one game in late July, Maris hit a home run to tie Mantle, who touched his teammate's hand in salute and then hit
one of his own to regain the lead.

The duel between the two sluggers was drawing capacity crowds
in a prolonged series of road games beginning in early July; in Chicago, Baltimore, Washington and Boston, the cheers for Mantle
and Maris matched those usually reserved for home-town heroes.
Their progress began receiving top billing over the outcome of the
games themselves. Yankees manager Ralph Houk announced that if
and when the team clinched the pennant, he would move them to
the top of the batting order to give them more chances to hit.

Amidst this excitement, Major League Commissioner Ford Frick
announced on July 17 that, because the American League was playing a 162-game schedule, Babe Ruth's record would not be considered broken if a player hit the decisive home runs after his club's
154th game. *Sports Illustrated*, among other sources, termed it "a
foolish, pathetic little statement, foolish because it makes so little
sense, pathetic because it will be ignored," adding that "it was
Frick himself who sanctioned the American League's 162-game
schedule, and if he had a statement to make regarding records that
might be broken because of the additional games, he should have
made it before the season began."

As public interest in the M & M boys' exploits reached a fever
pitch, Jack Olsen offered the following fanciful tableau in the September 11 issue of *Sports Illustrated:*

There may be one or two more important things going on in
the world as September ends, but only a few people will pay
them much heed.

TV and radio networks are arranging to break in with spot
announcements as the magic 60th homer comes in sight. Garry
Moore and Ed Sullivan and Perry Como are trying to sign
Maris and Mantle for appearances (asking price: $15,000 the
pair). Agents and hustlers are waiting in the wings with all

sorts of contracts. Ghostwriters are oiling up their typewriters to compose *How I Broke Ruth's Record*, byline pending.

During the final stages of the season, it became a one-man race as Mantle fell victim to a virus attack, his homer total stalling at fifty-four. Maris doggedly continued the quest, hitting three round trippers in games 150 through 154 to reach fifty-nine. After "tying" Ruth's record in game 158, his chances for taking sole possession of the mark came down to the final game of the season in New York against the Boston Red Sox. Maris flied out to left field in the first inning. In the fourth, he took the first two pitches for balls. The crowd, interested only in a home run, greeted both pitches with a chorus of boos. Pitcher Tracy Stallard then delivered a waist-high fastball down the middle which Maris parked into the lower right-field stands. *New York Times* reporter John Drebinger noted the events that followed:

> An ear-splitting roar went up as Maris, standing spellbound for just an instant at the plate, started his triumphant jog around the bases. As he came down the third-base line, he shook hands joyously with a young fan who had rushed onto the field to congratulate him.
>
> Crossing the plate and arriving at the Yankee dugout, he was met by a solid phalanx of team-mates . . . Smiling broadly, the usually unemotional player lifted his cap from his blond close-cropped thatch and waved it to the cheering fans. Not until he had taken four bows did his colleagues allow him to retire to the bench.

The chart below recapitulates, home run by home run, Maris' 1961 season:

| H.R. No. | Game No. | Date | Opposing Pitcher/Club | Home/Away |
|----------|----------|------|-----------------------|-----------|
| 1 | 10 | 4/26 | Foytack/Detroit | A |
| 2 | 16 | 5/03 | Ramos/Minnesota | A |
| 3 | 19 | 5/06 | Grba/Los Angeles | A |
| 4 | 28 | 5/17 | Burnside/Washington | H |
| 5 | 29 | 5/19 | Perry/Cleveland | A |
| 6 | 30 | 5/20 | Bell/Cleveland | A |
| 7 | 31 | 5/21 | Estrada/Baltimore | H |
| 8 | 34 | 5/24 | Conley/Boston | H |

| H.R. No. | Game No. | Date | Opposing Pitcher/Club | Home/Away |
|---|---|---|---|---|
| 9 | 37 | 5/28 | McLish/Chicago | H |
| 10 | 39 | 5/30 | Conley/Boston | A |
| 11 | 39 | 5/30 | Fornieles/Boston | A |
| 12 | 40 | 5/31 | Muffett/Boston | A |
| 13 | 42 | 6/02 | McLish/Chicago | A |
| 14 | 43 | 6/03 | Shaw/Chicago | A |
| 15 | 44 | 6/04 | Kemmerer/Chicago | A |
| 16 | 47 | 6/06 | Palmquist/Minnesota | H |
| 17 | 48 | 6/07 | Ramos/Minnesota | H |
| 18 | 51 | 6/09 | Herbert/Kansas City | H |
| 19 | 54 | 6/11 | Grba/Los Angeles | H |
| 20 | 54 | 6/11 | James/Los Angeles | H |
| 21 | 56 | 6/13 | Perry/Cleveland | A |
| 22 | 57 | 6/14 | Bell/Cleveland | A |
| 23 | 60 | 6/17 | Mossi/Detroit | A |
| 24 | 61 | 6/18 | Casale/Detroit | A |
| 25 | 62 | 6/19 | Archer/Kansas City | A |
| 26 | 63 | 6/20 | Nuxhall/Kansas City | A |
| 27 | 66 | 6/22 | Bass/Kansas City | A |
| 28 | 73 | 7/01 | Sisler/Washington | H |
| 29 | 74 | 7/02 | Burnside/Washington | H |
| 30 | 74 | 7/02 | Klippstein/Washington | H |
| 31 | 76 | 7/04 | Lary/Detroit | H |
| 32 | 77 | 7/05 | Funk/Cleveland | H |
| 33 | 81 | 7/09 | Monbouquette/Boston | A |
| 34 | 83 | 7/13 | Wynn/Chicago | A |
| 35 | 85 | 7/15 | Herbert/Chicago | A |
| 36 | 91 | 7/21 | Monbouquette/Boston | A |
| 37 | 94 | 7/25 | Baumann/Chicago | H |
| 38 | 94 | 7/25 | Larsen/Chicago | H |
| 39 | 95 | 7/25 | Kemmerer/Chicago | H |
| 40 | 95 | 7/25 | Hacker/Chicago | H |
| 41 | 105 | 8/04 | Pascual/Minnesota | H |
| 42 | 113 | 8/11 | Burnside/Washington | A |
| 43 | 114 | 8/12 | Donovan/Washington | A |
| 44 | 115 | 8/13 | Daniels/Washington | A |
| 45 | 116 | 8/13 | Kutyna/Washington | A |
| 46 | 117 | 8/15 | Pizarro/Chicago | H |
| 47 | 118 | 8/16 | Pierce/Chicago | H |
| 48 | 118 | 8/16 | Pierce/Chicago | H |
| 49 | 123 | 8/20 | Perry/Cleveland | A |
| 50 | 124 | 8/22 | McBride/Los Angeles | A |
| 51 | 128 | 8/26 | Walker/Kansas City | A |
| 52 | 134 | 9/02 | Lary/Detroit | H |
| 53 | 134 | 9/02 | Aguirre/Detroit | H |
| 54 | 139 | 9/06 | Cheney/Washington | H |
| 55 | 140 | 9/07 | Stigman/Cleveland | H |
| 56 | 142 | 9/09 | Grant/Cleveland | H |
| 57 | 150 | 9/16 | Lary/Detroit | A |
| 58 | 151 | 9/17 | Fox/Detroit | A |
| 59 | 154 | 9/20 | Pappas/Baltimore | A |
| 60 | 158 | 9/26 | Fisher/Baltimore | H |
| 61 | 162 | 10/01 | Stallard/Boston | H |

In retrospect, the unfulfilled promise characterizing the balance of Maris' career may have somewhat diminished his accomplishment. Constant harrassment by the media which Maris at that point in his career was completely unprepared for probably also contributed to lackluster seasons thereafter. But the fact remains that until another slugger breaks his record of 61, Maris is the greatest home run hitter to have played in the big leagues.

## BIBLIOGRAPHY

Allen, Maury. *Roger Maris: A Man for All Seasons*. Revised by Sue McGown. 1986.

Bingham, Walter. "Assault on the Record," *Sports Illustrated*. 17 (July 31, 1961) 8-11.

Bingham, Walter. "No. 60 and 61," *Sports Illustrated*. 15 (October 9, 1961) 14-17.

Cohane, T. "Roger Maris: Has He the Stuff for Stardom?," *Look*. 25 (June 20, 1961) 113-116.

Creamer, Robert W. "Mantle and Maris in the Movies," *Sports Illustrated*. 16 (April 2, 1962) 88-92ff.

Creamer, Robert W. "Roger Maris, 1934-1985," *Sports Illustrated*. 63 (December 23, 1985) 26.

Drebinger, John. "Maris Hits 61st in Final Game," In: *The New York Times Encyclopedia of Sports*, edited by Gene Brown. Volume 2: Baseball. New York: Arno, 1979. pp. 129-130.

Gould, Stephen Jay. "Mickey Mantle," *Sport*. 77 (December 1985) 74-78.

"I Tried Not to Think About It," *Life*. 51 (September 29, 1961) 97.

Kahn, Roger. "Pursuit of No. 60; the Ordeal of Roger Maris," *Sports Illustrated*. 15 (October 2, 1961) 22-25ff.

Koppett, L. "Mighty Mr. Maris," *Saturday Evening Post*. 234 (September 2, 1961) 24ff.

Lipsyte, Robert. "Grappling With Glory," *New York Times Magazine*. 134 (March 31, 1985) S62-66.

Mantle, Mickey, and Herb Gluck. *The Mick*. 1985.

Maris, Mrs. Roger. "My Husband," edited by D. Budge. *Look*. 26 (April 24, 1962) 89-90ff.

Maris, Roger, and Jim Ogle. "I Couldn't Go Through It Again; Excerpt from Roger Maris At Bat," *Look*. 26 (April 10, 1962) 38-40ff.

"Math Muscles in on the Race Against Ruth," *Life*. 51 (August 18, 1961) 62-65.

Olsen, Jack. "The Week They Try to Catch the Babe," *Sports Illustrated*. 17 (September 11, 1961) 18-21.

Wulf, Steve. "An Error for Baseball; Why Aren't Leo Durocher and Roger Maris in the Hall?," *Sports Illustrated*. 67 (August 10, 1987) 92.

# Mah Jong

Mah Jong, which took America by storm in 1923, appears to have been invented by an ancient fishing captain (c. 3,000-2,000 B.C.) to keep his crew contented in between schools of fish; he used tiles instead of cards so they would not blow off the windy deck. The game continued to evolve over the ages. A medieval general responsible for guarding the Great Wall is reputed to have adapted the game to keep his soldiers quiet between wars. His inventions included building the wall in the game itself as well as the incorporation of winds and dragons. A beautiful princess supposedly added flowers and seasons later.

Despite its survival in one form or another for at least 4,000 years, it was not until after the Boxer Rebellion that it gained popularity in the tea-houses; following the institution of the republic (1911) it became, practically, the national game of China. R. F. Foster reported on how it became an American fad in the Seattle *Daily Times:*

> . . . English-speaking residents in China soon became interested in the game which seemed to have such a fascination for the Chinese, especially among the merchant class in the teahouses, where most of the business with foreigners was transacted. Naval officers and their wives picked up the game from their servants, and all disputes were at once referred to the pantry for settlement. Representation of American firms, stationed in China, who were constantly brought into contact with the merchant class, also felt it incumbent upon them to learn the game in order to make themselves agreeable to their prospective customers.
>
> None of these, however, seems to have thought of introducing the game to America except sporadically, by sending a set to a friend or relative as a pretty gift, in a pretty box, which

was much admired, but never used. . . . It was not until Joseph P. Babcock, who was a representative of the Standard Oil Company near Shanghai, conceived the idea of sending sets to this country in large quantities, accompanied by printed rules for the game, that it became possible for large numbers of persons to become interested in the game.

The increased demand for sets caused a temporary crisis with respect to supply. As noted by the Springfield (Mass.) *Union*,

> . . . it developed that it is one thing to start a "craze" and an entirely different matter to supply the wherewithal to supply the craze. Orders began coming to China for sets of this Chinese game, and the Chinese manufacturer looked up from his workbench, where he was turning out "characters," "bamboos," and "circles," all deftly, but slowly, done by hand in the manner of his fathers, and said, "No can do," and went back to his work . . . And then there was another problem. . . . It seems that the white bone faces on the tiles can only be made from a small section (about seven inches in length) of the shinbone of the cow. . . . The Chinese dealer had these foreign buccaneers then. "No can get plenty bones!"

At this point, the major meat-packing companies such as Swift, Armour, and Libby began supplying the shin-bones while a group of Americans and Britishers in Shanghai founded the Mei Ren Company in Paoshan in mid-1923 which combined laborers possessing all of the needed skills to manufacture the game more efficiently under one roof.

The Seattle *Daily Times*, which published articles on an almost daily basis about the game during its peak of popularity, offered the following rationale for its appeal:

> First of all, Mah Jong is, with the exception of cribbage and picquet, the first satisfactory husband-and-wife game that has come along, because it can be played two-handed as well as three-handed, four-handed and five-handed.
> In some respects three-handed and four-handed are the most satisfactory forms; but those who have tried the two-handed

game have been amazed at its fascination and wonderful resources for amusement.

## BIBLIOGRAPHY

Allen, F.L. "Mah Jong in One Lesson," *Independent*. 112 (May 24, 1924) 283.

Bolitho, William. "Mah Jongg and the Idle Rich," *Living Age*. 320 (January 26, 1924) 184-185. Reprinted from the December 8, 1923 issue of *Outlook*.

Foster, R.F. "Clearing a Suit at Mah Jong," *Asia*. 24 (May 1924) 398.

Foster, R.F. "How Old Is Mah-Jong?," *Asia*. 24 (March 1924) 191-192.

Foster, R.F. "Mah Jong End Games," *Asia*. 24 (September 1924) 736-737.

Foster, R.F. "Some Fundamentals of Mah-Jong," *Asia*. 24 (April 1924) 305.

Harr, L.L. "Game of a Hundred Intelligences," *Asia*. 23 (August 1923) 595-596.

"How Mah-Jong Cured Seasickness, and Defeated Bandits," *Literary Digest*. 79 (October 13, 1923) 70-72.

"Insidious Mah Jong," *Literary Digest*. 80 (March 1929) 54-58.

Jefferies, N. "Pung-Chow," *Literary Review*. 3 (May 19, 1923) 710.

"Ma Jung, Game of Chinese Mandarins," *Literary Digest*. 75 (December 30, 1922) 38.

"Mah Jong Lyric," *Living Age*. 319 (December 8, 1923) 481.

"Making Mah Jongg Tiles Is An Important Chinese Industry," *Current Opinion*. 76 (March 1924) 357-358.

Merz, C. "Mah Jongg," *New Republic*. 35 (August 1, 1923) 255- 256.

Powell, J.B. "Mah Change: the Game and Its History," *Living Age*. 318 (September 1, 1923) 416-420. Reprinted from the June 30, 1923 issue of the *China Weekly Review*.

Winterbourne, E.M. "Construction of Mah Jong Sets," *Industrial Arts Magazine*. 13 (March 1924) 106-107.

# Mickey Mantle's Race with Ruth

Perhaps the best shot Mickey Mantle had of surpassing the immortal Babe Ruth's single season home run record of sixty came in 1956. More than that, however, it proved to be the year he came of age as a player.

In the spring training camp of 1951, Joe DiMaggio appeared to be fading fast and the Yankees, whose gate receipts had long been built upon a star system reaching back to Ruth and iron man Lou Gehrig, were frantically searching for new faces. Several long home runs of nearly 500 feet by young Mantle — only two years out of high school — ended that search and sent the Yankee publicity department in search of new superlatives. Under relentless pressure, Mantle seemed unable to fulfill his vast potential during his early campaigns. Prior to 1956, his best batting average in the major leagues was .311 and his highest home run total was thirty-seven (figures easily bettered by his center field rivals right in New York City, Willie Mays of the Giants and Duke Snider of the Dodgers).

In 1956, however, Mantle opened with a hot run, hitting ten homers in his first nineteen games. Talk immediately cropped up with respect to his chances of breaking Ruth's long-standing record. And he continued to excel; by mid-season he was leading the major leagues in batting average, runs batted in, runs scored, and hits, as well as homers. His success was attributed to his muscular physique (including a seventeen-and-one-half-inch neck, thick wrists and a back seemingly as "huge as Asia") and switch-hitting ability, the latter of which enabled him to get a bat on curves thrown by both left- and right-handed pitchers.

As public interest in Mantle's run at Ruth mounted, the entertainment world took note. On June 9, he was paid the then handsome sum of $1,000 for a ninety-second stint on the "Perry Como Show." By August, his fee for television appearances was up to $1,500. By September, he was featured on a best-selling recording with Teresa Brewer entitled, "I Love Mickey" (Coral). Newspapers and magazines seemed to cover his exploits in every issue.

A spurt in late August — eight homers in eleven games — carried Mantle to within striking distance of the record and whipped the public frenzy to an even higher level. With thirty-six games left, Mantle had hit forty-two home runs, three more than Ruth at the same point in 1927. Now, even his wife was besieged by offers, including an assignment to model brief shorts in a charity fashion show which was nixed by the slugger at the last minute.

Mantle's output tailed off in September, however, resulting in fifty-two round trippers for the season. At this point his accomplishment was overshadowed by the playoff's build-up (the second straight so-called subway series with the National League Dodgers featuring the revenge motive as the Yankees had lost to their cross-town rivals in 1955) and, ultimately, Don Larson's never-equalled World Series perfect game feat.

## BIBLIOGRAPHY

"Blackout at Home," *Newsweek*. (August 27, 1956) 63.
"Can the Young Yankee Beat the Babe?," *Newsweek*. (June 25, 1956) 63-67.
Lardner, John. "Toward Ruthlessness," *Newsweek*. (July 9, 1956) 63.

# Marathon Flying

What aviation historians call the golden twenties was truly a soul-stirring time for pilots and the American public. Flying airplanes higher, faster, and farther became an irresistible challenge — almost a Promethean defiance. By 1930, it was nothing to scoff at Jules Verne's around-the-world in eighty days; how about in fifteen or less? Marathon flying was tricky business. It required that the pilot burn every ounce of gas before refueling in an attempt to cover as many miles as possible, but it was also a kick in the pants. For the public it was vicarious adventure of the highest order. Just as Phileas Fogg and Passpartout dazzled the world with their exploits in Verne's fictional account, so too did their real life counterparts.

The men who flew long distance at their peril were primarily test pilots. Whatever problems they encountered during flight were brought back to the drawing board and analyzed. It was their sole mission to extend the limitations of flight, a mission they wanted to pursue in a quiet manner. Yet, their test flights became media events which created a dichotomous fad. Americans read with trepidation about the resultant fatalities of marathon flying, from which they experienced nightmares full of great silver birds falling from heaven to crash on the ground. But they also read with pride about American pilots as world-beaters, and being first at anything was always gratifying. Whether Americans expressed fear or boasted, navigating the skies to fly across the country or around the world was one of the most talked-about topics in the 1920s.

The first half of the decade started off with a bang. Only twenty years after the Wright Brothers, Lts. John A. Macready and Oakley G. Kelly piloted a Fokker T-2 monoplane from New York to San Diego in 26 hours, 50 minutes, to complete the first nonstop transcontinental flight. The next year (1924), four Douglas World Cruisers lived up to their name and covered 27,553 miles in 175 days circumnavigating the globe. This feat, and others, prompted *National Geographic Magazine* to devote its entire July 1924 issue to marathon flying. Three articles, "The Non-Stop Flight Across America," "America from the Air," and "Man's Amazing Progress in Conquering the Air" (altogether 122 pages) revealed how the miraculous was accomplished. The second article was certainly the most striking. It included never-before-seen aerial photographs; the subjects were Dayton, Ohio, the Washington Monument, and five snow-clad peaks in Washington State and Oregon. By 1927, pilots bragged about "globe-girdling" in a little over two weeks. Linton Wells held the record of 28 days, 14 hours, and 36 minutes established the year before, and he was out to prove that fifteen days was within reach. He and Lt. Leigh Wade were scheduled to break the old record that summer. *The Literary Digest* published their flight schedule: leave New York, 5 p.m., July 1; arrive New York, 5 p.m., July 16; distance, 20,000 miles at a high speed of 98 m.p.h., averaging 55 m.p.h. for the trip. Wells and Wade did not get to make the trip, but others did.

In the last years of the decade, the fad really came alive. Then marathon flying consisted of pilots circling an airport for days to establish refueling endurance records. Bemused people watched airplanes flying nowhere over the cities of Houston, Cleveland, Shreveport, Minneapolis, and San Francisco. Adroit refueling crews kept the airplanes aloft. Still, people scratched their heads not understanding that the "stunts" were scientific tests to determine how long man and machine could hold out before falling apart. Several pilots crashed which national newspapers were quick to editorialize about. The Philadelphia *Evening Public Ledger* lamented:

> Not one in a score of these dangerous flights or record-seeking performances has any real laboratory value. If successful, they open a golden door to personal profit for those that achieve them; if they end in total failure, they are laid at aviation's door.

On the other hand, the San Francisco *Chronicle* reassured:

> Endurance flyers learn something useful for aviation, even when they do not break records. . . . The hard treatment a motor gets in endurance flights shows up its weak points, then the manufacturer can correct them.

At decade's end, Dale "Red" Jackson and Forest O'Brine held the refueling endurance record by remaining in the air 420 hours, 21 minutes, and 30 seconds. Their effort earned them $31,000 +, a tidy sum of money which for some pilots was the real reason for risking life and limb. It would be remiss here not to mention Charles Lindbergh's solo transatlantic flight from New York to Paris (1927). He was the best known marathon flier, though not the most daring. His example of instant fame and fortune gave new impetus to the marathon flying fad. At times thrilling, at times foolhardy, the public did not know what to make of it. So much happened so quickly. It seemed long-distance flight had become a disturbing reality almost overnight.

## BIBLIOGRAPHY

"America's Marathons of the Sky," *Literary Digest*. 102 (August 10, 1929) 11.

"Beating Jules Verne by Sixty-Five Days," *Literary Digest*. 94 (July 2, 1927) 62-63.

"Flying 5400 Miles in Fifty Hours," *Literary Digest*. 63 (November 1, 1919) 19-20.

"The Non-Stop Flight Across America," "America from the Air," & "Man's Amazing Progress in Conquering the Air," *National Geographic Magazine*. 46 (July 1924) 1-122.

# Medical Electricity as a Tool for Fitness

"Medical electricity" enjoyed widespread popularity in America roughly between 1865-1900. The forces behind its rise included:

1. the more traditional "heroic" school of physicians were unable to counter the public tide of disbelief and anger with their methods, due in part to the continuing rancor within their own profession (homeopathic and, to a lesser extent, botanic physicians continued to thrive in the late nineteenth century, and a public intoxicated by new scientific discoveries interpreted the profession's internal disagreement as weakness)
2. the newly identified diseases of the era—in particular neurasthenia—seemed particularly unresponsive to traditional treatments
3. the small group of informed and semi-informed scientists of the pre-Civil War era who considered the human body electrical or magnetic in nature became much larger as chemists, physicists, and biologists progressively defined the essence of electricity.

The evolution of electrotherapeutic theory was, to a notable degree, based upon the concept that electricity and electromagnetism were, like magnetism, somewhat magical forces. One theorist within this school, W. R. Wells, asserted in *A New Theory of Disease* (1869) that all disease had "but one grand cause . . . a loss of balance of the two forces of electricity in the part or parts diseased." He argued that by applying electrical energy to those parts of the body diagnosed as out of balance, equilibrium and health could be restored.

In addition to explaining the origin and treatment of disease, electrotherapeutic theory appeared to unravel the mysteries of the universe, or at the very least its physical phenomena. Its employment of machines and measurement in a seemingly rigorous manner helped endow it with a contemporary, scientific aura. As up-to-date as it appeared, however, electrotherapeutic theory was heavily based upon earlier modes of thought. Emma Harding Britten's influential work, *The Electric Physician: or Self-Cure Through Electricity* (1875), adapted the concept of "grand positive magnetic poles" (brain, heart and lungs) largely from the magnetic poles identified in Henry Hall Sherwood's *A Manual for Magnetizing* (1845).

Perhaps of most importance to laymen, electricity offered hope that the perceptible trend of declining vitality might be reversed. It was somehow comforting to view the body as in a state of equilibrium when healthy, as well as logical to consider a man-made machine capable of correcting the body's imbalance and replenishing the store of energy depleted by the rigors of a new age. In short, electricity offered solutions to problems that previous generations had often considered inscrutable. For instance, cholera's visitations could be explained as "the rapid passage of electricity from the human frame," and as the "peculiarity of the atmosphere, known to exist during cholera" rather than as divine punishment.

Britten, like many other advocates of this theory, profited immensely from its application as a form of medical treatment. She and her husband ran an electromedical facility for many years in Brookline, Massachusetts. The relatively expensive treatments typically went as follows:

> For a "sick headache" . . . Britten advised home electricians to "apply a (metal) plate, (positive), across the loins, and another (negative), across the abdomen, (for) five minutes, then remove the back plate up between the shoulders lengthways . . . and the front across the diaphragm . . . (for) five minutes. Then apply the plate to the nape of the neck . . . and place the feet in a metal foot-tub with about an inch in depth of hot salt and water; into this drop the tin electrode . . . and keep adding hot water to keep up the temperature for ten minutes.

The whole apparatus—brass plates, electrodes, and the various cups and sponges of the typical medical electrical kit—would have been wired to a large wet cell. The current was always supposed to be "light," especially in the beginning of treatment, and a "seance" of treatment was not to exceed twenty to thirty minutes, lest the patient be "liable to reactionary fatigue, weariness, and pain." As with many other authors in this field, Britten offered not only advice and testimony for medical electricity but also a chance for readers to buy their own therapeutic device.

Many within the medical fraternity questioned the basic premises of the electrotherapeutic school. Henry Pickering Bowditch attacked the theory that "nerve force" and electricity were identical. J. H. Kellogg, while allowing that "when rightly used, [electricity] curative value is immense," opined that "it has fallen, unfortunately, almost entirely into the hands of quacks."

Despite these criticisms, the broad cultural enthusiasm for and confusion about electricity helped generate a variety of related but tangential theories about health and therapy. These theories in turn gave rise to a host of new products possessing questionable therapeutic value. Hall's Glass Castors, for insulating bedsteads, were reputed to halt the escape of electricity from the extremities during sleep (which explained feelings of "languor and exhaustion on rising in the morning") as well as protecting the sleeper from lightning. Brewster's Medicated Electricity advertised itself as "an infallible remedy for headache, neuralgia, hay fever, catarrh and cold in the head." One of the most popular of all expressions of the late nineteenth-century craze for electricity was the electric brush (Dr. Scott's, as advertised in the June 3, 1882 issue of *Harper's Weekly*, represented one particular brand), which probably gained its credibility due to the static electricity produced when hair was brushed with thermoplastic materials.

The medical electricity craze gradually lost momentum at the turn of the century as continued advances in medical knowledge, specifically speaking, and scientific research methods in general combined to discredit the school to a progressively larger portion of the populace.

## BIBLIOGRAPHY

"Application of Electro-Magnetism for Therapeutic Purposes," *Scientific American Supplement*. 58 (November 5, 1904) 24116.

"Crisp & Webb's Electric Belt," *Scientific American*. 64 (March 14, 1891) 163.

"Dry Cell Faradic Battery," *Scientific American*. 71 (October 20, 1894) 245.

"Electricity and Therapeutics," *Scientific American Supplement*. 57 (April 30, 1904) 23687-23688.

Faithfull, E. "Electrical Cure of Cancer," *Contemporary Review*. 61 (March 1892) 408-421.

Girdner, J.H. "Healing By Electricity," *Munsey*. 29 (April 1903) 85-87.

Green, Harvey. "Electricity, Energy, and Vitality," In: *Fit For America: Health, Fitness, Sport and American Society*. Baltimore: The Johns Hopkins University Press, 1988, c1986. pp. 167-180.

"Hartelius' Electrical Attachment For Rocking Chairs," *Scientific American*. 68 (May 6, 1893) 276.

Maude, A. "New Elixir of Life," *Current Literature*. 32 (April 1902) 410.

"Webb's Electric Belt," *Scientific American*. 68 (May 6, 1893) 277.

# Frank Merriwell

From 1896 to 1914, Frank Merriwell of Fardale Academy, Yale College and the world at large, performed unmatchable exploits on both the playing field and in everyday life on the pages of *Tip Top Weekly*, the most widely read nickel novel ever published. Merriwell represented virtually all of the qualities American readers might have wished to see embodied in a young man: truth, faith, justice, the triumph of right, friendship, loyalty, patriotism, duty, sacrifice, retribution, tolerance, honesty, modesty, and love of motherhood and the hearth fire.

According to Robert Boyle, Merriwell probably left a more enduring impression than any of the real-life athletic heroes who appeared on the American scene. Therefore, it was no surprise that his admirers reputedly included Jess Willard, Jack Dempsey, Fredric March, Christy Mathewson, Babe Ruth, Woodrow Wilson, Al Smith, and Wendell Willkie. Countless youngsters were also inspired by the Merriwell stories. Many followed his example by enrolling at Yale; Clarence Mulford consciously incorporated elements of Merriwell into his Hopalong Cassidy stories. Others have helped fuel a nostalgia boom for the character which includes fan clubs (e.g., the New York-based Friends of Frank Merriwell), a healthy business in the resale of old issues of *Tip Top*, and columns and features about the phenomenon (including the compilation of a plot synopsis for each story by Edward T. LeBlanc, editor of *Dime Novel Roundup*).

The character had its genesis in December 1895, when Street & Smith asked author Gilbert Patten, then twenty-nine and almost broke, to consider writing a weekly series for them:

> . . . something in the line of the Jack Harkaway stories, Gay Dashleigh series which we are running in *Good News* and the Island School series. . . . The idea being to issue a library containing a series of stories covering this class of incident, in

all of which will appear one prominent character surrounded by suitable satellites. . . .

It is important that the main character in the series should have a catchy name, such as Dick Lightheart, Jack Harkaway, Gay Dashleigh, Don Kirk, as upon this name will depend the title for the library.

The essential idea of this series is to interest young readers in the career of a young man at a boarding school, preferably a military or a naval academy. The stories should differ from the Jack Harkaways in being American and thoroughly up to date . . .

Patten enthusiastically took up the project, completing his first story in four days. Titled "Frank Merriwell; or, First Days at Fardale" (*Tip Top Weekly*, Volume I, Number 1), it appeared on April 18, 1896 under the Burt L. Standish pseudonym. Within a few months, the circulation of the periodical reached 75,000 copies, it ultimately reached an estimated level of 300,000 issues (the exact figures were kept a secret, perhaps because the publisher was paying Patten a straight salary, initially fifty dollars—and by 1914, $1,500—per week).

In 1914, after writing twenty million words for the series, Patten requested that someone else take over due to general fatigue. Written by a team of hacks, the series lasted three more years; Patten attributed its demise to the rise of movies. The character resurfaced in 1934 as a radio program. Patten, who continued to write novels, Hollywood scripts, and stories for adult adventure magazines throughout the 1920s and 1930s, contributed one final Merriwell work, a hard-cover novel entitled *Mr. Frank Merriwell*, in 1941. He died in early 1945 at the age of seventy-eight.

Patten himself assessed his contribution to the annals of sports literature in the following manner:

Did I love Merriwell? Not at first. Those early stories were more of a joke to me than anything else. But when it got so that half a million kids were reading him every week—and I think there were that many, when you stop to think how the stories were lent from hand to hand—I began to realize that I had about the biggest chance to influence the youth of this country that any man ever had. . . . Yes, I loved him. And I loved him most because no boy, if he followed in his tracks, ever did anything that he need be ashamed of.

## BIBLIOGRAPHY

Boyle, Robert H. "The Unreal Ideal: Frank Merriwell," In: *Sport—Mirror of American Life*. Boston: Little, Brown, 1963. pp. 241-271.
Cain, James M. "The Man Merriwell," *Saturday Evening Post*. (June 11, 1927).
Cutler, John Levi. *Gilbert Patten and His Frank Merriwell Saga*. Orono, Me: University of Maine, 1934.
*Dime Novel Roundup*. Edward T. LeBlanc, editor and publisher. Fall River, Mass. Monthly. Features regular studies in Merriwelliana.
Reynolds, Quentin. *The Fiction Factory*. New York: 1955.

# Them Amazin' Mets

Given the vantage point of hindsight, the New York Mets were a very successful expansion team. In the team's eighth year of existence, they won the World Series. However, the Mets set a major league record for futility during their debut season in 1962, losing 120 out of 160 games.

The late Bill Veeck observed,

> I never thought I would have an argument. I was always secure in the knowledge that when I owned the St. Louis Browns, I had the worst. Now it's different. You can say anything you want, but don't you dare say my Brownies were this bad. I'll prove it to you. There are still a few Browns in the major leagues and this is nine years later. How many Mets do you think are going to be around even two years from now? I'm being soft here. I haven't even mentioned my midget, Eddie Gaedel.

Many others — including journalists, former players and fans — concurred with this assessment.

The fact that the Mets were so bad could be attributed to the absence of any good players. The expansion process dictated that they be provided a list of expendable personnel by the other eight National League teams. The players chosen by the Mets included faded stars (e.g., first baseman Gil Hodges, center fielder Richie Ashburn), journeymen (e.g., first baseman Marvelous Marv Throneberry) and never-will-be's.

New York fans, grateful to once again have an alternative to the arrogant Yankees (the Brooklyn Dodgers and New York Giants had shifted their franchises to Los Angeles and San Francisco, respectively, prior to the beginning of the 1958 season), took the hapless Mets into their hearts. Certain players became almost legendary for their ineptitude, particularly Throneberry. In order to illustrate the strange things that happen when he plays, Jimmy Breslin recounted the events of the first game of a doubleheader against the Cubs at the Polo Grounds early in the season:

> In the first inning . . . Don Landrum of Chicago was caught in a rundown between first and second. Rundowns are not Throneberry's strong point. In the middle of the posse of Mets chasing the Cub, Throneberry found himself face to face with Landrum. The only trouble was Marvin did not have the ball. During a rundown the cardinal rule is to get out of the way if you do not have the ball. If you stand around, the runner will deliberately bang into you, claim interference and the umpire will give it to him.
> Which is exactly what happened to Marv . . . and that opened the gates for a four-run Chicago rally.
> Marv had a big chance to make good when the Mets came to bat. With two runners on, Marv drove a long shot to the bullpen in right center field. It looked to be a sure triple. Marv flew past first. Way past it. He didn't come within two steps of touching the bag . . . Ernie Banks, the Cubs' first basemen, casually strolled over to Umpire Dusty Boggess.
> "Didn't touch the bag, you know, Dusty," Banks said. Boggess nodded . . . Throneberry was standing on third . . . taking a deep breath and . . . proudly hitching up his belt when he saw the umpire calling him out at first.

Perhaps the most colorful Met was not a player at all. Manager Casey Stengel, 73, was considered too old to head the Yankees after guiding them to ten World Series in twelve years through 1961. The darling of reporters and fans alike due to his on-the-field antics and a peculiar form of rambling monologue, dubbed Stengelese, he won kudos for brilliant tactical maneuvering and extreme patience in the midst of wholesale ineptitude.

Despite this horrendous season, the franchise was committed to steady, solid development. Another Yankee castoff, General Manager George Weiss, stressed the building of a talented scouting corps in addition to a well-organized minor league operation rather than subscribing to a get-rich-quick philosophy. His good common sense and sound planning were rewarded with a world championship first in 1969, and then another pennant win in 1973.

## BIBLIOGRAPHY

Breslin, Jimmy. "Worst Baseball Team Ever," *Sports Illustrated*. 19 (1962) 22-24, 49-53.

"Casey at the Bat," *Time*. 79 (May 4, 1962) 46.

"Love those Mets," *Time*. 79 (June 15, 1962) 71.

Millstein, G. "Musings of a Dugout Socrates," *New York Times Magazine*. (August 26, 1962) 17ff.

Paxton, H.T. "Casey the Indestructible," *Saturday Evening Post*. 235 (April 7, 1962) 46ff.

Shecter, L. "Bring Back the Real Mets!," *New York Times Magazine*. (September 7, 1969) 66-67.

# Miniature Golf

Miniature golf—or, as it was variously called, "Tom Thumb golf," "half-pint golf" and "pigmy golf"—was the first major fad of the Great Depression, a period well known for its wealth of obsessions. By early fall 1930, some twenty million Americans were playing the game (four million on any given night) on 25,000 miniature links. A Department of Commerce report noted the following economic implications:

- increased trade for the golf club manufacturers, the cotton growers, the railroads, and the electric power companies;
- decreased attendance for the movies.

The majority of sources from that era credited Tennesseean Garnet Carter with creating the American offshoot of miniature golf (the game goes back to diminutive courses located in front of English inns which utilized natural grass with only trees, roots and a rolling lawn for hazards). He built the first American course (called Fairyland) in 1927 on Lookout Mountain near Chattanooga as a means of boosting the popularity of his hotel and standard length links. People crowded it in such numbers that Carter began charging a greens fee.

A major refinement ensued out of the destruction to turf (caused by the wear and tear of continuous play); Carter heard of a vegetable fibre substance patented by Fairbairn and McCart of Texas, who had accidently discovered the putting properties of cotton seed hulls when tapping a golf ball across the floor of a warehouse carpeted with these husks. In this form, the game spread through the Southern resorts, took fire in California, and, beginning in fall 1929, swept across the remaining portions of the nation. In New York, where vacant lots are scarce, miniature golf went indoors. In addition to commercial courses, there could be found many products of juvenile ingenuity constructed of bricks, boards, abandoned tiles, and drainpipes.

Many publications of that era speculated as to why the pursuit had become so popular. *The Nation* noted,

> The search for superiority is one [reason]. Golf is a gentleman's game — and who does not crave at least the accouterments of gentlemanliness? But golf links require many acres of rolling turf, and rolling turf is very scarce and beyond hope expensive.

The New York *Evening Post* stated,

> Altho it bears only the slightest resemblence to actual golf, it offers thousands of persons who have never had the opportunity to play, and who do not know the first thing about the game a chance to experiment with club and ball, and to feel that they are in on the real thing. Also the ingenious layout of these miniature courses, which leaves so much to Lady Luck, makes the game one of chance in which the golf novice may go around in par quite as easily as Bobby Jones himself.

In order to maintain interest in the game as well as to enhance its legitimacy as a sport related to genuine golf, promoters developed the National Tom Thumb Open Championship, first held at Carter's Fairyland course in October 1930. In its mania to forget the hardships engendered by the Great Depression, however, the American mind felt it necessary to manufacture a seemingly endless string of diversions. Despite a substantial drop-off in popularity from that watershed year, due at least in part to the appearance of new competitors, miniature golf has continued to attract players for well over a half century.

## BIBLIOGRAPHY

"All Thrills of Golf in Twenty-Five-Foot Ring," *Popular Mechanics*. 55 (April 1931) 533.

"Bobby Joneses of the Vacant-Lot Golf Clubs," *Literary Digest*. 10 (August 23, 1930) 32-34.

Davis, E. "Miniature Golf to the Rescue," *Harper*. 162 (December 1930) 4-14.

Evans, M. "Lilliput Putters," *Saturday Evening Post*. 203 (September 27, 1930) 12ff.

"Ever Crazier Hazards on the Tom Thumb Links," *Literary Digest*. 108 (January 24, 1931) 37.

Gelders, J.F. "That Giant, Midget Golf," *Review of Reviews*. 82 (November 1930) 77-78.

"Golf at the Fireside," *Literary Digest*. 108 (January 10, 1931) 35.

"Half-Pint Golf," *Outlook and Independent*. 155 (August 27, 1930) 656.

"In Honor of a Short One," *Commonweal*. 12 (August 27, 1930) 414.

Metzger, S. "Indoor Golf," *Country Life*. 59 (March 1931) 68.

"Midget or Colossus?," *Survey*. 65 (November 15, 1930) 197.

"Miniature Golf Again," *American City*. 43 (September 1930) 17.

"Miniature Golf and Public Policy," *American City*. 43 (August 1930) 17.

"Miniature Golf Helps Many Kinds of Business," *Business Week*. (September 3, 1930) 9.

Rice, G. "Small Game Hunters," *Collier's*. 86 (September 20, 1930) 19.

Seibert, C.F. "Miniature Golf on the Playgrounds," *Recreation*. 24 (March 1931) 662.

"Tom Thumb Golf," *The Nation*. 131:3399 (August 27, 1930) 215- 216.

Trevor, George. "Battle of Lilliput," *Outlook and Independent*. 156 (October 1, 1930) 194, 199.

In its heyday (the 1930s), socialites played miniature golf on country club courses like this one. They dressed smartly and spent a fine afternoon putting between talk of Wall Street and the next garden party. Later, when miniature golf came back in vogue, the rich disdained it as a lower-class pleasure.

# Monopoly

Monopoly might best be described as the board game which never went away. First produced by Parker Bros. in 1935, the company has sold between sixty and eighty-five million sets over the years.

Monopoly was invented in 1933 in Germantown, Pennsylvania by Charles Darrow, then an unemployed heating-equipment salesman. Reflecting on more prosperous times, he devised a game for his family and friends to play based upon his sketched-out representation of Atlantic City real estate on an oilcloth. To fill the demands of friends, he began making sets. As Monopoly sales quickly overtook his production capacity, Darrow decided to copyright the game.

When Philadelphia department stores began ordering Monopoly sets wholesale, he took the game to the Salem, Massachusetts firm of Parker Bros., the world's largest publisher of games. The company executives liked it, but felt the general public would not, because it took too long to play. In rejecting the game, Parker Bros. advised Darrow that it had "52 fundamental errors." The continued regional success of Monopoly led the company to reconsider and early in 1935 it offered Darrow an attractive royalty contract.

Parker Bros. refined the game, clarified the rules, and arrived at a version that could be played in less time. It was an immediate success and in 1937, at the age of forty-six, Darrow was able to retire to a farm in Bucks County, Pennsylvania for life. In its half century of life, Monopoly has far outsold all other proprietary games. Although the exact figures are shrouded in secrecy, it is generally agreed in the trade that Monopoly has been the top-selling game every year since it came out, with the possible exception of two years in the mid-1950s during the Scrabble craze and the year immediately following the introduction of Trivial Pursuit in the mid-1980s. Parker executives admit to continued annual sales of one million to two million sets per year. Few Americans have not tried the game at leat once. As noted by J. F. Wilkinson,

> You can go up to almost any literate American older than 10 and say: "Go directly to jail. Do not pass Go. Do not collect $200," and he will surely know that you are talking about Monopoly.

The appeal of Monopoly in the 1930s was felt to be largely a result of the fact that it gave the players a pleasurable illusion of wealth. However, since Monopoly now thrives amidst relative peace and plenty, *Fortune*'s assessment seems closer to the truth:

> . . . a game that caters to the most grindingly acquisitive instincts of every businessman. The idea is to squeeze out all your fellow players until you own the whole board. The more you own, the more you make.

Additional reasons given for the game's popularity include the fact that it appeals to the competitive nature of people as well as offering a release from the tensions of everyday life.

Regional variations of Monopoly have continued to spring up over the years, generally the brainchild of local chambers of commerce. Other spinoffs include Merit, developed to teach "the true Catholic way of life" and featuring plastic pieces in the likeness of Jesus, Mary, Joseph and the angels; and Trump, a monument to the real-life 1980s incarnation of an Atlantic City power broker.

Parker Bros. officials have noted a variety of interesting developments from the letters they receive, including the evolution of new ground rules (presumably the result of people playing by rules that have come down by word of mouth, long after the rules sheet has disappeared) and rise of sticklers (e.g., a Brooklynite asked whether he should play Monopoly according to New York state real-estate laws).

Editions of the game have been published in twenty-seven countries and in fifteen different languages. Darrow once saw natives playing it in New Guinea. While it represents the antithesis of Communism, Monopoly appears to be popular in Eastern Bloc nations as well. During the American National Exhibition in Moscow in

1959 — scene of the famed Nixon-Khrushchev kitchen debate — there were six Monopoly sets on display, all had been stolen by the time the exhibit was over.

## BIBLIOGRAPHY

Bongartz, Roy. "Pass Go and Retire," *Saturday Evening Post*. 237 (April 11, 1964) 26-27.

Brady, Maxine. *The Monopoly Book*. 1974.

"Child's Play: Merit; Catholic Monopoly," *Newsweek*. 66 (August 16, 1965) 56.

Kaye, Marvin. *The Story of Monopoly, Silly Putty, Bingo, Twister, Frisbee, Scrabble, Etcetera*. 1977.

"Monopoly," *Fortune*. 12 (December 1935) 40ff.

"Monopoly and Politics," *Time*. 27 (February 3, 1936) 68ff.

"Where Monopoly Is Not a Dirty Word: Parker Bros.," *Business Week*. (March 25, 1967) 180-182ff.

Wilkinson, J.F. "The Play-Money Game That Made Millions," *Sports Illustrated*. 19 (December 2, 1963) 52-59.

# Muhammed Ali

Boxer Muhammed Ali, born Cassius Clay in Louisville, Kentucky in 1942, remained a cultural phenomenon throughout a career spanning three decades. He claimed to be the most famous man alive, a point which no one chose to dispute. *Sports Illustrated* featured him on its cover a record thirty-one times during its first thirty-five years of publication (including the special 35th anniversary edition cover).

Four developments during his time in sport's center stage were perhaps most responsible for rendering Ali a household name:

1. his brash "I am the greatest" campaign aimed at securing him an early heavyweight title shot,
2. the controversial nature of his second bout with Sonny Liston,
3. his refusal to be inducted into military service in the midst of the Vietnam War,
4. the courageous return to the top of the boxing world following a forced hiatus which denied him the opportunity to ply his trade while in his prime.

After winning a gold medal in the 1960 Olympics, Ali began making waves early in his pro career for his wild behavior; e.g., reciting poetry (see Table I), prophesizing the round in which he would vanquish his opponent, mugging for crowds and photographers, an endless barrage of printable quotes ("Ain't I pretty? I'm too beautiful to be a fighter," "They all must fall in the round I call!" etc.). Ali was notable in that his conceits – did not outstrip his superb ring skills or bely his underlying shrewdness. At the outset of his career, Clay signed with a syndicate of reputable businessmen who gave him one of the most attractive contracts ever received by a young fighter up to that time as well as managing his earnings with respect to investments, tax payments, etc. The group allowed Ali to freely exercise the showmanship which quickly rendered him boxing's biggest draw outside of the heavyweight champion.

---

Table I
". . . I'm the greatest"
a poem by Cassius Clay

---

This is a story about a man
With iron fists and a beautiful tan.
He talks a lot and he boasts indeed
Of a powerful punch and blinding speed.
The fight game was dying
And promoters were crying
For someone to come along
With a new and different song.
Patterson was dull, quiet and sad,
And Sonny Liston was just as bad.
Then along came a kid named Cassius Clay,
Who said, "Liston, I'll take your title away,"
This colorful fighter is something to see,
And heavyweight champ he's certain to be.
You get the impression while watching him fight
That he plays cat and mouse, then turns out the light.
What a frustrating feeling I'm sure it must be,
To be hit by blows you can't even see.
Where was he first? Where was he last?
How can you conquer a man so fast?
I'm sure his opponents have tried their best,
But one by one on the canvas they rest.
Everyone knew when Cassius wasn't around,
For quietness descended on the town.
If Clay says a mosquito can pull a plow,
Don't ask him how —
Hitch him up!

---

Many ring historians have asserted that Ali's appeal was instrumental in saving boxing from abolishment by various state governments and ultimately, perhaps, by Washington. A series of ring deaths, most notably Davy Moore, in the early 1960s had provided the impetus for advocates of such a move. Ali actually spoke before the legislative committee which was considering terminating the sport in New York; the day following his appearance, the committeemen voted that boxing would continue.

Ironically, Ali's first heavyweight title defense in May 1965 against the dethroned champ Sonny Liston provided the grist for the next notable round of recriminations from the media and politicians. The suddenness and quickness of Ali's knockout punch in the first round — unseen by most fans in the arena as well as closed-circuit television viewers — led to widespread accusations of bout fixing. Tex Maule noted, in the fight's aftermath, that

> Bills to ban the sport were planned in several state legislatures. . . . Elderly ex-champions, among them Jack Dempsey and Gene Tunney, proclaimed the quick victory a fatal blow to boxing. . . . A promoter in San Antonio apologized to his theater TV customers and, on the basis that they had been defrauded by a "shameful spectacle," donated his take to boys' clubs. The California legislature, in session, received a resolution calling for an investigation by the state attorney general to determine if its closed-circuit televiewers had been fraudulently duped out of their money.

In actuality, Ali's performance was exceptional. Experts such as former heavyweight champion Floyd Patterson and the then light heavyweight champ Jose Torres lauded the knockout blow. It was perfectly delivered against an opponent who was moving toward it, resulting in the effect of a head-on collision.

The mid-1960s found Ali converting to Islamism (the first famous black athlete to do so) and consequently refusing induction into the army on religious grounds. His decision found both supporters and detractors in a nation already divided over the Vietnam experience. Groups within the Old and New Left as well as Black Power advocates argued that the immorality of this particular war justified the refusal by conscientious objectors to serve; on the other hand, conservatives noted that no single right could be absolute in practice, that a draft — necessary at times for the defense of the nation — is by its nature a coercive restriction of certain individual rights and freedoms. The latter point of view ultimately held sway in Ali's case as the fighter became involved in prolonged litigation while being stripped of his crown and license to box.

The changing attitudes of the nation as a whole during the late 1960s and early 1970s led many to reassess their feelings about Ali; he gradually emerged as a hero who had taken on an unfeeling, even immoral, government regarding his personal convictions. Freed to fight again, Ali—obviously no longer the marvelous athlete he once was (to some the greatest heavyweight ever)—began a slow trail back to the top. Despite detours—i.e., losses to Ken Norton and George Frazer—he regained the title he had never lost inside the ring from George Foreman in a stunning victory in 1974.

The remaining years as a boxer were undistinguished (save his epic win over Frazer in the "Thrilla In Manila") capped by the growing realization that Ali had a degenerative condition of the nervous system called Parkinson's Syndrome. Despite his slurred speech and awkward gait, Ali continued to attract fans throughout the world in the 1980s. He now appeared more heroic than ever to many, refusing to curtail his activities merely to accommodate his affliction.

## BIBLIOGRAPHY

"The Dissenting Champion," *National Review*. (May 30, 1967) 504-506.

Maule, Tex. "A Quick, Hard Right and a Needless of Protest," *Sports Illustrated*. 22 (June 7, 1965) 22-25.

Moses, Don. "Ride On, You Lip of Louisville," *Life*. 54 (February 15, 1963) 62-65.

"Theater of the Absurd," *Time*. 85 (June 4, 1965) 68-69.

# Muscular Christianity

The post-Civil War era witnessed an "Athletic Revival" which became linked with the continued strength of evangelical Christianity. Harvey Green summarized the underlying pattern of this development as follows:

> In the Northeast in particular, middle-class and wealthy Americans heeded the advocates of exercise and athletic competition because their environment had changed so radically from that of 1830. By 1860 nearly half the population of the Northeast lived in cities and towns. Many worked in sedentary, "brain work" occupations. The argument that theirs was a position superior to that of people of less developed civilizations appealed to them, as did the idea that physical activity— a positive action—would alleviate the ill effects of this advanced station. The idea that united the advocates and devotees of calisthenics, gymnastics, physical education, and sports was that the body was more than simply a container for the soul that should be kept free from disease; its form could be altered and perfected, and by doing so people could increase their energy and improve their life and, implicitly, their afterlife. Perfection of the body was an essential part of Christian morality in this system of thought and was perhaps the most vivid expression of the prewar millennial spirit, which had promoted the idea that human action could determine individual and social salvation.

Gymnasiums and playing fields were also popular because they served to bring people together. As rural populations moved to the large urban centers, the traditional mechanisms of social support and cultural continuity were virtually non-existent. Athletic activities such as gymnastics, calisthenics, baseball, football, track and field, rowing, boxing, tennis, and golf all achieved heretofore unparalleled popularity as focal points for people to get to know their neighbors and learn coping strategies for their unfamiliar environment.

Americans were particularly influenced by "Muscular Christianity," a movement which had its origins in England during the early 1800s. The English model of the "muscular Christian" was the fictional hero "Tom Brown," best known through Thomas Hughes' rendition of *Tom Brown's Schooldays*. Another popular English novelist, Charles Kingsley, coined the phrase; his most successful work, *Two Years Ago* (1857), had as its central tenet that morality was a function of muscularity as well as of piety, and that the best sort of Christians were physically fit. By 1870 it was noted in *Godey's Lady's Book* that muscular Christianity was "so popular with nearly all classes of people" that books on "bodily strength and skill will find abundant favor."

One devotee of muscular Christianity, Luther Gulick, was responsible for transforming the Young Men's Christian Association into a sports and fitness organization. By 1893 Frederick Jackson Turner would state that the frontier—the outlet through which the pressure of urban populations was eased—had disappeared; accordingly, organizations such as the YMCA came to be considered as instrumental in the maintenance of order.

Despite the continued viability of YMCAs, the Boy Scouts, and other like-minded organizations, the alliance of the moral and physical dimensions gradually lost its preeminent status in the public mind due to factors such as the increasing popularity of sports dominated by the colleges and professional leagues and the philosophy of winning no matter the costs. These trends fostered an elitism which ran contrary to the previously accepted notion that all individuals should strive for improvement via exercise.

## BIBLIOGRAPHY

Green, Harvey. "'Muscular Christianity' and the Athletic Revival," In: *Fit For America: Health, Fitness, Sport and American Society*. Baltimore: The Johns Hopkins University Press, 1988, c1986. pp. 181-215.

# "Broadway Joe" Namath

As early as 1966, Boston Patriots owner Billy Sullivan termed Joe Namath (a.k.a. "Broadway Joe" and "Joe Willie") "The biggest thing in New York since Babe Ruth." Namath, a native of Beaver Falls (a mill town located thirty miles outside of Pittsburgh, Pennsylvania), began his ascent to the sports world by quarterbacking the University of Alabama to three bowl games with seasons of 10-1, 9-2 and 10-1. On the heels of his 1964 national championship season with the Crimson Tide, New York Jets owner Sonny Werblin made him an instant media superstar by signing him to a $400,000 contract on January 2, 1965; a figure more than double that ever given to any other football player.

As the brightest star of the fledgling American Football League, Namath came to embody its hopes for achieving legitimacy in the eyes of its more established rival, the National Football League. His image also grew as a result of suspense which built as to whether he would be drafted for military service (he would flunk his physical), or whether his gimpy knee (he had undergone an operation on his knee in early 1965 to have a torn cartilage removed and a loose ligament tied) would enable him to play football at all. Satirist Robert Benton and David Newman supplied the hip line of the season in New York: "Sorry I can't make your party, Sybil, but I'm going to the tapping of Joe Namath's knee."

Namath's presence in the Jets' training camp at Peekskill, New York added to his notoriety. According to a *Time* account,

> He arrived toting a bag of golf clubs, buzzed around town in a green Continental convertible with the top down and jazz blaring from a tape recorder under the dash. His self-confidence knew no bounds. "Ah cain't wait 'til tomorrow," he cracked, admiring himself in the locker-room mirror, ' "cause ah get better lookin' every day."

Following a lackluster 1965 campaign, which he had begun relegated to the Jets' spotting phone on the sidelines, Namath set about proving that he was a throwing artist who would eventually come to rank with the best. Meanwhile, as his skills came into fruition, Namath remained a swinger. He lived in a penthouse on New York's Upper East Side, complete with a huge white llama-skin rug, an Italian marble bar, an elaborate stereo hookup, and a large oval bed. He cruised around the city in his convertible, the radio blaring, parking by fireplugs whenever possible, wearing tailor-made suits with tight pants and loud print lining, grabbing checks, spending approximately $25,000 a year ("On nuthin', man") and professing to be mystified as to why anyone might be offended at his carefree lifestyle.

Greater things, however, lay in store for Namath. After boasting over and over again that his Jets would whip the heavily favored Baltimore Colts in the 1969 Super Bowl—a game that up until then had not been won by the upstart American Football League—he spearheaded a 16-7 victory, thereby earning the appellation Super Joe. His time at the top was short-lived; in early summer NFL Commissioner Pete Rozelle, maintaining that Namath's Bachelors III restaurant was a hangout for known gamblers, ordered that the star either sell his interest in the night spot or retire from pro football. After a brief, tear-stained retirement from the game, Namath gave in to Rozelle's demands and agreed to sell his interest, noting that the problem had gotten out of proportion and was now affecting his family, his teammates, and the reputation of professional football. He added, "I still insist I haven't done anything wrong. I'd stand on my principle if it was only me alone."

Namath remained a top draw in the NFL until the mid-1970s, finishing out his career with the Los Angeles Rams. He remained in the public eye as an actor and sports commentator. When these endeavors stalled, Namath wrote his autobiography in the late 1980s; by then a thoroughly domesticated animal (married, with kids), he demonstrated a more subdued form of self-assurance while making the promotional rounds on television talk shows, no longer appearing drawn to the limelight.

# BIBLIOGRAPHY

Astor, G. "Namath the Game," *Look*. 30 (November 29, 1966) 115-118.

"Bachelors II," *Time*. 94 (July 25, 1969) 49.

"Battle of the QBs," *Time*. 86 (September 17, 1965) 96.

"Blues for Broadway Joe," *Newsweek*. 73 (June 23, 1969) 109-110.

"Broadway Joe's Return," *Newsweek*. 74 (July 28, 1969) 72ff.

Cant, G. "Joint for Next Season," *Sports Illustrated*. 22 (February 8, 1965) 38-41.

"Demi-God; Symposium," *Esquire*. 72 (October 1969) 103-113ff.

"$400,000 Knee," *Time*. 85 (February 5, 1965) 53.

Jenkins, Dan. "The Sweet Life of Swinging Joe," *Sports Illustrated*. 25 (October 17, 1966) 42-44ff.

"Joe's Tearful Good-By," *Newsweek*. 73 (June 16, 1969) 66.

Johnson, W. "Mod Man Out," *Sports Illustrated*. 30 (June 16, 1969) 10, 20-23. Includes editorial comment.

Lake, J. "Two for the Football Show: the Swinger and the Square," *New York Times Magazine*. (November 5, 1967) 40-41.

Long, B. "Joe Namath," *Vogue*. 149 (February 1, 1967) 156-157ff.

Mathis, B. "Joe Namath," *Esquire*. 70 (September 1968) 122-125ff.

Maule, Tex. "Say It's Say, Joe," *Sports Illustrated*. 30 (January 20, 1969) 10-15.

"Mr. Big of the Bonus Baby War," *Life*. 58 (January 15, 1965) 56D-57.

"Namath of the Jets," *Newsweek*. 74 (September 15, 1969) 57- 58ff.

O'Neil, P. "Broadway Joe," *Life*. 66 (January 24, 1969) 24-29.

Shrake, E. "Joe Passes the Big Test in a Breeze," *Sports Illustrated*. 30 (January 6, 1969) 16-19.

Skow, J. "Joe, Joe, You're the Most Beautiful Thing in the World!," *Saturday Evening Post*. 239 (December 3, 1966) 99-103.

Smith, S. "Broadway Joe: Rebel With a Nightclub for a Cause," *Life*. 66 (June 20, 1969) 22-27.

Underwood, J. "Another Good Joe for the AFL," *Sports Illustrated*. 23 (August 9, 1965) 46-49.

# North/South Horse Races

Four North/South horse races had already been run before the great contest in 1845, that of Fashion vs. Peytona. Earlier in 1823, the northern horse Eclipse beat the southern Sir Henry in part setting up the final determining series of races. Twice a northern horse had won and twice a southern. So it remained for either Fashion or Peytona to break the tie. The Long Island races in New York hosted the glorious duel with spectators lining the course before 8 a.m. Trains from every direction brought in more people. The morning hours passed slowly as the scene grew gayer. A New York *Herald* reporter described the festivities:

> Business in the tents—the wigwams—the culinary camps and conventicles commenced at an early hour, and was carried on with a briskness that betimes looked like voracity, and fears were occasionally excited that the impetuosity of the hungry crowd might find a melancholy end in the prodigious tubs of lemonade and brandy punch that lay in elegant negligence around the tables, whose extended surfaces supported masses of ham, sandwiches, lobsters, loaves, decanters, glasses, and all the paraphernalia of drinking that could be condensed into the space.

Near race time, the crowd by best estimate numbered 30,000. "Betting and gambling and guzzling went on at a rapid rate, and the work of Satan here progressed with a celerity and promptitude that must have been greatly pleasing to his infernal highness."

About half past two, the northern mare Fashion stood nose to nose with the southern mare Peytona. Their riders leaned forward for the first of three heats to determine equine supremacy of the United States. Considerable pride was on line, not to mention a stable full of money. Peytona won the first heat by two lengths, sprinting the four miles in 7 minutes 39 seconds. Immediately, betting odds changed from near even to 50-30 on Peytona. The odds-makers knew their business, for Peytona took the second heat by a length in 7 minutes 45 seconds. No need for a third race, twenty minutes later, after resting, the two horses again trotted onto the course and Peytona was formally crowned queen of the turf.

> The Southerners appeared perfectly beside themselves with joy, and afforded quite a striking contrast to the Northerners, whose lengthened faces were indicative of the shortening their purses and fame had undergone within the last few minutes. . . . The cost of travelling and other expenses of the strangers, may be fairly estimated to have been a million dollars — and the value of the time and money of all, wasted or expended, cannot be supposed at less than two million. The amount of the bets can only be guessed at — it is very possible that they exceeded a million; for the 'sporting world,' from the extreme East to the extreme West, and the extreme North to the extreme South of the United States, was engaged in this affair!

Fashion vs. Peytona marked the high point of North/South horse racing. In contrast to the equally popular sport of harness racing, which depended more on the expert lead of the sulky driver for victory than on sheer animal speed and endurance, the simpler two-horse race stripped away any artificiality making the whole affair more of a three-round prize fight. A portent of darker days to come, the fad amplified the rivalry between North and South that soon turned into hatred. Less than two decades later, northerners and southerners spilled each others blood in earnest.

## BIBLIOGRAPHY

"Eclipse Bested Sir Henry at Union Course, Long Island in 1823." *Niles Weekly Register*. (May 31, 1823) 193-194.

"The Great Contest: Fashion v. Peytona (1845)." In: *The American Sporting Experience* edited by Steven A. Riess. New York: Leisure Press, 1984. pp. 91-103.

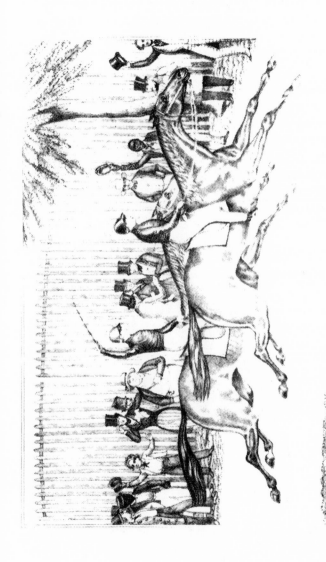

GREAT RACE BETWEEN PEYTONA & FASHION, FOR $20,000!!!

On the New York Union Course. May 13, 1845. Won by Peytona 1st Heat 7:44¾ — 2d Heat 7:45¾ —

Printed and published by N. Currier. Nassau St. N.Y.

Sperited in the Clerks Office for the Southern Districts; New York June 10, 1845.

North/South horse races excited the passions of a youthful America moving inexorably toward civil war. Northern horses won two races and southern two, before Peytona, in the last great confrontation (1845), broke the tie, giving the South the edge.

# The Notre Dame Mystique

The Notre Dame Mystique can be found residing in many places. There are approximately two hundred alumni clubs and countless other fugitive groups, the "subway-prairie-mountain-swamp alumni" who live only for the school's next gridiron triumph and know nothing of its excellent academic reputation. Beano Cook, currently a sports analyst for ESPN, observed that "Notre Dame is the only team in the country that never plays a road game."

At the university's campus in South Bend, Indiana, people ascribe football-like characteristics to local landmarks. A statue of Father Corby near Sorin Hall—the aging bronze mold of a man holding up his right arm—is referred to as "old fair-catch Corby." Another statue, Moses, located near the library, depicting the Old Testament patriarch with an arm uplifted, forefinger gesturing to the heavens, is interpreted as saying, "We're No. 1." A huge mosaic on the library showing Christ raising both arms is called "Touchdown Jesus."

The sports pages explain it all. Notre Dame's spectacular entrance upon the big time college football scene came in 1913 with a resounding 35-13 victory over a powerful Army team which would end the season with only that one defeat on its record. The school has since produced fourteen teams that have won national championships, over 120 All-Americans, seven Heisman Trophy winners, and countless legends (e.g., the Four Horsemen and Seven Mules) and coaching geniuses such as Knute Rockne (best remembered now for his "win one for the Gipper" speech), Frank Leahy, Ara Parseghian, and the most recent restorer of the glory that was, Lou Holtz.

Perhaps most notable of all has been Notre Dame's refusal to fall prey to the many pitfalls afflicting the rank-and-file football factories; e.g., almost all of its players graduate, its teams have never been sanctioned by the NCAA for rules violations. Many observers felt that Notre Dame's refusal to participate in post-season bowl games between 1925 and 1970 was the result of its desire to remain aloof from the rest of the pack. (The need for funds to aid a program for underprivileged students as well as the opportunities to reward players, enhance ratings, and recruit new prospects caused school officials to reconsider during the 1969 campaign, leading to a Cotton Bowl invitation to play Texas on January 1, 1970.)

On the heels of its 1989 national championship season, Notre Dame was ranked number one on all college football polls up to late November 1989 and in possession of the longest winning streak in its history (twenty-three). Whether due to divine intervention of the Blessed Virgin or a result of the luck of the Irish, Notre Dame has continued to add to its famed legacy up to the present day. (See Tables I-VIII.)

Table I: Number of Times Ranked No. 1, 1936-1984
------------------------------------------------------------

1.  Notre Dame.....69
2.  Ohio State.....62
3.  Oklahoma.....50
4.  Southern California.....47
5.  Texas.....38


------------------------------------------------------------
        Table II: Number of Times Ranked, 1936-1984
------------------------------------------------------------

1.  Notre Dame.....443
2.  Ohio State.....406
2.  Texas.....406
4.  Michigan.....396
5.  Southern California.....387


------------------------------------------------------------
Table III: Notre Dame's AP National Championships (1936-)
------------------------------------------------------------

    1943
    1946
    1947
    1949
    1966
    1973
    1977
    1988


------------------------------------------------------------
Table IV: Notre Dame's UPI National Championships (1950-)
------------------------------------------------------------

    1966
    1977
    1988


------------------------------------------------------------
       Table V: Consecutive Times Ranked, 1936-1984
------------------------------------------------------------

 1.  Michigan.....160 (1968-1980)
 2.  Notre Dame.....159 (1964-1975)
 3.  Oklahoma.....156 (1971-1981)
 4.  Oklahoma.....125 (1947-1960)
 5.  Penn State.....118 (1967-1976)
13.  Notre Dame.....79 (1941-1949)

------------------------------------------------------------
     Table VI: Notre Dame's Year-By-Year Won-Lost Record
------------------------------------------------------------

```
1887-1888.....0-3
1888.....1-0 (Overall: 1-3)
1889.....1-0 (2-3)
1890.....no football
1891.....no football
1892.....1-0-1 (3-3-1)
1893.....4-0 (7-3-1)
1894.....3-2-1 (10-5-2)
1895.....3-1 (13-6-2)
1896.....4-3 (17-9-2)
1897.....4-1-1 (21-10-3)
1898.....4-2 (25-12-3)
1899.....6-3-1 (31-15-4)
1900.....6-3-1 (37-18-5)
1901.....8-1-1 (45-19-6)
1902.....5-2-1 (50-21-7)
1903.....8-0-1 (58-21-8)
1904.....5-3 (63-24-8)
1905.....5-4 (68-28-8)
1906.....6-1 (74-29-8)
1907.....6-0-1 (80-29-9)
1908.....8-1 (88-30-9)
1909.....7-0-1 (95-30-10)
1910.....4-1-1 (99-31-11)
1911.....6-0-2 (105-31-13)
1912.....7-0 (112-31-13)
1913.....7-0 (119-31-13)
1914.....5-2 (124-33-13)
1915.....7-1 (131-34-13)
1916.....8-1 (139-35-13)
1917.....7-1 (146-36-13)
1918.....3-1-2 (149-37-15)
1919.....9-0 (158-37-15)
1920.....9-0 (167-37-15)
1921.....10-1 (177-38-15)
1922.....8-1-1 (185-39-16)
1923.....9-1 (194-40-16)
1924.....9-0 (203-40-16)
1925.....7-2-1 (210-42-17)
1926.....9-1 (219-43-17)
1927.....7-1-1 (226-44-18)
1928.....5-4 (231-48-18)
1929.....9-0 (240-48-18)
1930.....10-0 (250-48-18)
1931.....6-2-1 (256-50-19)
1932.....7-2 (263-52-19)
1933.....3-5-1 (266-57-20)
1934.....6-3 (272-60-20)
1935.....7-1-1 (279-61-21)
```

```
1936.....6-2-1 (285-63-22)
1937.....6-2-1 (291-65-23)
1938.....8-1 (299-66-23)
1939.....7-2 (306-68-23)
1940.....7-2 (313-70-23)
1941.....8-0-1 (321-70-24)
1942.....7-2-2 (328-72-26)
1943.....9-1 (337-73-26)
1944.....8-2 (345-75-26)
1945.....7-2-1 (352-77-27)
1946.....8-0-1 (360-77-28)
1947.....9-0 (369-77-28)
1948.....9-0-1 (378-77-29)
1949.....10-0 (388-77-29)
1950.....4-4-1 (392-81-30)
1951.....7-2-1 (399-83-31)
1952.....7-2-1 (406-85-32)
1953.....9-0-1 (415-85-33)
1954.....9-1 (424-86-33)
1955.....8-2 (432-88-33)
1956.....2-8 (434-96-33)
1957.....7-3 (441-99-33)
1958.....6-4 (447-103-33)
1959.....5-5 (452-108-33)
1960.....2-8 (454-116-33)
1961.....5-5 (459-121-33)
1962.....5-5 (464-126-33)
1963.....2-7 (466-133-33)
1964.....9-1 (475-134-33)
1965.....7-2-1 (482-136-33)
1966.....8-0-1 (490-136-33)
1967.....8-2 (498-138-33)
1968.....7-2-1 (505-140-34)
1969.....8-1-1 (513-141-35)
1970.....9-1 (522-142-35)
1971.....8-2 (530-144-35)
1972.....8-2 (538-146-35)
1973.....10-0 (548-146-35)
1974.....9-2 (557-148-35)
1975.....8-3 (565-151-35)
1976.....8-3 (573-154-35)
1977.....10-1 (583-155-35)
1978.....8-3 (591-158-35)
1979.....7-4 (598-162-35)
1980.....9-1-1 (607-163-36)
1981.....5-6 (612-169-36)
1982.....6-4-1 (618-173-37)
1983.....7-5 (625-178-37)
1984.....7-5 (632-183-37)
1985.....5-6 (637-189-37)
1986.....5-6 (642-195-37)
1987.....8-4 (650-199-37)
1988.....12-0 (662-199-37)
1989.....11-1 (673-200-37)
```

---
---

### Table VII: Notre Dame's Undefeated Seasons

---

1888
1889
1892
1893
1903
1907
1909
1911
1912
1913
1919
1920
1924
1929
1930
1941
1946
1947
1948
1949
1953
1966
1973
1988

---
---

### Table VIII: Notre Dame's Losing Seasons

---

1887-1888
1933
1956
1960
1963
1981
1985
1986

# BIBLIOGRAPHY

Callahan, Tom. "Shaking Free of the Thunder," *Time*. 126 (December 9, 1985) 77. Re head coach Gerry Faust.

Cohane, Tom. "Do They Expect to Win Them All at Notre Dame?," *Look*. 23 (March 3, 1959) 78ff.

Cohane, Tom. "Rockne, Parseghian and the Fighting Irish," *Look*. 29 (November 2, 1965) 88-89ff.

Jenkins, Dan. "Knute Would Have Agreed, Ara," *Sports Illustrated*. 31 (December 22, 1969) 26-31.

Jenkins, Dan. "That Legend Is Loose Again," *Sports Illustrated*. 25 (November 7, 1966) 70-80.

Leerhsen, C. "The Damnation of Faust," *Newsweek*. 106 (December 9, 1985) 65.

Moore, K. "Somebody Up There May Be Listening," *Sports Illustrated*. 61 (November 5, 1984) 24-28ff.

# Ouija Board

In combination, the French and German word for yes, "oui" and "ja," give this diversion its name. The playing board is a flat polished sheet of wood or wood derivative about 18″ by 12″ with the alphabet, A through Z, enscribed in a wide half-moon lengthwise. A heart-shaped pointer mounted on tiny castors operates the board. Called a game by some and an oracle by others, the ouija board works in this manner: two people place their fingertips on the pointer which rests on the lettered board. Activated by deep concentration (most evident when the two participants are in direct sympathy with one another) the pointer moves from one letter to another spelling out words and making sentences in answer to a question; but if the participants lack sufficient mental energy and are impatient, the pointer might just move to a designated "yes" or "no" corner of the board and be done with it. Part of the mystery of ouija is knowing whether the participants moved the pointer or some master spirit hovering in the room. Playing by candlelight on a rainy night accentuated the "divine" experience. Around 1920, the ouija board was at its height as a fad for communicating with "the other side," which in itself was a fad manifested in an ever growing interest in the occult. Players reasoned that what ouija spelled out had to come from a third party, and that third party had to be one of the dead since no one else was in the room.

Lending credence to ouija during this time, the Belgian poet, Maurice Maeterlinck, and the English scientist, Sir Oliver Lodge, lectured at length on psychic revelations. The news media imbued their every word with the utmost importance, so much so that people discussed their notions of the "unseen" in the same breath with politics, religion, and the economy. The ouija board capitalized on this frenzy and was soon called, with affection, Mother Ouija. And a frenzy it was according to one journalist:

Everybody's doing it. It is the new fairyland. It is the universal amusement. The Cabaret of Ghosts is running performances day and night. . . . Telephones are rapidly falling into the discard; men, women, and children ring up Hyperspace and talk with their ancestors and their prenatal souls. Books are being written with the aid of 'controls'; the stock market has abandoned the ticker for the ouija pointer; the weather forecaster has tossed his maps and wind-measures into the river and gets his predictions from the spirits.

Fascination for Mother Ouija engendered debate between scientists and occultists. Dr. Eleanor Crosby Kemp, a consulting psychologist, believed that ouija was "but a natural phenomenon"; the unconscious mind made itself known through the fingertips. But she thought it folly for anyone to believe that Mother Ouija could provide a direct line of communication with the dead.

. . . mental energy aroused in the conscious or unconscious mind seeks normal expression through the musculature. . . . Let the ouija board, if you will, entertain you and interest you, by revealing to you your unconscious mind, but expect through it no communication with worlds unknown.

Actually, Dr. Kemp's real message was for everyone to forget about such time-wasters as the ouija board because, "Work is the order of this our day of reconstruction, and if real pleasure is to be ours let us honestly study some of the great simple facts which science has revealed." The occultists likewise lamented that Mother Ouija had gone too far, but that Dr. Kemp had no right to discount genuine psychic research. "The evidences of survival of bodily death and of communication with the unseen are too great to be lightly swept aside with ouija boards and charlatans," so ran the argument. Of course, the dispute regarding bona fide communication with the dead could have been settled by asking none other than Mother Ouija herself. Except that a scientist and an occultist could not have played at the same time because of the "direct sympathy" requirement.

# BIBLIOGRAPHY

Johnson, B. "Revelation" *Harper's Monthly Magazine*. 141 (August 1920) 401-402.

Kemp, E.C. "Folly of the Ouija Board" *Outlook*. 124 (April 28, 1920) 758-759.

Matthes, E.L.C. "'The Folly of the Ouija Board' — A Reply" *Outlook*. 125 (June 23, 1920) 394-395.

"Ouija Board, Bolshevik of the Spirit World" *Literary Digest*. 64 (January 31, 1920) 64-67.

"Ouija, Ouija, Who's Got the Ouija?," *Literary Digest*. 66 (July 3, 1920) 66-68.

Throughout the 1920s it would have been an insult to call the Ouija board a game. "Mother Ouija" answered questions of the heart, gave investment advice, and foretold the future — all in one evening of serious fun.

# Parachuting

Between 1958 and 1959, the number of parachute enthusiasts in the U.S. doubled from 1,500 to 3,000. Greater media attention and the founding of parachute clubs in about seventy cities were responsible for the increase. Once people learned that falling out of an airplane at 10,500 feet per minute, descending at the rate of 125 m.p.h., and trusting one's life to an oversized umbrella stashed in a backpack was safe, they became less fearful. The Sport Parachuting Center in Orange, Massachusetts served as the focal point of the emerging sport. A 30-year-old, French-born American, Jacques Andre Istel, who ran the Center, proselytized every chance he got. In his words:

> The parachutist has a sense of purpose, a sense of conquest impossible for most people to achieve in other ways. There are too many restrictions in modern life. A young man can't do anything without breaking some law. In parachuting he has complete freedom, including freedom of the choice to save his own life. If he fouls up, he is dead.

Not exactly comforting, Istel threw out a challenge to men and women of backbone. By mid-1959 there were four recorded deaths from parachuting, but Istel quickly replied, "You can do everything wrong and still make a fairly good jump." In the public mind military statistics loomed large; during 1956 U.S. paratroopers made more than 200,000 jumps, resulting in 440 injuries and 36 deaths. That sounded like certain danger to most; although the ratio of safe driving to highway accidents made parachuting appear to be the way to get to work.

Parachute clubs required every new jumper to pass a physical exam. Weather conditions had to be right for jumping, and all equipment in perfect order. On the ground, the novice practiced the spread-eagle stance or "stable position" until it felt natural. Throwing the body out of the plane spread-eagle allowed the jumper to remain parallel to the earth "back arched, head thrown back and arms flung wide in the swan dive to end all swan dives." An expert jumper supervised the first five jumps with the use of a static line (a strap hooked inside the plane that pulls the chute open after only a four-second fall). The jumper who failed to assume the stable position usually tumbled and looped uncontrollably in a disorderly fall. Doing a forward somersault just after exiting the plane was not trick parachuting. The disorderly faller might stabilize by rolling over with his or her back to the earth, but then a new danger presented itself. In that position the air feels like one big featherbed and the jumper might relax too much and forget to time the jump. Even for an experienced parachutist the seductive sensation of free-falling was the main cause of fatalities. A 28-year-old Texas jumper, who was supposed to pull his rip cord after a 20-second fall, smashed against the ground. His undamaged watch read 26 seconds.

Many first jumpers reported that parachuting was the most dangerous thing they could do with any reasonable degree of safety. Brazen on the ground, "As they ride up to bail-out altitude beside the yawning open door their gaze becomes fixed, their faces sweat, they only nod numbly in response to the cheerful chatter of the jumpmaster." Those who attempted parachuting just to prove their courage or for the heady thrill of it, rarely returned for a second jump. Parachuting appealed most to those interested in lively weekend recreation or a demanding sport. And as a team sport some observers in 1959 predicted its inclusion in the Olympic Games. Five-man jumping to form precise geometric shapes against a blue sky was a gorgeous sight. One jumper followed seconds later by another holding a baton with the intention to catch up and pass the baton, required aerial dexterity and split-second timing. The open gore chute (one with a pie-shaped section of the canopy removed) permitted much greater accuracy in steering through the air to land on an "x" every time. All of this and more was part of competition. International matches, especially with the French, who excelled at parachuting, attracted large crowds.

The prediction proved wrong. Parachuting never made it as an Olympic sport. As with other faddish recreations that ceased to amuse, it was just too expensive. Good gear, lessons, and airplane lifts were not cheap. The danger factor both attracted and repelled the curious and kept parachuting from achieving solid acceptance unlike another risky sport, snow skiing. Now that snow skiing is outrageously expensive, maybe the cheaper thrill of parachuting will make a comeback.

## BIBLIOGRAPHY

Brown, Donnie MacNab, and Tilly L. Hoagland. "Jump!," *Mademoiselle*. 50 (March 1960) 134 + .

Kerr, Carson. "Bailing Out for Fun," *Popular Mechanics*. 111 (May 1959) 65-69, 284, 286.

Wainwright, Loudon. "Growing U.S. Fad: Falls for Fun," *Life*. 47 (August 10, 1959) 100-114.

# Parlor Disguises

Before and after the American Civil War, the parlor served as the scene for many lively recreations, one of which involved family members donning disguises. Widely read storybooks told tales about giants and other fabulous beings, so why not have one visit in the flesh? To construct a giant, a boy sat on the shoulders of an adult, both hidden under a very long overcoat. The boy's face was visible and adorned with a curly black mustache and a top hat. One short arm held an extra-long walking cane to complete the disguise. A witness to the fun had this to say about the unseen adult:

> It is, indeed, an ordeal rather severe, after partaking heartily of Christmas dinner, and, perhaps, generously of wine, to walk about a hot room with a warm boy on your shoulders, and your entire person — head, face, and all — enveloped in a heavy cloak or overcoat, and not a breath of fresh air to be taken under penalty of spoiling the giant.

Another merry disguise was the backward walking man. The person performing it put on a loose coat and vest buttoned on his back — not the usual way in front — with his arms stretched out behind him. He fastened a false face to the back of his head and put a wig on over his own face. A top hat slanted toward his heels also gave the impression that his body was in two parts: from the waist up he looked backwards, but from the waist down he moved forward in normal fashion. A little skip in his walk added just the right comedic touch.

Animal disguises were equally amusing. For the tiger-dog, a household pet was painted with stripes to resemble a wild and ferocious creature. The pet, not knowing it had been transformed into a jungle terror, upon hearing a familiar whistle from its master ran into the parlor. The tiger-dog jumped on everyone eliciting shrieks of horror when it only wanted love and affection. Another favorite, especially with children, was the lumbering elephant. Two adults bent forward, the rear one rested his head on his partner's lower back while placing his arms straight out in front of him to touch his partner's ribs. The adult in front assumed the same position, though held in his hands a grey shawl or tablecover rolled up to represent the elephant's trunk. He swung it about to achieve a lifelike effect. A large piece of grey material covered the two adults. For eyes, two pieces of round paper were cut with black dots painted in the center of them. Old gloves were sewn on for ears. Long pieces of twisted white paper pinned to the inside of the shawl made fine tusks. The final bit of deception was for the two adults under the grey hide to wear thick rubber overshoes on their feet and the elephant was ready to lumber through the parlor. Children anxious to ride the beast bounced up and down on its back.

Each of these disguises only made their appearance after a lot of preparatory talk. For instance, the tiger-dog setup required getting the audience to envision an imaginary excursion to the heart of Africa. The narrator told a harrowing tale of discovering the tiger-dog feasting on human remains. There was no limit to what the tiger-dog might do, and it loved to nibble on children's ears before gobbling up both arms. Parlor disguises were faddish amusement for families before seductive store-bought toys and more sophisticated diversions became readily available.

## BIBLIOGRAPHY

Bellew, Frank. *The Art of Amusing.* New York: Arno Press, 1974. (Orginally published in 1866.)

# Pedestrian Events

These great running and walking contests originated in England, crossing over to America in the 1820s. While the British dominated, a field of international "peds" competed against time and one another for fat purses — sometimes for thousands of dollars. The distances they covered varied but were usually of a length and difficulty that tested the whole man. American pedestrianism came into its own in 1835 with a much-publicized event at the Union Race Course on Long Island. Promoter John Stevens offered a prize of $1,000 to any ped who could run ten miles in less than an hour, and an additional $300 if only one man did it. On April 22nd — a cold windswept day — an unbroken line of spectators marked the road between Brooklyn and the Union Course. Another 20,000 to 30,000 people packed the stands at the track. To the delight of those assembled, a Connecticut ped, Henry Stannard, outran the foreign entries to win the entire purse of $1,300. If Stannard's feat of running ten miles under 60 minutes does not seem that impressive, consider the wind stiff-armed him as he ran, the road was primitive, and scientific distance training was unheard of. But the best was yet to come.

At Boston, in 1843, Thomas Elsworth defeated Simon Fogg by walking one thousand miles in forty days. Then, at Beacon Race Course near Hoboken, a series of races commenced to fortify ped mania. Billed as American against the best British runners, and also as white against the red man, throngs of people attended all four races. The cream of British peds arrived in good health ready to sweep the races. John Steeprock of the Seneca tribe entered as the top Indian ped; he ran in a loping gait "as if he were going through underbrush." Forgetting the British momentarily, betting men feared Steeprock's natural talent would overpower the other runners. On June 3, older but still feisty Henry Stannard won the first ten-miler, sprinting home the last few hundred yards. He celebrated by mounting a horse and whipping it around the track at breakneck speed. Four months later, in a more grueling footrace a stocky ped from New York City, John Gildersleeve, just did nudge out the British favorite, John Greenhalgh. Ped fans went wild; that made it America 2 to 0. The next month, November, John Barlow came through for Brittania and set a new ten-mile record: 54 minutes, 36 seconds. All of a sudden Britain was back in it and Barlow had broken the record, as if the first two races were mere warm-ups.

For the last contest, in December, fans clamored to see a rematch of Gildersleeve and Greenhalgh who, running neck-and-neck, had provided the most excitement so far. A relief to many though a disappointment to some, John Steeprock had proven inferior to white peds, quieting that controversy. Dramatically, the distance was upped to twelve miles; Gildersleeve and Greenhalgh would have to go extra to claim the winner-take-all purse of $1,000. After ten miles both men perspired heavily despite the near-blizzard conditions. As anticipated, with one mile left, Gildersleeve and Greenhalgh began their sprint together, locked in a mad dash for the finish line. The delirious crowd shouted encouragement to Gildersleeve. Somehow Greenhalgh forged slightly ahead to win, then nearly collapsed from exhaustion in the arms of the officials. The Beacon races made news everywhere; people across the country wanted to see the same type of thrilling series in their home state. For the next fifteen years they got their wish—John Gildersleeve even turned up in the new state of California (1850-1851), where he won two ten-mile races.

During these years, other native Americans toed the starting line and the rivalry between Britain and the U.S. increased in fervor. Before long, the red man did indeed outrun the white man to vindicate Steeprock, especially at greater distances. And what a spectacle it was. The white runners ran strictly upright with elbows close to the body and wore bright silk costumes like their counterparts on horseback—the jockeys; while the Indians leaned forward to scurry across the miles and kept on their feathers and moccasins or scampered barefoot. The recurring question of racial superiority was either settled or unsettled each race depending on the outcome. There was always the next contest and the one after, if the wrong party won. For Americans a sure blow to national pride emerged in the lithe figure of an English ped, William Howitt. Standing 5'2" and weighing 103 lbs., he was also known as "William Jackson" and mis-christened "The American Deer." Until the beginning of the American Civil War, Howitt was the premier distance runner on both continents, winning thousands of dollars in prize money and wagers. His running prowess was such that he extended the challenge to race any runner from two to twenty miles for a purse of $1,000 or more — spotting distance as well. Howitt rarely lost and was the first man to run eleven miles under one hour. Among his many world records he held the ten-mile mark at 51 minutes, 20 seconds.

Due to the war and the rise of post-bellum participation sports, after 1860 interest waned in ped events that involved running. The new rage was for walking ped events, and as with so many other emerging sports one man intoxicated the public mind. Edward Payson Weston, or "Weston the Walker," lived to the ripe old age of 90. He believed that man could do anything he set his mind to, and walking was to be proof of his simple belief. In 1861, at age 22, Weston accepted a bet to walk from Boston to Washington in ten days to hear Abraham Lincoln's inauguration speech. It took him half a day longer, but his effort made headlines. Six years later, he agreed to a challenge from a ped club to attempt a walk of 1,326 miles from Portland, Maine to Chicago in thirty consecutive days. Prior publicity inspired heavy betting that he would not make it. Weston breezed in one hour and 20 minutes early and the press immediately hailed him as America's greatest walking phenomenon. Also in the blink of an eye Weston had a new career. He spent much of the rest of his life engaged in competitive walking, either against the world's best or himself.

To validate ped mania British and American promoters established the six-day walking race held indoors around a track. This was to be the supreme pedestrian event — the world series of walking. Imagine that being tried today when the last vestige of competitive walking seen in the Olympic Games induces more laughter than admiration. But in the 1870s spectators fought for tickets so they could eat, drink, and doze right there in the arena. Weston did lose a few of these grand challenges. Still, the hubristic British had to admit he was a "nervy little beggar of a Yankee" who could keep up with them stride for stride. In London (1876), two hundred thousand Brits paid to see Weston walk 1,015 miles in just five weeks; and for a "farewell appearance" he traversed 127 miles in 24 hours to set a speed walking record of 5.29 m.p.h. Forty years after the Portland to Chicago walk, Weston, at age 67, told the world he would do it again. This time he covered the same ground plus nineteen miles, breaking his 1867 record by 29 hours. Impassioned, America followed his example by taking to the roads. Not everyone could run like John Gildersleeve or hike like "Weston the Walker," but of the two activities striding at a rapid clip was possible for the average person. Attired in the clothes of a dandy—jacket with colored piping; matching hat, gloves, and scarf; tight black britches; horsewhip in hand to strike his leg; and, most importantly, low-heeled boots—Weston cut quite a figure. For the man who wanted to be the "propagandist for pedestrianism," walking was never faddish recreation.

## BIBLIOGRAPHY

Bernstein, Walter, and Milton Meltzer. "A Walking Fever Has Set In," *The Virginia Quarterly Review*. 56 (Autumn 1980) 698-711.

Lamb, Edward. "'Weston the Walker' Made Pedestrianism a Way of Life," *Smithsonian*. 10 (July 1979) 89-98.

Moss, George. "The Long Distance Runners of Ante-Bellum America," *Journal of Popular Culture*. 8, no. 2 (1974) 370-382.

A "Great Six Days' Walking Match," held in either New York City or London, packed in the crowds. America's foremost pedestrian, Weston the Walker, waves to his fans before outstriding the best British competitors. Whereas Weston had to keep going left-right-left, the spectators napped, went out for beer, or reluctantly returned to their jobs. 1870s.

# Pelota

Better known as jai-alai, meaning "merry festival" in Basque language, pelota (Spanish for ball) was introduced in the United States during the 1904 World's Fair in St. Louis. Watching those first matches must have been thrilling. To see agile athletes throwing the pelota at up to 150 miles per hour against a stone wall, then catching the pelota to smash it again against the wall—what a sight. By 1904, the game had evolved from Aztec days (pre-Cortez) when players used their bare hands to slap a less lively ball, to swatting the pelota with a flat bat, to hurling the pelota from a short basket, to the final weapon. The "cesta," then and now, is a long curved wicker basket tightly strapped to the player's wrist; in this manner it becomes part of the hand which at the end of a strong shoulder creates a rifle arm. A skilled player hurls the pelota—a hard rubber ball covered with goatskin a little smaller than a baseball—faster than the eye can see. That is, for the spectator. The players follow every movement of the pelota usually leaping high in the air, arms outstretched, to make spectacular catches.

To begin play the server fires the pelota against the front wall causing it to rebound and land in fair territory. The opponent must catch the pelota either on the fly or after only one bounce and return it to the wall in a single motion, also keeping it within bounds. Play continues at a furious pace until one or the other player misses. Most games, though, are for doubles to insure even more explosive action. Whichever individual or team scores seven points first wins the match. At 176' long, 50' wide, and 39' high, the court is five times larger than that for tennis. The court or building used for pelota is called a fronton. It has only one side wall; the other side is open for the spectators to view the game.

After sampling pelota in 1904, Americans did not get to see much of it again until 1924, the year the game opened in its first arena in Miami, Florida. In the latter 1920s, Chicago, New York

City, and New Orleans also acquired arenas and promoters thought the sport was off and running. Crowds loved pelota for its thrill-a-minute play, and also for its ample opportunity to bet on a series of matches — not just one — making the betting as frenetic as in horse racing. The arenas were full to the rafters almost every night until the gambling laws changed a few years later. Once the states declared betting on pelota illegal, the new sport came to a standstill except in Florida. In 1933, Florida legalized pari-mutuel betting on horses, dogs, and jai-alai; and because of Miami's Latin population and proximity to Latin countries, the sport gained a stronghold which continues to this day. Other attempts to establish jai-alai beyond fad status have occurred over the years. During the 1970s, frontons were built in the Connecticut cities of Bridgeport, Milford, and Hartford, and in Newport, Rhode Island. To stay alive these frontons had to have the best players in the world and to allow betting. Still, the sport lacks national recognition. Only an occasional visitor to Miami reports having seen a jai-alai match to friends who consider him Marco Polo for having witnessed something so exotic. Why jai-alai has never made it as a major sport in America might be due to the fact that Americans find the action too hard to follow.

## BIBLIOGRAPHY

Brown, Gene, ed. *The New York Times Encyclopedia of Sports*. Volume 11: Indoor Sports. New York: Arno Press, 1979.

"Chicago Adds a Sport to Its Winter Program," *Literary Digest*. 96 (March 17, 1928) 54-56.

Cohen, O.R. "Pronounced Hi-Li," *Saturday Evening Post*. 205 (August 13, 1932) 15 + .

Menke, Frank G., ed. *The Encyclopedia of Sports*. 5th rev. ed. South Brunswick and New York: A.S. Barnes, 1975.

"Shall We Be Jai Alai Fans, Like the Aztecs?," *Literary Digest*. 103 (October 5, 1929) 72-76.

# Perestroika in Pro Sports

In 1989, the incorporation of star Soviet athletes into the fabric of American professional sports became a reality. The triggering force was Soviet Gorbachev's program of economic restructuring, which required that sports federations in the U.S.S.R. pay more of their own expenses. To bring in funds, Soviet athletes were granted permission to participate in a wide variety of Western pro venues, including U.S. harness racing, European bicycling, Japanese wrestling, the National Hockey League, U.S. boxing, European soccer, and the National Basketball Association.

Given the Soviets' preeminence in the world arena in hockey, it was perhaps no surprise that their most visible penetration took place in that sport. In late March, Sergei Priakin became the first athlete from the U.S.S.R. to be given permission by his government to play in a North American pro league, and consequently made his debut with the NHL's Calgary Flames.

Many observers felt, however, that the front door did not swing open wide until the highly talented twenty-year-old winger Alexander Mogilny defected to the Buffalo Sabres in May 1989. This move, coupled with the resolve of some veteran Soviet players to be rewarded for their years of service, appears to have spurred the U.S.S.R. sport bureaucracy to reconsider its traditional stand of noninvolvement with Western pro teams. Accordingly, eight Soviets were granted permission by their country to perform in the NHL during the 1989-1990 season. They included right wing Sergei Makarov, 31, one of the game's most dynamic talents, who joined Priakin on the Flames; Vladimir Krutov, 29, a left wing, and Igor Larionov, a center, the Vancouver Canucks; defensemen Viacheslav Fetisov, 31, and Sergei Starikov, 30, the New Jersey Devils; Sergei Mylnikov, 31, goalie, Quebec, and Helmut Balderis, 37, a wing, the Minnesota North Stars.

The impact of these athletes — as well as those from other sports — would appear to include:

1. the introduction of new talent into North America;
2. the exposure to higher quality play; and
3. resentment on the part of native players, both due to jobs lost to Soviets and a lingering cold war antipathy.

Perhaps of even greater import, however, would be the potential for positive developments in the larger geopolitical sphere. As noted by Peter Stastny, a Czechoslovakian and teammate of Mylnikov's on the Quebec Nordiques:

> This is so nice. I really believe this and other things that we hear are happening over there tell us that we are heading into a nice peaceful period in the history of mankind.

## BIBLIOGRAPHY

Greenberg, Jay. "The Honeymooners," *Sports Illustrated*. 71:16 (October 9, 1989) 44-50, 86-87.
"Perestroika in Sports," *Sports Illustrated*. (1989) 11.

# Personal Watercraft

"Personal watercraft"* (PWCs) were developed as early as 1968, beginning with Bombardier's "water scooter." It proved to be ahead of its time and quietly disappeared following several seasons on the market. PWCs began to reappear in the 1980s; however, the first models—e.g., Ultranautics Wetbike and the standup Kawasaki Jet Ski—required practice and a reasonable degree of athletic skill.

Then a revolution took place in the latter part of the decade with the appearance of low-to-the-water, sit-down PWCs which enabled people to simply insert the key and blast off. One of the first was Wetjet, made in Paynesville, Minnesota, which debuted in 1984. Yamaha followed into the sit-down PWC market with its Waverunner; perhaps more than any other craft, it sparked the ensuing boom in PWCs. By, 1988 more than 100,000 units were being sold annually and new designs and models were, according to *Popular Mechanics* writers, Joe Skorupa, "popping up like umbrellas in a rainstorm." Even Bombardier's 1968 trail-blazer—under its official name, the Sea-Doo—was resurrected in 1988 and achieved almost instant success.

Despite the unqualified success of PWCs, the picture was not entirely rosy. Legislation began appearing aimed at either banning or controlling them. In New Hampshire, as of October 1, 1988, personal watercraft were prohibited from operating on any body of water less than seventy-five acres and on fifteen specified lakes more than seventy-five acres. Many other governing bodies also began deliberating the restriction of PWC use by forcing them to operate at least 150 feet from shore, or at least 150 feet apart.

---

*The term personal watercraft is defined by the Coast Guard as the primary source of propulsion and operated by a person sitting, standing or kneeling on the craft rather than in the conventional manner of boat operation.

ABC's "20/20" aired a segment in 1988 which was sharply critical of their use in public places.

Supporters of PWC replied that safety did not appear to be an issue. Skorupa noted that "There is no body of data showing that accidents and injury are occurring at levels higher than that of pleasure boats in general." He added that the *real* reasons PWCs were being attacked included (1) they are the new kid on the block (windsurfers experienced a similar backlash in the early 1980s), and (2) the failure of some operators to be courteous and observe basic rules.

The PWC industry attempted to counterattack by focusing upon the promotion of safe operation. Its umbrella organization, the Personal Watercraft Industry Association (PWIA), developed safe operational guidelines that it distributed in copious quantities (i.e., "Fun With Safety On Your Personal Watercraft"). Manufacturers also assisted, many distributing instructional videos on safety.

By late 1989, the ultimate fate of PWCs remained unclear. However, it appeared likely that the vehicles would eventually achieve more widespread acceptance as greater numbers of Americans came to use them.

## BIBLIOGRAPHY

Ashley, S. "Agile Aqua-Scooter," *Popular Science*. 232 (January 1988) 42.

Cinque, Chris. "Are Water Bikes a Menace?," *The Physician and Sports Medicine*. 17 (June 1989) 31.

Cole, T.H. "Yamaha's New Water Sleds," *Popular Mechanics*. 164 (March 1987) 40.

Davis, D. "Summer Toys for Big Boys," *Motor Boating & Sailing*. 162 (August 1988) 36-39.

De Gaspari, John. "Safety is Key Issue for Personal Watercraft," *Boating Industry*. 52 (April 1989) 14-17.

Gauthier, Michele M. "Preventing Injuries Among Water Craft Paddlers: Steady as You Go!," *The Physician and Sports Medicine*. 17 (June 1989) 162-167.

Lydecker, Ryck. "Legislators Compare ATVs with Personal Watercraft," *Boating Industry*. 52 (March 1989) 15.

Skorupa, Joe. "Invasion of the 'Water Snatchers,'" *Popular Mechanics*. 166 (April 1989) 39, 43.

Skorupa, Joe. "Jet Ski's Big Brother," *Popular Mechanics*. 164 (July 1987) 12.

Skorupa, Joe. "New Wave Watercraft," *Popular Mechanics*. 165 (September 1988) 79-81, 106.

Skorupa, Joe. "Wet and Wild Toys," *Popular Mechanics*. 165 (August 1988) 24.

Toy, S. "Take Off on a Jet Ski Built for Two," *Business Week*. (October 20, 1986) 138.

# Pick Up Sticks

In less than a year after its introduction, around Easter 1936, nearly 3,000,000 sets of Pick Up Sticks had been sold. A deceptively simple game, there were 41 seven-inch sticks painted yellow, red, green, blue, and black packed in a canister with a set of rules. The first player held all the sticks in his or her fist perpendicular to the surface of a table or rug, then released them. The sticks fell and intertwined forming a haystack from which the player had to pick up one stick at a time without disturbing the others. Each color was worth a different amount of points; the lone black stick counted the most. As soon as the first player either made a false move or picked up all the sticks cleanly, the next player released a fistful and so on.

Eugene Levay, a toy buyer for Gimbel Brothers, purloined the game from Hungary, where it was known as Marokko. He interested a toymaker, O. Schoenhut Inc., in manufacturing Pick Up Sticks even though the owners, Otto and George Schoenhut, thought it too frivolous to excite the American public. They were pleasantly surprised to have been so wrong. Once R. H. Macy of Manhattan and Woolworth's started beating the drum for Pick Up Sticks, the Schoenhuts had trouble filling orders. At the height of the craze, Otto and George had 400 employees producing 200 gross of the game a day.

The name, Pick Up Sticks, came from a childhood rhyme: "One, two, button my shoe; three, four, shut the door; five, six, pick up sticks." A comedienne of the day, Beatrice Lillie sang the ditty differently about hiking with campfire girls: "One, two, three, tickle my knee; four, five, six, pick up sticks; seven, eight, nine, girls halt!" For some inexplicable reason hearing this silly rhyme on the radio prompted people to buy the game. At the same time, and equally inexplicable, Ethiopia and Italy were enmeshed in a bloody war. With the Italians winning, Ethiopian emperor Haile Selassie had to flee his country and take refuge in England. Selassie's personal peril and his country's disarray became embodied in Pick Up Sticks. The lone black stick represented Selassie surrounded by the rest of the sticks which stood for precarious circumstances. Thus the simple game assumed new and more worldly significance.

## BIBLIOGRAPHY

"4-5-6 Pick Up Sticks," *Fortune*. 15 (May 1937) 18.

# Ping-Pong

Ping-Pong took American society by storm in the early days of the twentieth century. An indoor ball game similar in principle to lawn tennis and played on a flat table divided into two equal courts by a net fixed across its width at the middle, Ping-Pong employs a hollow ball made of either celluloid or a similar plastic which is propelled back and forth across the net by small rackets (bats or paddles) held by the players.

*The New York Times* provided the following report on the origins of Ping-Pong:

> . . . the game started with cigar-box lids for bats, champagne corks for balls and a row of books for a net. That was early in the '80s. Afterward, organized efforts were made to bring tennis to the dining room table. In time a venerable sports goods house of London put out celluloid balls, vellum battledores and a lower net and called the game ping-pong, after the sound the little ball made when it struck. That was in 1900. Then a way was found to make the balls without seams and the improvement was reflected in increased popularity, and almost before it realized what had happened the firm found itself in the midst of the biggest boom of its 200-year history. It is said that never did a game attain such popularity so quickly.

Few homes were without a set during this period. Then came a lull in which it was played only by the highly skilled.

Ping-Pong underwent a revival in the 1920s largely as a result of the efforts of a group of enthusiasts to bring the U.S. in line with a movement to restore it as an international sport abroad. The old Ping-Pong Association (originally formed in 1902 and subsequently disbanded in 1905) was revived in 1921, adopting the new appellation "table tennis." Ping-Pong equipment assumed leadership among those for indoor sports.

All along, America had noted the English fad but did not take it seriously until 1925. Then, Parker Brothers of Salem, Massachusetts copyrighted the name "Ping-Pong," for its complete line of "official" equipment; and formed the American Ping-Pong Association, conducting national tournaments for almost a decade. In 1931, another governing body came into existence, the New York Table-Tennis Association, which sponsored its own national tournament in competition with Parker Brothers. After three years of having two national championships and much confusion, the equipment manufacturers (Parker Brothers no longer had a monopoly) joined together to support the newly formed United States Table Tennis Association. Now it was time to convince the American public that table tennis or Ping-Pong—depending on whether you bought Parker Brothers equipment—was the great new spectator sport and home recreation.

It took a few more years and a young Hungarian named Victor Barna to raise Ping-Pong to the status of a national obsession. Table tennis was the number one sport in Hungary, its star athletes equivalent in prestige to American heavyweight boxers. As Barna toured in this country he amazed people with his skill. Oddly, he stood five to ten feet from the table and smashed the ball with all his might, blistering it across the net in a winning blur. His pet shot, the "Barna flick," played off the backhand with or without topspin and nearly impossible to return, had never been seen before or even dreamed of. During an exhibition, he continually hit a dime placed on his opponent's side of the table at the far end. In competition the best Americans used a chop-shot which slowed the ball allowing Barna to flick them to death. After Barna, the Americans dropped the chop-shot and began to imitate his searing, slashing play. This advancement worked wonders for the game, lifting it from what was thought of as a sissy sport to one of hawklike concentration and endurance. Most assuredly, the new Ping-Pong raised a sweat and made muscles sore.

The expansion of Ping-Pong in the 1930s (an estimated 10,000,000 addicts, 5,000,000 tables in private homes, the most popular intramural sport in large universities, a Chicago tournament drawing 22,000 entries, given an "A" ranking along with golf and tennis) subsided with the advent of World War II, but has had sporadic outbursts in years since then.

The game has remained a popular form of recreation and an international sport up to the present day. Players from more than 100 nations belong to the International Table Tennis Federation (ITTF), which holds a world championship tournament every two years.

Ping-Pong has also left its mark upon the geopolitical sphere. In April 1971, an American Table Tennis team was invited to visit the People's Republic of China. Because the invitation had represented a diplomatic initiative, the term "Ping-Pong diplomacy" was applied to the subsequent Chinese-U.S. consultations that paved the way for President Richard Nixon's trip in February 1972 concerned with normalizing Sino-American relations.

## BIBLIOGRAPHY

"Bouncing Game: Table-Tennis Speeds Up, Crowds Out Old-Fashioned Playing Styles," *Literary Digest*. 123 (May 29, 1937) 33-34.

"Concerning Ping-Pong," *Harper's Weekly*. 46 (May 3, 1902) 577.

"Game of Ping-Pong," *Current Literature*. 32 (March 1902) 332.

"A Ping Pong Era Is Upon Us," In: *The New York Times Encyclopedia of Sports*, edited by Gene Brown. Volume 11: Indoor Sports. New York: Arno, 1979. p. 38.

"The Ping-Pong 'Menace,'" *Literary Digest*. 112 (March 19, 1932) 42-43.

Purves, Jay. *Table Tennis*. New York: A.S. Barnes and Company, 1942.

# Platform Tennis

Played predominately in winter on a moveable wooden court, platform tennis grew out of playground paddle tennis which Frank P. Beal invented in 1898. Beal devised the game as a substitute for lawn tennis, one that could be set up practically anywhere with minimal expense: in a backyard, gymnasium, or on the street. The first courts were one-quarter the size of a regular tennis court, and were used to teach the rudiments of tennis. Tape marked the boundaries with a simple net stretched across the middle of the court. The players hit old tennis balls with solid wood paddles scoring the same as in tennis. The game achieved enough popularity that in 1923, the United States Paddle Tennis Association was formed. In 1928, Fessenden S. Blanchard and James K. Cogswell changed the game by enlarging the court size, employing slower balls, and erecting a chicken wire fence around the court to keep the ball in play. They liked platform tennis because it got them outdoors on wintry days to bat a ball on a platform raised above the snow and slush. Under frigid conditions they could get in a good workout safe from the cold and damp.

A few years later, Blanchard and Cogswell changed things again. This time they increased the court size to 30' × 60', lowered the net, and raised the wire fencing to 12'. Their final improvement was the one-service rule, thereby disallowing dominance by a strong server as in tennis. Also different from tennis, four players (doubles) played most of the time, with singles as the exception. In 1934, Donald K. Evans solved the problem of erratic bounces off the fence by installing adjustable tension bars. These three men were part of a coterie who delighted in playing paddle matches in private before the exclusive tennis clubs caught on to the game's appeal. The clubs, wanting to offer year-round sport, accepted the design and rules of Blanchard and Cogwell and the game flourished.

Over the next thirty years, platform tennis slowly gained more participants and followers, though still centered mainly in the Northeast. Few, if any, of these elevated miniature tennis courts surrounded by fencing appeared elsewhere. In the early to mid-1970s, promoters attempted to break the game wide open and sell it to the public. They wanted to create a strong interest in platform tennis that would translate into millions of dollars. They tried to accomplish this by sponsoring more tournaments and garnering greater publicity. A national championship, then a world championship, at least notified America that platform tennis was a legitimate sport. Coca Cola spent $40,000 to inaugurate a professional tour to demonstrate the game. Publishers located book writers to explain how to play "America's fastest-growing racquet sport." The texts were engaging enough but the photographs of players in action were a turnoff. Attired in fashionable sweaters, turtlenecks, and jackets, wearing long pants and spotless tennis shoes, with neat haircuts, the players looked exactly like the stockbrokers, lawyers, and accountants they were. For the rest of the club-less country not born to the manor, the game appeared too blue blood. Bob Callaway and Michael Hughes, in their book *Platform Tennis*, put in a strong bid to entice the over-thirty competitor:

> The sport has since its inception been a sanctuary of sorts for the middle-aged athlete. The average age of the thirty-two men qualifying for the world championships in 1977 was thirty-four. The average age of the thirty-two women competitors was thirty-five. . . . Paddle is principally a doubles game (there are no singles tournaments), reducing the physical demands on the individual player. The compact court size reduces the need for great speed and extended running. And the high screens surrounding the court keep the ball in play, giving the player a second chance to make the play as the ball ricochets off the wires.

Even with this endorsement the game lacked fire. After the big push in the 1970s to turn platform tennis into a popular sport, in the 1980s only an occasional article in a sports magazine informed readers of its existence. It was like starting over again, since the articles related history and how to play the game as if no one knew.

## BIBLIOGRAPHY

Callaway, Bob, and Michael Hughes. *Platform Tennis*. New York: J.P. Lippincott Company, 1977.

Paige, Edward P. "Platform Tennis: A Winter's Tale," *World Tennis*. 33 (February 1986) 72-73.

Squires, Dick, ed. *The Complete Book of Platform Tennis*. Boston: Houghton Mifflin Company, 1974.

Sullivan, George. *Paddle: The Beginner's Guide to Platform Tennis*. New York: Coward, McCann & Geoghegan, Inc., 1975.

# Pushball

The first pushball was made in Newton, Massachusetts in 1894, thus making the game an American inspiration. The ball was large, at least the height of an average man, and because of its round shape it looked as if it could bowl over a set of human ninepins with ease. To construct the ball, four leather hides cut in six sections were used to cover a wooden frame held together with belting hooks. Inside the frame, a bladder made of rubber cloth also cut in sections and cemented together allowed the ball to be inflated. The cost of a pushball was about $175, a tidy sum in those days. The final requirements for competition were a field with a goal at each end and two opposing teams striving to shove the ponderous pushball through a goal for a score.

During the 1910s, college athletes popularized the sport by playing it for fans who liked watching their comic capers. The robust young men resembled ants grappling with a crumb of food. They huffed and puffed to get the ball rolling, which once in motion was hard to control. Players got steamrolled, and the sight of the pushball sailing toward the fans drew shouts of merriment. Even the preliminaries were amusing as the athletes wore themselves out inflating the ball. Pushball rules and records appear not to have survived, so it is difficult to get a clear picture of the dimensions of the sport. Most likely, rival colleges got together for an afternoon of fun by appropriating the closest football field to play on. The score probably did not matter all that much, as long as everyone had a good time. A variant of the game played on horseback in the Western states differed in that the horses pushed the ball with their heads and bodies, while their riders merely directed them. A vintage photograph of Western style pushball shows a full grandstand cheering six or eight cowboys on horseback maneuvering for position to attack the ball. As dust flies, the stiff-necked horses seem unsure of what their masters have gotten them into, having to ram their heads against a six-foot-high leather ball for no apparent reason.

Pushball was still around in 1916, but little heard of after that. The expense of making the ball and the few manufacturers who would set up shop to do so caused the sport to fade quickly. Furthermore, World War I brought an end to such pre-war frivolity, clearing the way for the roaring twenties and its more advanced foolishness.

## BIBLIOGRAPHY

"Pushball — The Biggest Plaything," *St. Nicholas*. XLIV (November 1916) 80-81.

# Quoits

Presumably of French origin, with written references dating back to the 1400s, quoits involved tossing flat rings of iron or rope to encircle a stake. This popular European pastime reached our shores earlier than 1920-1940 but did not become a fad until then. At first, country people played quoits or, as the game was known to them, "barnyard golf." It provided a much needed respite between stints of hard labor.

> In the old game, according to common belief, the players stepped off a convenient distance in the barnyard, drove pegs, hunted up a pair of old Dobbin's cast-off shoes, and calmly and neighborly tested their skill. The best players curled a sinewy finger around the heel calk of the shoes and pitched a rapid whirling, flat-floating shoe. Ringers were rare, greeted with whoops of joy; arguments over leaners were common causes for dispute, and on a close decision a stick or branch off a tree measured which shoe was the nearer.

Using "old Dobbin's cast-off shoes" gave quoits a new name — horseshoes. Perhaps it was only a matter of time before the game would emerge from the barnyard, but when photographers captured President Warren G. Harding (1921-1923) pitching horseshoes, the nation took notice. Opportunistic manufacturers presented Harding with a nickel and a copper pair of shoes, his name engraved on both. On April 18, 1921 the National Horseshoe Pitchers' Association (50,000 members) announced that their Honorary President was to be none other than Warren G. Harding. There was no better endorsement for a recreation than to have the leader of state an enthusiast. Also in 1921, the Minnesota State Fair hosted a world championship tournament, which was fitting since barnyard golf's greatest popularity was in the mid-West states. Prizes for the event included gold medals set with diamonds, gold watches, silver loving-cups, nickel-plated horseshoes in leather cases, and other trophies, in addition to cash totaling $2,000.

Recalling that quoits were originally unbroken rings, the open shoe became the standard for modern play. The resourceful player who first picked up a horseshoe to pitch at a stake because he did not have a quoit, probably did not realize the importance of that action. The break in the ring added finesse to the game.

> Distance, direction, the proper arc and the delivery of the open shoe are the four pelots of success in quoit tossing. The best combination of these essentials is possessed by the champion tosser. The longer the arc or projectile path of the shoe, the more it will turn in the air. Perfect-timing of the easy, graceful pendulum swing of the arm in delivery is essential.

With organized play came structured rules, such as if a double-ringer lands on top of the opponent's double-ringer, the opponent loses the points. Players had special pitching shoes designed just for barnyard golf. The weight had to feel right in the hand for an accurate pitch. National championships were played on clay courts so that courtkeepers could maintain the clay around the stake at the consistency of putty to hold the shoes where they dropped. During the fad's hot streak, newspapers reported the results of horseshoe tournaments right along with football and baseball, and magazines included feature articles on what they still called quoits.

Minnesota was a good place to pitch horseshoes in the summer, but come winter the master players moved to Florida. Some of these now unheard of heroes were Blair Nunamaker, "Putt" Mossman, and C. C. Jackson. Enraptured spectators watched from the grandstands as they piled up statistics. At a tournament in Lake Worth, Florida, Blair Nunamaker won the best individual exercise record by tossing 5,632 shoes thus handling 7 tons, 80 pounds of steel. Altogether he walked 26.68 miles. Health nuts bathed in the glory of Nunamaker's performance, claiming for the sport a brighter mental outlook and increased longevity. Before the fad subsided (World War II), there were enough tournaments yearly to occupy a professional's time. Pages of official records were logged and an official paper, "Barnyard Golf," appeared and disappeared. Clay and sand courts dotted the nation. There were thirty-five alone at Waterfront Park in St. Petersburg, Florida.

To point out a difference in the times, as with Harding before him, photographers snapped shots of current President George Bush pitching horseshoes. But instead of launching a craze this time, Bush's interest in the game seemed to confirm him as a wimp — a derogatory label he was branded with during his campaign for the presidency. Now the public considers horseshoes a sissy game. How quickly we forget the feats of Blair Nunamaker!

## BIBLIOGRAPHY

Bulger, B. "Pitch Horseshoes and Live Long," *Saturday Evening Post.* 204 (February 20, 1932) 34 + .

Dacy, George H. "Barnyard Golf," *Hygeia.* 5 (February 1927) 87-89.

Hodge, M.H. "Organized Horseshoe Pitching," *Playground.* 23 (July 1929) 241-243.

"Horseshoe Pitchers to the Fore," *Literary Digest.* 70 (September 17, 1921) 53-54.

Leighton, B.G. "Establishment of Official National Horseshoe Pitching Records," *Playground.* 18 (December 1924) 550-551.

Wood, M.T. "Hour's Pitchin,'" *American City.* 29 (August 1923) 151-152.

# "The Refrigerator": William Perry

William "Refrigerator" Perry, the most refreshing story of the 1985 NFL season, appears to have owed his fame to the revenge motive. On October 13, against the San Francisco Forty-Niners, Perry carried the ball on the last two plays of the game for a net gain of four yards. The ploy was openly criticized as Mike Ditka's heavy-handed payback to San Francisco head coach Bill Walsh, who had employed Guy McIntyre, a 271-pound guard, in the backfield in the Forty-Niners' 23-0 victory over the Bears in the previous year's NFC title game.

The former Clemson star and first-round draft choice of the Chicago Bears in 1985 seemed destined at the start of the season to wallow in obscurity on the bench. Buddy Ryan, then the Bears' defensive coordinator, dismissed Perry as "a wasted draft choice" when he came into training camp weighing 330 pounds.

Although logging little playing time as a defensive lineman—his intended position—Perry gained increasing fame as a spot offensive performer following the San Francisco game. During "Monday Night Football" on October 21, Perry tossed opponents aside like rag dolls in clearing a path for two Walter Payton scoring plunges and then plowed into the end zone for a touchdown of his own as the Bears defeated Green Bay 23-7. *Chicago Sun-Times* columnist Ray Sons called it "the best use of fat since the invention of bacon."

Perry's popularity appeared to be as much a result of his demeanor as his size. He always acted natural and was unfailingly pleasant, with a smile that *Sports Illustrated* termed "as wide and innocent as a kid's jack-o'-lantern." With respect to his October 21 heroics, he stated,

When Coach first asked me if I'd play fullback in short-yard-age situations, I laughed. I carried the ball a couple of times back in high school in Aiken, South Carolina, just having fun. I'll do anything to help the Bears win. Offense. It seems like they have fun all the time.

Ryan continued to fight against using him on defense, feeling that he lacked the technique, knowledge, endurance, and waistline of a professional. At one point he quipped, "Hell, he's exciting when he's on offense. Must be easier than defense."

The November game against the Packers provided yet another wrinkle in the ongoing saga of the "Refrigerator's" exploits. Down 3-0 in the closing moments of the first half, with a second down and goal at the Packer four, Ditka again called on Perry. This time, instead of bulldozing ahead at the snap, he sidestepped a startled linebacker and caught a soft pass for a TD. By now, all football fans drooled at the possibilities each time the Bears neared an opposing team's end zone.

Generally overlooked in the brouhaha surrounding Perry was the fact that he possessed extraordinary athletic ability despite his great size; he could run the forty-yard dash in 5.05 seconds, bench press 465 pounds, and — at a height of 6'2" — dunk a basketball with ease. Perry seemed impervious to continued efforts by the Bears to get him to lose weight (e.g., assigning him to a nutritionist); he noted that he — like all members of his family — was simply big, weighing thirteen and one-half pounds at birth and never dipping below 300 since junior high school.

Mid-season found Perry enjoying the fruits of celebrity. The majority of television talk programs — Carson, Letterman, "The Today Show" — wanted him and his agent was deluged with lucrative offers to endorse various products (most notably, both GE and Whirlpool were interested in getting Perry to talk about refrigerators).

As the Bears steamrolled toward an eventual Super Bowl win, anecdotes about Perry began to reach almost legendary status. Beer was declared the diet pill in his slimming program. As Perry noted, "You drink it, see, and it fills you up. So you don't eat. Then the next day you sweat it out in practice, and you don't gain weight."

During a road trip he put the fear of weight into his roommate, 185-pound cornerback Les Frazier. After watching a horror flick on television, Perry began sleepwalking, finally coming to rest on Frazier's bed. Said Frazier, "It scared me to death. He pounced on my bed. A man of that size . . ."

Whatever momentum Refrigeratormania did not lose over the off-season was dissipated when Perry landed in Ditka's doghouse during the 1986 campaign due to his ongoing weight problems. Driven to the point of exasperation, Ditka publicly acknowledged that Perry had an eating disorder which threatened to end not merely his career but his very life. Pulled from his offensive duties, Perry promptly fell into relative obscurity although he has continued to perform in a defensive supporting role for the Bears throughout the latter 1980s.

## BIBLIOGRAPHY

"At 302 Pounds, Hot 'Fridge' Ready To Cool It On Diet," *Jet*. 69 (December 16, 1985) 49.

Callahan, Tom. "Hurry, Hurry, Step Right Up," *Time*. 126 (November 11, 1985) 83.

Frank, J. "'The Refrigerator' Fills Up On Cold, Hard Cash," *Business Week*. (November 25, 1985) 124.

"The Refrigerator," *People Weekly*. 24 (December 23/30, 1985) 40-41.

"The Refrigerator Is Hot," *Newsweek*. 106 (November 18, 1985) 83.

"'Refrigerator' Will Stock Up On Coke in Ad Campaign," *Jet*. 69 (December 9, 1985) 47.

Tolander, Rick. "Monster of the Midway," *Sports Illustrated*. 63 (November 4, 1985) 42-44, 49.

Unger, N.O. "Bears' 'Refrigerator' Comes Down in Size and Gains Popularity," *Jet*. 69 (November 18, 1985) 46-47.

Wolmuth, R. "Warming Up the Fridge: the Bears' William Perry Melts Down for First Down," *People Weekly*. 24 (September 9, 1985) 107-108.

# Jackie Robinson
## and Baseball's Color Line

The early years of professional baseball coincided with the emergence of segregation as an American institution. While the rules of play had become fairly standardized by the late nineteenth century, regulations varied from one league to another. With regard to the admission of blacks in baseball, only a patchwork of local decisions existed. During the 1880s, as many as two dozen blacks played on professional teams. A pair of brothers, Moses and Weldy Walker, played briefly with Toledo of the American Association (then a major league) in 1884. However, in 1887 a sequence of events — the folding of The League of Colored Base Ball Clubs (recognized as a minor league by the National League's National Agreement in 1879) and a growing crescendo of complaints by whites about their black teammates as well as segregationists (which led the International League to ban future contracts with blacks) — led professional baseball irrevocably down the path to Jim Crow. By the turn of the century, blacks could no longer be found at any level in the major and minor leagues.

Unrest over the color line was muted somewhat by the formation of professional Negro Leagues; however, increasing anti-segregationist sentiments, a general shortage of males, and the success blacks experienced during exhibitions with big-leaguers gave rise to isolated efforts to break down the barrier during the World War II era. In 1944, Bill Veeck attempted to buy the Philadelphia Phillies, with the intention of signing several black stars for the struggling club, but his purchase was not completed. When the Boston Red Sox gave a tryout to three black stars in the same year, two city councilmen threatened to strip the Sox of exemptions from Sunday blue laws.

One of the three players given the standard line, "Don't call us, we'll call you," by the Red Sox was Kansas City Monarchs star

Jackie Robinson. A four-letter man at U.C.L.A. in the early 1940s, Robinson would prove to be the perfect man with which to attempt the integration of the major leagues. Contacted by Brooklyn Dodgers executive Branch Rickey, Robinson reported to the club's top farm franchise, Montreal, in 1946. "I had to do it for so many reasons," Robinson would comment later. "For black youth, for my mother, for Rachel [his wife], and for myself. I even felt I had to do it for Branch Rickey."

Rickey decided to bring Robinson up to the parent club at the start of the 1947 season. After a relatively tranquil start, he and those around him were thrust into a period of unrelenting crises and tension beginning in late April. Opening a home stand against the Phillies, Robinson was subjected to the racial taunts of the opposing team's manager, Alabaman Ben Chapman. Sportswriter Harold Parrott noted,

> At no time in my life have I heard racial venom and dugout abuse to match the abuse that Ben sprayed on Robinson that night. Chapman mentioned everything from thick lips to the supposedly extra-thick Negro skull . . . [and] the repulsive sores and diseases he said Robinson's teammates would become infected with if they touched the towels or the combs he used.

The verbal assault led fans to write letters of protest to Commissioner Happy Chandler and newsman Walter Winchell attacked Chapman on his national Sunday night radio broadcast. Rickey would later claim that this incident, more than any other, cemented Dodger support for Robinson.

Such taunts, along with other distractions — thousands of invitations to make in-person appearances, hate mail, the refusal of Philadelphia's Benjamin Franklin Hotel to lodge him, an alleged plot by National League players, led by the St. Louis Cardinals, to strike against him, etc. — caused Robinson to enter into a hitting slump. However, he proved to be a magnet to fans, causing attendance records to be set in Philadelphia and Chicago during May. "Jackie's nimble/Jackie's quick/Jackie's making the turnstiles click," wrote Wendell Smith in the Pittsburgh *Courier*. Jimmy Cannon hailed him as "the most lucrative draw since Babe Ruth."

By late May, however, Robinson's batting began to steadily climb. More important, his obvious intelligence, self-deprecating wit, and public willingness to forgive and understand his tormentors, made him an American hero, to blacks and whites alike. His dynamic performance instilled a sense of pride in black Americans and led many whites to reassess their own feelings. The affection for Robinson grew so widespread that at the end of the year, voters in the Pittsburgh *Courier*'s annual public opinion poll named him the second most popular man in America (behind Bing Crosby). For his accomplishments as a player he became the recipient of baseball's first Rookie of the Year Award.

Robinson's success immediately opened the door for others. Larry Doby, one of fourteen blacks signed by Bill Veeck's Cleveland Indians in the early years of integration, became the first black to play in the American League late in 1947. With the arrival of a host of black stars upon the major league scene by the late 1940s (e.g., Satchel Paige, Roy Campanella, Don Newcombe, Monte Irvin), the issue faded forever from America's social consciousness. Within a few years all other major professional sports in America were integrated as well. In a broader sense, as noted by Rickey, "integration in baseball started public integration on trains, in Pullmans, in dining cars, in restaurants in the South, long before the issue of public accommodations became daily news."

## BIBLIOGRAPHY

Frommer, Harvey. *Rickey and Robinson: The Man Who Broke Baseball's Color Barrier*. New York: 1982.

Robinson, Jackie, as told to Alfred Duckett. *I Never Had It Made*. New York: Putnam, 1972.

Schlossberg, Dan. "The Color Line," In: *The Baseball Catalog*. Middle Village, N.Y.: Jonathan David, n.d. pp. 100-102.

Tygiel, Jules. *Baseball's Great Experiment; Jackie Robinson and His Legacy*. New York: Oxford University Press, 1983.

# The Pete Rose Gambling Scandal

Pete Rose's gambling habit became front-page news following baseball commissioner Peter Ueberroth's announcement on March 20, 1989 that his office was conducting a "full inquiry into serious allegations" about the Cincinnati Reds manager. Ueberroth's move seeded the media clouds, and the deluge that ensued drenched Rose — and baseball — in a torrent of stories divulging Rose's relationships with convicted felons, his alleged substantial betting losses, and his handling of lucrative memorabilia sales and autograph signings.

While Rose continued to proclaim his innocence, a wealth of evidence seemed to contradict him. Allegations to the contrary included the following:

- Alan Statman — a lawyer for Ron Peters, a Franklin, Ohio restauranteur, described as Rose's "principal bookmaker" — approached *Sports Illustrated* in hopes of selling Peters's story and said he had told baseball investigators that he and Peters had evidence to show that Rose had bet on baseball.
- *Sports Illustrated* also reported discussing the purchase of a story about Rose's baseball betting with Paul Janszen, a bodybuilder friend then serving a six-month sentence in a Cincinnati halfway house for evading taxes on income derived from the sale of steroids.
- A former employee at Gold's Gym in the Cincinnati suburbs alleged that Tommy Gioiosa, an ex-manager of the gym, and Janszen both placed bets on Rose's behalf. Several other witnesses supported these contentions.
- A source with access to Gold's telephone records told *Sports Illustrated* that during the first eleven months of 1986, 104 calls were made from the gym's office phone to Jonathan's,

the restaurant owned by Peters. Gioiosa and Janszen were alleged to do their betting through Peters.

• The Dayton *Daily News* reported that federal investigators were looking into "tax and gambling issues" involving Rose, including income he derived from the sale of personal memorabilia.

• The New York *Post*, quoting an unidentified source, said Cincinnati police estimated that at present Rose owes bookies between $500,000 and $750,000. The Cincinnati *Post* quoted a former Reds official as saying that Rose had gambling debts of "close to half a million" when he signed with the Philadelphia Phillies as a free agent in 1978. The official added that the Cincinnati management reported cash brought in from Japan.

*Sports Illustrated* summarized its case against Rose by noting,

> There have always been two sides to Rose, and last week's revelations focused attention on the less appealing one. As a player for 24 years, Rose was a relentless overachiever who played with unmatched abandon. But off the field his aggressiveness sometimes manifested itself as greed and coarseness. Over the years Rose let nothing faze him, not a 1979 paternity suit while he was playing for the Phillies, which was settled out of court, not a '79 interview with *Playboy*, in which he admitted using amphetamines, not even increasing concern over his often shadowy associations and indications that his passion for betting might be excessive.

Despite all this, public sympathy for Rose appeared to run high during the summer of 1989. Many felt that the media—as in cases involving other public figures—were overstepping the bounds of propriety in the search for a story. Others felt that the severity of the penalty—Rose faced the likelihood of lifetime banishment from organized baseball if found guilty of betting on the sport—was unwarranted. Related to this perception was the fact that Rose had become a symbol not just of gambling but also of the social toleration of it. *Time* assessed just how prevalent the practice had become, noting,

Sports betting is not even the largest or fastest-growing type of gambling. Christiansen/Cummings Associates in New York City, a leading consulting firm to the gaming industry, figures that all kinds of wagering (except friendly bets between individuals) have increased a thumping 57% in the past five years. Casinos took in more than half of all bets, or $164 billion; sports gambling was a distant second with a $28 billion take, up 57% from 1983. Though impressive, that increase was dwarfed by a 98% jump in the coins clinked into slot machines, a 103% rise in legal bookmaking and a 228% leap in money wagered in cardrooms.

Even these figures understate the spread of gambling fever. The biggest jump is in gambling state and local governments not merely tolerate but promote.

Despite some eleventh-hour legal wrangling in which a sympathetic Hamilton County Court of Common Pleas judge issued a temporary restraining order barring the new baseball commissioner, Bart Giamatti, from holding a disciplinary hearing in mid-summer (in the meantime, the Ohio Supreme Court forced the release of the 235-page investigative report to Giamatti upon which the commissioner's final decision was expected to be largely based), Rose ultimately agreed to striking a bargain with Giamatti. As a result, in late August, Giamatti announced that Rose was banned from baseball for life for betting on his own team. Rose, however, appeared at a press conference shortly thereafter, reiterating his innocence and promising to apply for reinstatement to baseball in August 1990, the first legal opportunity he would have to do so.

In the end, with many of the press and fans disillusioned with his recent conduct (e.g., the night before Giamatti's announcement, he was hawking autographed baseballs on the Cable Value Network at $39.94 apiece and selling uniforms with his old number 14 on them, the same number he used with his bookie), Rose could only hope that his on-the-field exploits — e.g., the records set for hits (4,256), games played (3,562) and 200-plus-hit seasons (ten), along with three National League batting titles and the N.L. MVP in 1973 — would, in the end, outshine his seamier activities in the minds of later generations.

# BIBLIOGRAPHY

Carlson, Margaret. "Charlie Hustle's Final Play; an Unrepentant Pete Rose Is Banned from His Beloved Game," *Time*. (September 4, 1989) 64.

Church, George J. "Why Pick on Pete?," *Time*. (July 10, 1989) 16-20.

Neff, Craig, and Jill Lieber. "Rose's Grim Vigil," *Sports Illustrated*. 70:40 (April 3, 1989) 52-59.

Neff, Craig, ed. "Rose Probe (Cont.)," *Sports Illustrated*. 13-16.

Wulf, Steve. "Score One for Integrity," *Sports Illustrated*. 71:10 (September 4, 1989) 172.

# Babe Ruth Calls His Shot

Babe Ruth performed many heroic feats on the ball field during his twenty-two years as a major leaguer. Among his exploits were:

1. 714 career regular season home runs — a total that remained unsurpassed for forty years;
2. a lifetime .342 batting average — a figure within the top eight all-time;
3. a season total of sixty homers in 1927 — a total which, while eclipsed by Roger Maris in 1961, continues to be a record for a 154-game season; and
4. an outstanding record as a pitcher — ninety-four wins and forty-six losses during the regular season (3-0 in World Series play) along with a microscopic 2.28 ERA.

He is perhaps best known, however, for calling a home run in the 1932 World Series. In a highly charged situation — a two balls-two strikes count in the fifth inning of the third game of the Series, with a hostile crowd screaming epithets at him and the opposing Chicago Cubs team taunting him as a fat, over-the-hill, has-been — Ruth pointed toward the center field bleachers and walloped the next pitch in the vicinity of where he had gestured. It was the longest round tripper ever hit in Wrigley Field, and it effectively put a lid on any Chicago hopes to win the Series. The Yankees went on to a four-game sweep.

Because eyewitnesses cannot agree on what really happened, a controversy has raged for over half a century as to whether Ruth really called his shot. The feat almost defies belief with respect to even the most objective observer; i.e., did the slugger actually have the audacity to leave himself open to the ridicule which would have ensued had he struck out or been retired in some other ineffectual manner? The evidence includes some of the following testimonies:

• Media accounts of the game were inconclusive. Most papers ignored the incident altogether. Those noting the occurrence made the following comments in print:

> . . . with the Cubs riding him unmercifully from the bench, Ruth pointed to center and punched a screaming liner to a spot where no ball had ever been hit before. (Joe Williams, *New York World Telegram*)

> . . . in no mistaken motions, the Babe notified the crowd that the nature of his retaliation would be a wallop right out of the confines of the park. (John Drebinger, *The New York Times*)

> It was the most defiant, and the most debated, gesture in World Series history. Chicago pitcher Charlie Root threw a called strike past the Babe and the Cub bench let the big fellow have it. Babe, holding the bat in one hand, held up the index finger of the other to signify that it was indeed a strike. Root threw another called strike. Ruth held up two fingers and the Cub bench howled in derision.
>
> It was then that the big fellow made what many believe to be the *beau geste* of his entire career. He posted in the direction of dead center field. Some say it was merely a gesture toward Root, others say he was just letting the Cub bench know that he still had the big one left. Ruth himself has changed his version a couple of times but the reaction of most of those who saw him point his finger toward center field is that he was calling his shot. Everybody agrees that Babe did point in the direction of center field and that he did hit a home run there and that's good enough for me. (Tom Meany, sportswriter in the press box that day who wrote a definitive biography of Ruth)

• True believers at the scene included:

> George Pipgras, Yankee pitcher: "Yes, sir, he called it. He pointed toward the bleachers and then he hit it right there. I saw him do it."

> Joe Sewell, Yankee third baseman: "I was there. I saw it. I don't care what anybody says. He called it."

Lou Gehrig, Yankee first baseman: "What do you think of the nerve of that monkey? Calling his shot and getting away with it."

Pat Pieper, Wrigley Field public address announcer: "Don't let anybody tell you differently. Babe definitely pointed to center field."

Ruth himself: "I swung from the ground with everything I had . . . and that ball just went on and on and on and hit far up in the center field bleachers in exactly the spot I had pointed to."

• Skeptics on the scene included:

Charlie Root, Cub pitcher: "Ruth did *not* point at the fence before he swung. If he'd made a gesture like that, I'd have put one in his ear and knocked him on his ass."

Burleigh Grimes, Cub pitcher: "He never called it. Forget it."

Charlie Grimm, Cub manager and first baseman: "He didn't call his shot. He was shouting to pitcher Guy Bush, who was in our dugout. Bush was his chief heckler and he was yelling to Bush that he'd like to see him out there pitching. As he yelled that to Bush, he pointed toward the pitcher's mound."

Gabby Hartnett, Cub catcher: "Babe waved his hand across the plate toward our bench, which was on the third base side. One finger was up. I think only the umpire and I heard him say, 'It only takes one to hit it.' He didn't point out at the bleachers. If he had, I'd be the first to say so."

All said, it would appear that the eyewitness accounts, albeit biased in tone, are too contradictory to draw any absolute conclusions. What can be stated with sureity, however, is that Ruth's feat has captured the imagination of generations, having shifted beyond the domain of established fact into the realm of myth and legend.

# BIBLIOGRAPHY

Creamer, Robert W. *Babe: The Legend Comes to Life*. New York: Simon and Schuster, 1974. Paperback edition by Penguin, 1983.

Daniel, Dan, and H.G. Salsinger. *The Real Babe Ruth*. St. Louis: The Sporting News, 1963.

Meany, Tom. *Babe Ruth: The Big Moments of the Big Fellow*. New York: Barnes, 1947. Paperback edition by Bantam, 1948.

Ritter, Lawrence S., and Mark Rucker. *The Babe: A Life in Pictures*. New York: Ticknor & Fields, 1988.

Smelser, Marshall. *The House That Ruth Built*. New York: Quadrangle, 1975.

Sobol, Ken. *Babe Ruth & The American Dream*. New York: Random House, 1974.

Wagenheim, Kal. *Babe Ruth: His Life and Legend*. New York: Praeger, 1974.

Weldon, Martin. *Babe Ruth*. New York: Crowell, 1948.

Babe Ruth in his last appearance at Yankee Stadium reminded his adoring fans of the day he had called his shot. No one else in baseball history had been able to predict hitting a home run to a particular field and live up to the boast. But "The Sultan of Swat" had done just that, enrapturing Americans everywhere.

# Scandals in College Athletics

College athletics — particularly Division I-A football and basketball programs — suffered countless scandals during the late 1980s. The list included:

- the Chicago trial of sports agents Norby Walters and Lloyd Bloom, who were ultimately convicted of bribing amateur athletes.
- a rash of unlawful incidents involving University of Oklahoma football players in early 1989, including drug dealing, rape, and assault and battery, which led to the resignation of Head Coach Barry Switzer.
- the testimony of two former University of Iowa football players that they took such puff courses as billiards, watercolor painting and recreational leisure.
- two published articles in *Sports Illustrated* — one by a key player on the NCAA championship Villanova basketball squad, the other by a lineman on the University of South Carolina football team — which detailed cases of serious drug abuse (cocaine in the former case, steroids with respect to the latter).
- an NCAA investigation of the University of Florida program in fall 1989 — where (1) Gator basketball coaches stood accused of having paid players, (2) former athletes allegedly purchased drugs while playing for Florida, (3) the starting quarterback and one of his backups were booted off the team for betting on games, and (4) the football coach resigned for having violated NCAA rules — seemed likely to result in the imposition of the "death penalty" (given the 1984 firing of the head coach in football for infractions that included improper recruiting activities and payments).
- the forced resignation in 1989 of North Carolina State basketball coach Jim Valvano as Wolfpack athletic director, the

result of a state investigation of academic and other abuses in his basketball program, followed by evidence — suppressed for one and a half months by Valvano — that nine current or former members of the wrestling team had assaulted two men and a woman near campus.

- the sentencing of ex-Memphis State basketball coach Dana Kirk to a year in prison for income tax evasion.
- the investigation of a former University of Kentucky assistant coach for reportedly sending $1,000 through the mail to the father of a recruited player.
- the placing of many other big-time programs (e.g., USC, Oklahoma State, Texas A&M, the University of Houston, Texas Christian, Kansas, Clemson, the University of Texas) on NCAA probation for assorted violations.

The primary rationale put forward for the sheer number of violations was that the major sports, whose popularity was fueled by ever-increasing television coverage, had proved to be first-rate money-makers. While the traditional argument that a winning team attracts alumni donations to academic departments had by then been largely disproven, many college administrators and governing boards remained convinced athletics were invaluable as (1) a recruiting tool, (2) a means of increased national visibility and prestige, and (3) a traditional form of entertainment in high demand by students, graduates, and the surrounding community.

In addition to the eternal question of whether winning justifies cheating, college athletics were now being criticized for perpetuating a form of slavery; i.e., student athletes were being asked to devote the bulk of their energies to performing in a particular sport without any legal opportunity for financial renumeration. To the colleges' defense that athletes received payment in the form of a free education, skeptics argued that many — particularly those from disadvantaged backgrounds, who often arrived in need of extensive remedial work — lack either the ability or motivation (typically viewing intercollegiate competition as a necessary prelude to the pros) to survive the rigors of the classroom. Even the most motivated students have been severely taxed keeping up academically while practicing as much as thirty hours a week and missing a significant number of classes due to road games.

Critics of the status quo have offered countless prescriptions, ranging from the hiring of professionals to perform under the school banner to the dismantling of intercollegiate competition altogether (substituting in its place some form of intramural program). Noting that scandals have always been around and that the present system has much that is worth saving, *Time* offered a somewhat more conservative list of recommendations in early 1989 aimed at minimizing the chief problems at the heart of college athletics:

1. Colleges should have the same entrance and academic requirements for athletes as for other students, while reaffirming their commitment to admitting minority and disadvantaged students.
2. Athletic dorms should be abolished. They only reinforce the separation of players from the rest of the university community.
3. Practice time should be reduced.
4. All freshmen should be ineligible to practice or play.
5. Games should be scheduled on weekends only.
6. Coaches should be paid on the same scale as faculty members and made eligible for tenure. As long as their jobs are tied to win-loss records, their self-interest may be pitted against the interests of the students in their charge.
7. A greater portion of revenues from sports should go into the general university coffers rather than remain within the athletic departments.
8. The NCAA should require coaches to come forward when they learn of violations. Penalties should be stiffened for all rule breakers.

Both the National Collegiate Athletic Association and college administrators have thus far been slow to propose significant reforms. However, given the very real threat of legislative action as well as disillusionment on the part of the public in general, more substantial efforts at curbing abuses would appear likely in the 1990s.

# BIBLIOGRAPHY

"Big-Time College Sports: Behind Scandals," *U.S. News & World Report*. 92 (April 5, 1982) 60-61.

Guy, Ted. "Foul!," *Time*. (April 3, 1989) 54-60.

Kirshenbaum, Jerry, and others. "A National Disgrace," *Reader's Digest*. 135 (August 1989) 136-142.

Lederman, Douglas. "The Pressure to Win Leads to Unethical Conduct in Many Programs, Sports Officials Say," *The Chronicle of Higher Education*. 35 (July 5, 1989) A27.

McKenzie, Richard B., and E. Thomas Sullivan. "Does the NCAA Exploit College Athletics? An Economic and Legal Reinterpretation," *Antitrust Bulletin*. 32 (Summer 1987) 373-399.

Nack, William. "This Case Was One for the Books; Jan Kemp Won $2.58 Million in a Suit That Bared Academic Abuses Involving the Athletes at Georgia," *Sports Illustrated*. 64 (February 24, 1986) 34-38.

Naison, Mark. "Scenario for Scandal, Sports in the Political Economy of Higher Education," *Commonweal*. 109 (September 24, 1982) 493-496.

Neff, Craig, ed. "Brawls and Barbecues," *Sports Illustrated*. 71:18 (October 30, 1989) 17.

Oberlander, Susan. "Scandal-Plagued SMU Requires Players to Take Course on Issues in Sports; Topics Include Abuses That Led to Stiff Penalties at Their Institution," *The Chronicle of Higher Education*. 35 (May 10, 1989) A33.

Sanoff, Alvin P. "College Sports' Real Scandal: Athletes Make the Grade in the Games But Not in Class," *U.S. News & World Report*. 101 (September 15, 1986) 62-63.

Sanoff, Alvin P. "It's Cleanup Time for College Sports," *U.S. News & World Report*. 99 (July 1, 1985) 62-64.

Sullivan, Robert. "Gambling, Payoffs and Drugs," *Sports Illustrated*. 71:18 (October 30, 1989) 40-45.

Wall, James M. "Institutional Greed Taints College Sports," *The Christian Century*. 102 (May 1, 1985) 35-36.

# Scrabble

In Christmas 1953, shoppers could obtain the standard three-dollar Scrabble set in only two ways: they could place their names on long waiting lists, or they could stand for hours alongside a retail counter until a new shipment of the game arrived, at which time they were likely to become engulfed in a wave of desperately groping humanity. At that point in time there were approximately 1.1 million sets in the U.S. and perhaps ten million players, with countless converts appearing every hour. Scrabble was alleged to be selling more rapidly than any board game in the history of the trade.

The game was not new at the peak of its popularity. It was invented in 1933 by a New York architect named Alfred Butt when he found himself temporarily unemployed. Disliking dice games, which are almost entirely luck, and feeling that all-skill games were too highbrow for the general public, he combined both elements into a pursuit modeled after his love of anagrams and crossword puzzles (see Table I). He and his wife played the game through the 1930s and 1940s, and made some 500 sets for their friends and the odd purchaser.

In 1948, a social worker named James Brunot, who had played the game with the Butts many times over the years, arranged to produce and distribute the game. He named it "Scrabble" (dictionary definition: "to scrape, paw or scratch with the hands or feet") and began assembling the game parts (produced by various manufacturers) in his Newtown, Connecticut home. The operation continued to lose money up until the third quarter of 1952, when sales leaped from a second quarter of eighteen a day to 107 (then to an average of 411 per day in the fourth quarter).

Brunot attributed its sudden success to word-of-mouth promotion combined with the particular lifestyle of many early enthusiasts. Purchasers were generally well-to-do, and were in the habit of spending their summer at various resorts throughout the country.

When the other summer colonists returned to their homes and tried to buy Scrabble sets at their local stores, the big rush began.

After a couple of production relocations proved to be merely a stopgap measure in the face of orders for hundreds of thousands of games, Brunot approached the Selchow & Righter Co. of New York with the aim of broadening the distribution of Scrabble. The company produced almost one million sets between May and December 1953. Scrabble clubs convened throughout the nation and the game was seen everywhere in public.

In addition to the standard game, the Scrabble craze engendered many other merchandising bonanzas. Brunot contracted with the Cadaco-Ellis Company of Chicago to allow the production of a game called "Skip-a-Cross" which differed from Scrabble only in minor manufacturing respects — its tiles were made of cardboard rather than wood, its playing board was a part of the box rather than a separate unit, and its price was two dollars. Cadaco-Ellis sold approximately 250,000 units prior to the end of 1953.

At the upper end, Brunot developed a deluxe ten-dollar set which enabled him to maintain his own little business. It sold 30,000 in the latter half of 1953. It included a red, leather-like case, white plastic tiles and built-in scoring devices on the racks which hold the tiles. Also, half a dozen companies were producing imitations of Scrabble by 1953, following the lines of the original game as much as the copyright laws would permit.

Brunot professed to have received vast quantities of mail at the time, a substantial portion of which concerned itself with various spin-off ploys. These included timing devices, turntables, tile-turning instruments and boys to hold the letter tiles. M. K. Enterprises, Inc. of Chicago was particularly successful in pressing its proposals with Brunot, winning the right to produce both a turntable (consisting of two pieces of fiberboard joined by a pivot, working like a Lazy Susan) and a device for turning the tile over. Brunot also authorized two books, both published by Grosset & Dunlap, and written by Jacob Orleans and Edmund Jacobson. One, *How to Win at Scrabble*, was concerned with strategy, while *The Scrabble World Guide* was a dictionary-like guide to 30,000 useful words (sans definitions). Many dictionary publishers approached Brunot about lending his endorsement to one work or another as the official Scrabble dictionary.

Brunot's refusal to overexpose the game may well have contributed to its ultimate staying power. After a couple of years as America's best-selling board game, it went on to become an institution like Monopoly, Parchesi et al.

---

Table I
Rules of the Game

---

The July 20, 1953 issue of *Time* offered the following summary of how the game was (and continues to be) played:

> A player gets seven counters in the draw, each with a letter and a number. The numbers relate to the letters' frequency of use. The five vowels count only one point each, while "z" counts ten. A player moves by spelling out a word on the board, and his score is the numerical value of the counters plus the value of any premium squares on the board; e.g., hitting a blue square can double or triple the value of the letter used.
>
> The next player must build another word on the original, but only in such a way that every combination of adjoining letters which he makes forms some word. Short, recondite words like gnus and zax have a habit of appearing. Scrabble starts easily, but by the time the board is well covered, the addition of one letter usually involves trying to form two well-nigh impossible words. It is then that dictionaries are consulted and frustrated word-coiners denounce the rigidity of the English tongue.

---

# BIBLIOGRAPHY

"Board Games Kids Liked Best," *Consumer Reports*. 46 (November 1981) 36-37.

Chamish, Barry. "Masters of the Tiles: Even to Initiates, Scrabble Has Yet to Yield Up All Its Secrets," *The Atlantic*. 259 (June 1987) 54-58.

Finkelstein, Alix. "The Very Best Board Games Ever; Tried, True — or New —

These Games Promise Your Entire Family Hours of Fun," *Parents' Magazine*. 61 (August 1986) 60-65.

Gilligan, Eugene. "Classic Toys Sport New Look," *Playthings*. 80 (July 1982) 34-36.

"Gnus, Nix, Zax, Tut," *Time*. 62 (July 20, 1953) 17.

Hobson, L.Z. "Speaking of Scrabble," *Saturday Review*. 36 (August 22, 1953) 5.

Kohl, Louise. "Laying Down the Word," *MacUser*. 4 (January 1988) 50. An analysis of a microcomputer program, Scrabble, from Electronic Arts, for the Apple Macintosh.

Martin, Douglas. "Scrabble: Obsession Over Tiles," *The New York Times*. 138 (August 2, 1989) A13, B1. Covers the New York scene.

"Only the Beginning; History of Scrabble," *New Yorker*. 29 (May 30, 1953) 17.

Rabow, Gerald. "The Cooperative Edge: New Versions of Scrabble, Bridge and Basketball Help Teach Us the Advantages of Cooperation in Play and Real Life," *Psychology Today*. 22 (January 1988) 54-58.

Wallace, Robert. "A Man Makes a Best-Selling Game — Scrabble — and Achieves His Ambition (Spelled Out Above)," *Life*. 35 (December 14, 1953) 101-112.

Wallace, Robert. "Scrabble: Little Business in the Country," *Reader's Digest*. 64 (April 1954) 109-110. Abridged version of the article appeared in the December 14, 1953 issue of *Life*.

# Skateboarding

After a fitful start which had some observers comparing it to the hula hoop, skateboarding has gone on to achieve a seemingly permanent place in the pantheon of American sports. It grew hesitantly along California beach walks in the early 1960s, assuming the dimensions of a nationwide craze by late 1964.

A combination of skiing and surfing, skateboarding became big business in 1965. The total sales for the two-by-four scooters reached $100 million that year; one leading manufacturer, the Roller Derby Skate Corp. of Litchfield, Illinois, grossed eight million dollars on its lines of five models (ranging in price from $1.79 to $14).

In addition, the sport boasted its own music, magazine, national championship tournament and jargon. Jan and Dean, leading proponents of the so-called "California Sound," had a top-twenty hit with "Sidewalk Surfin'" in fall 1964. Patrick McNulty instituted *Quarterly Skateboarder,* with 50,000 charter subscribers in 1965. The sport's credibility received added impetus with the holding of the First Annual National Skateboard Championships in Anaheim, California on May 22-23, 1965. Tie-in merchandising had already reached a fever pitch at this event, with manufacturers distributing products such as T-shirts and "720" shoes (for a skateboarding term meaning two complete revolutions on a board). Other colorful terms used by enthusiasts included "kick-out" (to remove front foot and push forward with the back foot so that the board skitters into the air and enables the rider to catch it), "heelie" (standing on the front of the board, thereby riding on the front wheels only), and "hang ten" (to hang both feet — i.e., all ten toes — over the board's front edge).

The continued growth of skateboarding, however, was severely curtailed by a backlash fueled by parents and other authority figures. The California Medical Association termed the sport "a new medical menace," noting that a lack of control was the key to the hazards of skateboarding.

> [the skateboard] consists of a plank of wood about two feet long with a pair of roller skate wheels attached at either end — no steering handle, no brakes, and no means of control other than the agility of the rider, who stands on the board and propels himself by pushing off with one foot or by letting gravity send him down a hill.

The National Safety Council attempted to take a somewhat more moderate line, issuing a list of rules for safe skateboarding:

> Stay off streets and driveways inclining into streets; use paved playgrounds, noncongested sidewalks, or especially designated areas; confine maneuvers to your level of skill; make your watchword control, not speed; examine your board regularly for mechanical soundness; don't leave your board on walks, driveways, or stairs; and finally, for parents of skateboarders, make sure your child can understand these rules.

Nevertheless, harassed municipal officials searched frantically through old ordinances in the name of protecting bystanders from skateboarders. Bountiful, Utah Police Chief D.O. Anderson confiscated all visible skateboards out of hand, calling them a common public nuisance. In Jacksonville, safety patrolmen impounded them under an "impeding traffic" ordinance, while in Wisconsin the highway department applied a rule prohibiting roller skates on public highways.

In the face of widespread restrictions and poor construction, the popularity of skateboarding dropped off precipitously in the latter half of the 1960s. However, a diehard core of California enthusiasts stuck with the sport. Then, in 1972, they discovered that urethane roller skate wheels, when placed on old boards, gripped the riding surface better and provided more flexibility than the previously employed steel or clay ones.

On the basis of this improved technology, the sport underwent a phenomenal rebirth in the mid-1970s. By 1976, skateboarding was a 250-million-dollar industry catering to approximately ten million

Americans; at least 150 manufacturers were turning out models priced between twenty-five and seventy dollars (including one with blades for ice rinks). Tournaments again began springing up, including the first World Masters Invitational in New York in June 1976 and the first Open World Invitational in California in September 1976, which offered $50,000 in prize money.

While the new equipment was much safer than in the 1960s (when one quarter of all participants were estimated to have been injured at one point or another), the number of hospitalized skateboarders soared to 27,522 Americans in 1975. As communities began considering another repressive wave of rulings aimed at restricting skateboard use, enthusiasts fought back by pushing for traffic-free boarding areas as well as the mandatory use of kneepads, elbow pads and helmets. Russ Howell, a professional making $50,000 a year for appearances on skateboard safety, noted,

> The most dangerous thing about skateboarding is that most communities don't provide a safe area to do it in. I'd like to see skateboarding introduced into school systems. Conventional sports aren't arousing kids' interest any more.

Other supporters pointed to such advantages as the fact that it strengthened thigh, calf, and hip muscles and represented a cheap mode of transport (Emery Air Freight in Los Angeles used skateboarders at the time for small deliveries).

The vogue has remained strong throughout the 1980s, generating countless fanzines, a merchandizing bonanza, and new fashions (e.g., jammers, a cross between the deck pants and bermuda shorts of the 1960s) as well as intermingling with rock music to produce the "thrash rock" lifestyle.

## BIBLIOGRAPHY

—Early Phase
"Here Come the Sidewalk Surfers," *Life*. 56 (June 5, 1964) 89-90.
"A New Sport, or a New Menace?," *Consumer Reports*. 30 (June 1965) 273-274.
"Sidewalk Surfing," *Newsweek*. 65 (April 5, 1965) 71.
"Skateboard Mania," *Life*. 58 (May 14, 1965) 126C-128ff.

"Skateboard Skiddoo," *Newsweek*. 65 (May 10, 1965) 40ff.

"Skateboarding: Hazardous New Fad for Kids," *Good Housekeeping*. 161 (August 1965) 137.

"Skateboards, Fun But Dangerous," *Consumer Bulletin*. 48 (August 1965) 13-14.

"Taking the Plunge," *Newsweek*. 65 (May 24, 1965) 110ff.

—Later Phase

Arthur, G.J. "Ocean Bowl Story," *Parks & Recreation*. 11 (December 1976) 14-17ff.

Hiss, A., and S. Bart. "Free as a Board," *New York Times Magazine*. (September 12, 1976) 40-41ff.

Kellogg, Mary Alice. "Rebirth of the Boards," *Newsweek*. 87 (June 21, 1976) 56-57.

Kesselman, J.R. "Skateboard Menace," *Family Health*. 8 (August 1976) 34-35ff.

McClintock, M. "Surfing on Concrete," *Popular Mechanics*. 145 (June 1976) 94-95ff.

Schildkraut, M.L. "Tips That Help Get the Danger Out of Skateboarding," *Good Housekeeping*. 183 (October 1976) 236.

# The Slam Dunk

The growing impact of the dunk shot — that is, jamming the basketball through the hoop — was the result of a number of factors:

1. the increasing percentage of tall, highly coordinated players;
2. the aura of showboating came to be viewed less in negative terms;
3. the greater tolerance of coaches with respect to allowing players more freedom of expression (many of the former seemed to feel it represented the only realistic strategy in order to attract the more athletic recruits who learned their game in a freewheeling urban playground milieu); and
4. coaches, athletic directors, general managers, etc., recognized that it was boffo at the box office — and money has always been the name of the game in college as well as the pros.

The decision of the NCAA to outlaw the dunk beginning with the 1967-1968 season (it was repealed after the 1975-1976 season), represented an effort to curb the growing domination of the big man in basketball. It proved to be a failure in that tall players continued to hold an inherent edge over smaller participants while the game was robbed of (1) a fan-pleasing display, and (2) the highest percentage shot if done in a straightforward way.

The early 1980s saw the ascendancy of a new variant of the shot, the slam dunk. The most renowned practitioner in the NBA was Darryl Dawkins, whose capacity for splintering backboards became a staple of the television highlight films. The college game had the University of Houston's Phi Slama Jama, which included Akeem Olajuwon, Clyde "the Glide" Drexler, Larry "Mr. Mean" Micheaux, Michael Young and Greg "Cadillac" Anderson. In 1984, Dan Gehringer observed that the Houston style of play caused a sensation:

> [In 1980] the university bookstore was not doing a land-office business, as it is today, in Phi Slama Jama Twenties-style "we

bad'' caps and painter's caps and old-timer's caps and $18.95 caps wired for sound and blinking lights (batteries not included) and $94.95 TEXAS' TALLEST FRATERNITY jackets and Phi Slama Jama T-shirts and sweat shirts and mugs and sweatbands and towels (red-and-white checked, just like the one Coach Lewis wipes his sweating face with at the games) and Phi Slama Jama taffy.

It is notable that Houston failed to win the NCAA championship with the Phi Slama Jama contingent despite reaching the final four three times during the early 1980s. John Garrity seemed to offer an explanation for this failure in a column he wrote for *Sports Illustrated*. He criticized the show-off dunk as a combination of bad sportsmanship and bad tactics; i.e., it indicated that scoring wasn't enough, a shorter player (or one rushing the shot) often would hit the heel of the rim, and—while missed layups often were tipped in by a trailer—not so dunks. He proposed exacting one or another of the following penalties for missed or overly showy dunks (after all, doesn't football penalize players who indulge in sack dances or spiking the ball?): (1) deduct two points; (2) call a technical foul; or (3) simply award the opposing team free throws.

Whether or not all coaches and fans are enamored of the dunk, it appears to be here for the long run (short of some drastic measure such as an outright ban or raising the rim four feet higher). Recognizing its crowd appeal, the pros have legitimized it by holding slam dunk contests in conjunction with the NBA All Star Game each year; this contest tends to pull in higher ratings than the game itself.

## BIBLIOGRAPHY

Axthelm, Pete. "It Takes Discipline to Dunk," *Newsweek*. 101 (April 18, 1983) 48.

Bloom, S. "The Right Stuffs," *TV Guide*. 36 (February 6/12, 1988) 30-31.

Garrity, John. "Too Much Silly Stuff; Show-Off Slam Dunking Is Junking Up Basketball," *Sports Illustrated*. 68 (March 14, 1988) 96.

Gehringer, Dan. "Phi Slama Jama," *Rolling Stone*. (March 29, 1984) 89-97.

Sakamoto, B. "The Supreme Slam Dunk Contest," *Sport*. (New York, N.Y.). 79 (March 1988) 71.

# Slave Fights

Plantation owners in the South of antebellum days employed Negro slaves not only in every working capacity, but also for their own amusement and recreation. There are no exact figures tabulating the number of organized fights that occurred in which neighboring owners pitted their stoutest slaves against each other. On record, though, is evidence of the practice and most likely it was widespread. Southern white males took great pride in possessing the finest horseflesh and man flesh around. If they were not racing the former, they prodded the latter into bare-knuckle fistfights with no rules to speak of. Wagering on the outcome of these rough-and-tumble affairs added spice to the spectacle of watching muscular field hands fight for the honor of their masters. The pugilists did not box, spar, and mix it up in a gentlemanly manner; they brawled, grappled, and collided. If the owner desired to make the contest even more interesting, he promised his slave freedom in exchange for thrashing the opponent. One such pact involved a slave, Tom Molineaux (1784-1818), the son of Zachary Molineaux, now credited with having founded boxing in the United States. Father taught son everything there was to know about heads-up boxing so he would not enter a fight flailing away to no advantage.

At around sixteen, Tom's owner promised him $100 and his freedom if he could defeat the slave of a rival planter. Tom whipped his opponent and walked off a freeman. Zachary, who had died a few years before, was not there to witness the great day. An unanswered question arises at this point: If Zachary Molineaux was the father of boxing in this country, from whom did he learn the art? Boxing historians suggest that young southern males, while in England for their education, observed boxing firsthand. The sport in England marked its beginning in 1719 with the opening of James Figg's pugilistic academy in London. From 1785 to 1825, British bare-knuckle boxing was at its zenith, so that a visitor had ample opportunity to see any number of matches. Home again, the southern males instructed their slaves. Zachary Molineaux must have absorbed all of this secondhand teaching and combined it with his own and Tom's natural talent.

Not sure what to do next, Tom drifted to New York where he worked on the docks and earned extra money fighting waterfront challengers. In a short time he had knocked down enough opponents to win the spurious title around New York as America's boxing champion. Because he was an ex-slave, a fierce competitor (200 lbs. with enormously long arms), and seemingly unbeatable, Tom excited audiences and bare-knuckle boxing became all the rage. In 1809, Tom sailed to London to really prove himself by challenging the British boxing champion, Tom Cribb. But first, he had to battle several opponents before Cribb would consider him worthy of a championship match. Tom won the matches preliminary to what was to be the first international prize fight. On December 10, 1810, the two Toms met at Coptoll Common on a miserable day of weather (the fight was outdoors). Molineaux pounded Cribb for 29 rounds; but after a ruse to gain more rest for Cribb and Molineaux taking a chill during the wait, the Englishman went on to knock out the American in the 40th round. Cheated of the world title in the premiere, Molineaux also lost in a rematch. The few years remaining to the ex-slave were sad ones indeed. Tom wasted energy in street brawls, took to drink, and got hopelessly out of shape. In 1815 another British boxer, George Cooper, defeated him in less than twenty minutes. Tom then wrestled but failed at that too, dying a penniless beggar in Galway, Ireland, far from his lovely Virginia birthplace.

Meanwhile, in the United States the fad of bare-knuckle fistfights without rules sputtered along, unorganized and savage. The British had long followed Broughton's rules of the ring which curbed "American excesses" such as gouging, hitting below the belt, and kicking a man when he was down. As a result, the art of boxing developed rapidly in England. But here mercenary promoters controlled the fights and bloodbaths continued devoid of any artistry. In fact, the secret of Tom Molineaux's success on the waterfront in New York was that he had learned self-defense from his father, elevating him above the common brawler he met. It was not until

1849 that a bare-knuckle champion of the United States emerged, Tom Hyer. The slow evolution was due to the savagery of anything-goes fighting which all states eventually outlawed early in the nineteenth century. However, the aristocratic privilege of slave fights proceeded distinctly separate from organized British and brutal northern fisticuffs. Other slaves may have won their freedom and drifted up North, but Tom Molineaux was the only one who made boxing history.

## BIBLIOGRAPHY

Fleischer, Nat S. *Black Dynamite: The Story of the Negro in the Prize Ring from 1782 to 1938*. 5 vols. New York: C.J. O'Brien, c1938-1947.

Fox, Richard K. *The Black Champions of the Prize Ring from Molineaux to Jackson*. New York: Self-Published, 1890.

Henderson, Edwin Bancroft. *The Negro in Sports*. Washington, D.C.: The Associated Publishers, Inc., 1939.

# Snow Bat

In emulation of baseball, this winter sport gave kids a chance to play America's favorite game year round. As in baseball the batter held a bat, though at the end of it, making a round hitting surface, there was attached a 10″ disk composed of thin, light material such as plywood, fiber board, pressed wood, or even fabric. Behind the batter a catcher crouched holding a "snow catcher" (called the target) securely with both hands. It was a 24″ disk, often the hard cover from a bushel basket. The racquet-like bat and the much larger circular snow catcher completed the equipment needs. Opposite the batter, some 30′ away, the thrower might start with only fifteen snowballs, or more depending on local rules. The object was for the thrower to hurl each snowball past the batter and at the same time hit the snow catcher. The catcher had to keep both hands firmly affixed to the target, but could move the target around within the batter's circle to intercept the snowballs. Of course, the batter's job was to pulverize each and every white missile.

Now here is where the rules got complicated. As soon as the first pitch was thrown, a runner — not the batter — started off speeding around an elliptical course skirting the pitcher's circle, then back to the batter's circle. One full circuit of the ellipse constituted a score of one point. The runner did not stop running until the batter missed smashing a snowball whereas the thrower hitting the target signalled the batter was out and the next batter took his place. Three outs and the teams changed places. The thrill in snow bat was for the thrower to pitch as rapidly as possible to stop the breakneck runner from scoring points. Behind the thrower, two snowball makers worked diligently to keep the supply of ammunition coming. This was a distinct advantage for the thrower who could literally bombard the batter with a flurry of snowballs. So to even things up the thrower could use only one hand to hurl with — no double throws; and the catcher had to maintain contact with a stick behind him by pressing his foot against it at all times. This restricted his ability to move the target in extreme directions away from the batter. Of equal advantage to both teams, a snowball that split or burst in the air before contact did not count, and time-out could be called to bring in a fresh mound of snow for making snowballs.

Snow bat was one of those marvelous sports, inventor unknown, that kids of lesser means could play by utilizing found objects. A full afternoon of throwing and batting at such a reckless pace wore them out happily, and at the same time satisfied their budding aggressive natures without doing anyone any harm.

## BIBLIOGRAPHY

"Fast and Exciting New Winter Game Played with Snowballs," *Popular Science Monthly*. 122 (January 1933) 62.

# Spirit of the Times

William Trotter Porter began *Spirit of the Times* in 1831 to fill a gap in American magazine publishing. He modeled his sporting newspaper after *Bell's Life in London*, which showcased turf news (horse racing) but also offered a miscellany of other reports and stories. Porter could have contented himself with just reporting English and local (New York) turf news, but because of his love for horse racing he sent correspondents down south and into the western regions. His desire to publish sporting news happily coincided with the crescendo and peak of American horse racing in the 1830s. Whether *Spirit of the Times* nutured the horse-racing craze, or whether Porter simply capitalized on its apparent popularity, is a matter of conjecture. What is certain is that Porter's magazine was the first to report American sporting news at length, inaugurating a faddish interest in turf details and statistics.

Before Porter, subscription periodicals were full of "fine writing," i.e., belles-lettres. They were meant for educated readers who appreciated such things. Because not everyone in the 1830s could read, a good circulation rate for any periodical was perhaps a few thousand. At the height of its popularity, *Spirit of the Times* sold to around forty thousand customers. Porter was one of those educated readers and did include in his magazine some fine writing, but it was his addition of the very bone and marrow of the turf that attracted a wider range of readers and non-readers. Although based in New York, Porter should have established his paper in Richmond or Atlanta. Horse racing was king in the South, and the first American sport that galvanized people to think, talk, and live it.

Early issues of *Spirit of the Times* contained items common to other publications: reprinted articles from English and American periodicals; police reports for New York, Philadelphia, and London; extracts from speeches; poems and local occurrences. The ground-breaking items were: reports on game laws and hunting;

articles on horses and sports club meetings; notes of horse races; lists of winners in races; lists of stallions; articles on the training of race horses; betting tips; and advertisements for horse medicines, veterinarians, gunsmiths and the like. Porter himself was an avid angler, but did not allow his passion for fishing to cloud his editorial judgement — turf came first. Readers devoted to the turf and its underpinning — gambling — leafed through the pages with great delight. Finally, here was a practical sheet. High-flown rhetoric and pretty words be damned.

During his journalistic career, Porter had his share of troubles. He was forced to sell and then re-buy *Spirit of the Times*. The paper was a stand-up success, published almost continuously from 1831 until 1858; if not owner, Porter served as editor for most of those years. *Spirit of the Times* was read as far away as Europe and on the western frontier. Read, yes, but not always paid for. Porter's subscribers held onto their money. So at the close of the 1830s "not the first red cent" was his. Porter was partly at fault; he had increased the price of *Spirit of the Times* to as high as ten dollars a year, an uncompetitive sum back then. He charged more so that he could add pages to the publication and costly steel engravings of famous racehorses. When turf mania subsided at the beginning of the 1840s, Porter had a dying magazine on his hands. Always the vigilant editor, he recalled that some local color sketches had elicited letters of congratulations. Porter, the father of American sporting news, soon became the father of "The Big Bear School of Writing." Upon its publication March 27, 1841, the "Big Bear of Arkansas," a tale by Col. T. B. Thorpe, reinvigorated *Spirit of the Times*. Tall tales from the wooly West whipped up a new faddish reading interest among civilized Easterners. Just that simply, Porter had found uncharted journalistic territory to explore, and thereafter American humorists could count on him to supply a medium and an audience.

Porter assessed his own influence on horse racing in an April 1843 issue of *Spirit of the Times*. He felt that his paper had made horse breeders rich by boosting sales of thoroughbreds, lessened the prejudice of the Puritan North against horse racing, and shown the British that American horse racing was on near-equal standing with their own. Porter's death in 1858 brought to a close publication of the paper. His biographer, Francis Brinley, wrote of him: "As a turf-writer, he was without rival in this country, or even in England, where sporting literature had been cultivated for years by men of taste and education."

## BIBLIOGRAPHY

Brinley, Francis. *Life of William T. Porter*. New York: D. Appleton, 1860.

Mundt, Shirley M. "William Trotter Porter," In: *Dictionary of Literary Biography. Vol. 43: American Newspaper Journalists, 1690-1872*. Edited by Perry J. Ashley. Detroit: Gale Research Co., 1985.

Yates, Norris W. *William T. Porter and the 'Spirit of the Times.'* Baton Rouge: Louisiana State University Press, 1957.

# Spiritualism

Several fads of the 1920s relied heavily on the credulity of the average American. The in-vogue thing was to visit a psychic or medium to talk to a dead relative, to seek advice before making an important decision, or to test the powers of the spiritualist. Harry Houdini, the famous magician and escape artist, made it his personal mission to expose these tricksters. He revealed that spiritualists relied heavily on radio transmission for their secret information. A psychic or medium might place an antenna in the sole of her shoe, under a nearby rug, or in a bouquet of flowers. A headphone hidden inside her wig or headdress received messages from a confederate, who had learned inside information earlier from the client. This simple ruse allowed the spiritualist to greet a perfect stranger by name and tell that person his or her past history in detail. Houdini also explained how easy it was to plant a telephone receiver in a statue to make it speak, or even in a kitchen kettle. Another favorite subterfuge was to have confederates wait at police stations, hospitals, and newspaper offices to get all the fast-breaking news. Once ascertained, the confederate would radio in facts for the psychic or medium to tell her clients. Later that evening or the next morning after the news was public knowledge, those who had heard it "first" from the spiritualist were amazed and reverential.

Table-tipping, -tapping, or -turning were also popular pastimes. A group of people sat at a table with their outspread fingers touching one another to form a circle on the tabletop. In this communal manner they waited in silence for the table to speak to them. The big moment came when the table seesawed, tapped the floor, moved its position, or lifted in the air. Three knocks signified "yes," one knock "no." This deception was simple to produce, yet powerful in performance. The operator made the table move by lifting a leg with the sole of his or her shoe, or with the help of a confederate seated opposite, causing the table to really jump around. Why such a transparent deception enthralled people is hard to understand, except to say they wanted desperately to believe in it.

Another fraud was automatic writing. Even more simple than table-tipping, it was also more potent. The psychic or medium, already aware of the answer to a client's question, started to tremble with uncontrollable muscle agitation prompted by the "psychic self." Her hand then scrawled letters on paper forming words, until her fingers went limp, drained of supernatural energy. The mystic scrawl told her client everything, making the evening well worth the investment of time and money. By conjuring up her psychic self instead of just vocalizing the message, she provided a real service full of otherworldly, incontrovertible truth.

Fads associated with spiritualism were not new to the 1920s. Perfected in Europe, table-tipping and automatic writing had obsessed credulous Americans long before. But given the radio for transmission of secret information, psychics and mediums advanced to greater heights of glory and fraud. Interestingly, a new development—the emergence of the amateur spiritualist—irritated the gifted ones who had been "trained" in Europe. The true spiritualists warned the public that false prophets were out to cheat them. Amateurs misinformed and wrongfully built up hopes. The authentic mental telepathists, table-tippers, and automatic writers did not want the imposters to give the industry a bad name. What makes spiritualism fads so fascinating is that even though Houdini and others did their best to expose the nonsense, people still flocked to the garish parlors. One reason given for belief in spiritualism after 1918 was that many people had lost loved ones in World War I. The need to communicate with the recently departed was so overpowering that any method appeared worth a chance. Then again, perhaps spiritualism was one manifestation of what made the 1920s roar.

## BIBLIOGRAPHY

Gerould, Gordon H. "Ghost and Devils, New Style," *Scribner's Monthly*. 71 (April 1922) 428-32.

"Ghosts that Talk by Radio," *Literary Digest*. 75 (October 21, 1922) 28-29.

"The Modern Flood of Amateur 'Psychics' Shocks the Professionals," *Literary Digest*. 64 (March 20, 1920) 74-76.

Randi, James. *Flim-Flam: Psychics, ESP, Unicorns, and Other Delusions*. Buffalo, N.Y.: Prometheus, 1982.

Slosson, E.E. "Mediums and Tricksters," *Scientific Monthly*. 15 (September 1922) 285-287.

In various "reincarnations" spiritualism entranced Americans for almost two decades. Clients went to mediums to contact their dearly departed. World War I boosted business and the rampant fraud perpetrated angered no less an authority on deception than Harry Houdini, who exposed any and every sham practice.

347

# Sting Ray Bicycles

The sting ray bicycle represented the wish fulfillment of young boys emulating the hot rod styling then popular with driving-age teens. Do-it-yourself customizing—i.e., removing the basket, fenders, and chain guards from standard issue models and then raising the seat and handlebars—led manufacturers to hit upon the basic design: a compact, lightweight bike usually with only twenty-inch wheels; high, looping handlebars ("ape hangers"); and a long, narrow seat ("polo saddle").

Making its appearance in the mid-1960s, the sting ray was particularly big in California, accounting for more than ninety percent of all bike sales in that state. In 1966 alone, approximately one million were purchased across the nation. "Man, talk about fads!" exclaimed John Lea, owner of a bike shop in Marin County, California. "Everybody wants it."

*Newsweek* attributed the sting ray's appeal to "its power to make a seven-year old come on like Steve McQueen aboard his Triumph." Its low center allowed for the performance of such stunts as "wheelies" (pulling up on the handlebars, leaning back and riding on the rear wheel only) and "jumpies" (jamming on the brakes with the result that the bike flies for several feet or more). Sting ray owners borrowed from the dragsters in spraying their frames with "diamond flake" paint and placing wildly hued slip covers over the saddle seats as well as by utilizing treadless tires ("racing slicks" on the rear wheels for faster starts).

Since its initial high-interest phase, the sting ray has gone on to become an established model for all major American bicycle manufacturers, including Schwinn and Murray. It remains a steady seller with a high visibility on the nation's streets and playgrounds.

# BIBLIOGRAPHY

"All About the New Look in Bicycles," *Good Housekeeping*. 161 (November 1965) 180.

Wall, A. "Look What's Happening to Bicycles," *Popular Science*. 187 (August 1965) 108-111ff.

"Wheelies and Jumpies," *Newsweek*. 67 (February 7, 1966) 54.

# Streaking

Oh, what the hell. They're just a bunch of foolish kids. And I was a foolish kid once, too.

So said 74-year-old Fred R. Pierce, presiding justice of the California Court of Appeals, about romping nude in public. In 1918, at Stanford, he had crawled naked through a chest-high ditch behind a sorority house to win a $5 bet.

Streaking in 1974 was not quite as timid. Mostly college men, and a few coeds, dashed about naked in full view of an audience. Their private parts dangled and bounced and shocked no one to any great extent. It was the total surprise of the event that made streaking fun to do and watch. When least expected, a naked guy sprinted across campus or through a cafeteria or down main street. At Harvard two streakers, naked except for surgical masks, interrupted a packed amphitheater of students taking a first-year anatomy test. At the University of Missouri, attired only in sneakers, socks, and hats, a group of 35 men streaked through "Greek Town"; not to be outdone, 15 coeds responded by running naked outside their dormitory while 25 others jiggled their bare flesh behind windows. A trumpeter in the crowd of 1,500 seized the moment and played the Missouri fight song. Creativity came to the fore at Stanford when seven nude males interrupted a fraternity man entertaining a coed in his room; they all carried golf bags and asked, "May we play through?" At the University of South Carolina a streaker entered the library and inquired if *The Naked Ape* were in the collection. At Princeton University a candidate for vice president of the class of '76, who also romped in the nude, adopted the campaign slogan, "Vote the Streaker — If Elected He Will Run." At the University of Georgia and the University of Illinois, students jumped from airplanes wearing only parachutes.

Collegians did not win all the glory. A bank employee ran naked down Wall Street in observance of a bare market. A male passenger on a jumbo jet flight from London to New York streaked up and down the aisles. Both naked, a 67-year-old man and his 46-year-old female companion strolled leisurely through the public square in Lima, Ohio; when arrested the pair said they were "snailing" because of their age. And on national television, with millions of people watching, a lone streaker shot across the stage during the Academy Awards ceremony. Hollywood itself could not have topped the improbability of such an eye-opener.

How and why did streaking begin? No one really knows; its birth was spontaneous. The University of Maryland claimed the distinction, as did several other universities once the word got out. The Rhode Island Historical Society was quick to report that streaking went back as far as 1776. The Society had papers that described an incident in the spring of that year in which Continental Army soldiers went on a streaking rampage. At their camp near a millpond in Brooklyn, New York, they would "come out of the water and run to the houses naked with a design to insult and wound the modesty of female decency." General Nathanael Greene scolded his troops, reminding them that "our enemies have sought to fix a stigma upon the New England people as being rude and barbarous . . . for heaven's sake don't let your behavior serve as an example to confirm these observations." For the "why" part of the question, psychology professors were asked to comment on the streaking mania.

> College students are irreverent toward social values. This is an attack on dominant social values. (Philip Zimbardo, Stanford University)
>
> It's spring, the weather is warm, it's something to do. (Arthur Yehle, Memphis State University)
>
> . . . a form of escapism that doesn't seem sexual in nature. Students are working harder in school, and this is letting off steam. (Dorothy Hochreich, University of Connecticut)
>
> . . . an impulse that comes to frustrated persons who are afraid of being conformists. (Mike Nichols, Emory University)

A Yale student answered why by saying simply, "We're college students and college students are supposed to have fun." And fun they had participating in the "epidermis epidemic" until tragedy struck. A streaker on a motorcycle died in a collision. Another one trying to cross the Dallas-Fort Worth turnpike was hit and killed. Less tragic were the many arrests for public disturbance, fines, and jail time. Some universities censured streaking, others vowed "noninterference." Luckily, naked females were left alone except for an occasional running through a gauntlet of fingers. Surprisingly, there were no major rape incidents.

Soon everyone got in on the act. President Richard Nixon when asked by a reporter if his hair was graying at the temples quipped, "They call that streaking." And the Seminole Health Club, a nudist colony in Davie, Florida, staged a "Gnikaerts" ("streaking" spelled backwards); they ran around Davie fully clothed. Perhaps streaking was just spontaneous fun, but its outbreak in 1974 coincided with a number of national news stories that might have triggered such screwball behavior. The year before the Vietnam cease-fire agreement was signed, bringing an end to the most unpopular war in U.S. history. Later in 1973, Vice President Spiro T. Agnew resigned in the face of certain conviction for income tax evasion. August 9, 1974, the Watergate Affair climaxed with Richard Nixon's resignation of the presidency. Then Nixon's appointee as Vice President, Gerald R. Ford, who became president after August 9, granted Nixon a full pardon for all federal crimes. These events were hot topics on college campuses. With the end of war and the dismissal of "tricky Dick," what better way to celebrate than to run nude in a show of ecstatic happiness, or in the case of the pardon, to release pent up frustration at a perceived miscarriage of justice.

## BIBLIOGRAPHY

"Blue Streaks," *Newsweek*. 83 (February 4, 1974) 63.
"The Founding Streakers," *Newsweek*. 83 (May 20, 1974) 120.
"Streaking: One Way to Get a B.A.," *Newsweek*. 83 (March 18, 1974) 41-42.
"Streaking, Streaking Everywhere," *Time*. 110 (March 18, 1974) 58-59.

When Robert Opal streaked behind David Niven during the televised 1974 Oscar ceremony, the dapper and quick-witted Niven replied, "Isn't it fascinating that probably the only laugh this man will ever get in his life is by stripping off his clothes and showing his shortcomings."

# The John L. Sullivan Mystique

John L. Sullivan began his reign as World Heavyweight Champion by knocking out Paddy Ryan in the ninth round at Mississippi City on February 7, 1882. While a succession of victories over foreign challengers during the next couple of years added considerably to his appeal, what finally raised Sullivan to the pinnacle of popularity was a tour of the United States, during which he offered one thousand dollars to anyone who could remain standing in the ring with him for four rounds. His prescribing of gloves for these matches popularized their use throughout the nation.

During his reign, Sullivan continued to mingle world tours, formal and informal exhibitions, meeting-all-comers stunts, and vaudeville appearances with his regular professional career, progressively adding to his renown. When Sullivan defeated Jake Kilrain in seventy-five rounds at Richburg, Mississippi—the last bare-knuckle championship bout (under the London Prize Ring Rules which had held sway since their appearance in 1838)—Sullivan solidified the general consensus that he was the greatest fighter of all time. One notable poet was moved to reflect in verse:

> When I was nine years old, in 1889,
> I heard a battle trumpet sound.
> Nigh New Orleans
> Upon an emerald plain
> John L. Sullivan
> The strong boy
> Of Boston
> Fought seventy-five rounds with Jake Kilrain . . .
> "East side, west side, all around the town
> The tots sang: 'Ring a rosie'

'LONDON BRIDGE IS FALLING DOWN.' "
And . . .
John L. Sullivan knocked out Jake Kilrain.

—Vachel Lindsey
*John L. Sullivan, the Strong Boy of Boston*

Following the defeat of Kilrain, Sullivan became as much an American institution as "strawberry shortcake, fireworks on the Fourth of July, and the high-wheeled bicycle." In the ring or out, he was the biggest drawing card of that era. He barnstormed the nation successfully as the hero of a melodrama entitled *Honest Hearts and Willing Hands*. His reputation as a free spender did not lessen his popularity; nor did his well-known habit of entering a saloon, ordering everyone a round of drinks, and announcing that he could lick any blankety-blank son-of-a-so-and-so in the place.

Three years elapsed before Sullivan entered the ring except for exhibitions. By the time he faced off against Gentleman Jim Corbett on September 7, 1892 in New Orleans, idleness, the enervating life of the stage, and long nights spent carousing with boon companions had combined to sap vitality and substantially increase his girth. In contrast to Sullivan's braggadocio and overconfidence, Corbett had figured a way to exploit his opponent's weaknesses; i.e., to make the slugger miss often, fool him with quick footwork, and gradually wear him down. When Sullivan dropped from sheer exhaustion in the twenty-first round, America's working millions entered into a profound malaise. Their hero had been a symbol of national glory, a manifestation of America's greatness. A long period elapsed before Corbett was able to overcome the prejudice engendered because he had had the audacity to pull John the Great from his pedestal.

Sullivan, for his part, continued to be uniformly successful in vaudeville and on the lecture platform. Those of a later generation came in droves to see him as had their fathers, even though Sullivan eventually swore off drinking and became a lecturer on temperance. His fame was such that—despite his inferiority to some heavyweight title holders—many call him the Champion of Champions.

# BIBLIOGRAPHY

Cox, James A. "The Great Fight: 'Mr. Jake' vs. John L. Sullivan," *Smithsonian*. 15 (December 1984) 152ff.

Durant, J. "Yours Truly, John L. Sullivan," *American Heritage*. 10 (August 1959) 54-59ff.

Fleischer, Nat. *The Heavyweight Championship; An Informal History of Heavyweight Boxing from 1719 to the Present Day*. New York: Putnam, 1961. pp. 77-103 (Chapters 7-9).

Lawless, Ken. "Last But Not the Least; the Final Bare-Knuckle Title Fight Was a Bloody Battle," *Sports Illustrated*. 71 (July 3, 1989) 69-70. A retrospective look at the John L. Sullivan-Jake Kilrain bout of July 8, 1889.

Smith, S.D. "Duel in the Sun," *New York Times Magazine*. (April 9, 1964) 72-73.

Ward, Geoffrey C. "The Boston Strong Boy," *American Heritage*. 39 (September-October 1988) 12-13. Column providing a tribute to Sullivan.

JOHN L. SULLIVAN,
CHAMPION PUGILIST OF THE WORLD.

Born at Boston, Mass. 1858.      Height, 5 ft. 10 ½ ins.      Weight, 196 lbs.

Beat Donaldson, with hard gloves. at Cincinnati O. Dec. 28th. 1880. Purse $500.   Beat Flood on the Hudson" May 16th. 1881. Purse $1000.
Beat Ryan at Mississippi City. Miss. Feb 7th 1882. $2.500 a side.   Knocked out Elliott in 3 rounds. glove fight; New York. July 4th. 1882.

The most picturesque fighter of his day, John L. Sullivan attracted new fans for boxing wherever he entered a ring. Not even his defeat in 1892 at the hands of James J. Corbett could diminish his stature. Sullivan was also the last of the bare-knuckle boxers, which explains much of his fascination for manly crowds.

# Surfing

Of all surfing fads perhaps the most bizarre was wearing a Nazi swastika. Also called the Iron Cross, and later the Surfer's Cross, California's most outrageous motorcycle gang, the Hell's Angels, wore them first. The Angels' purpose was to look at least as mean as the World War II German hoodlums, the Nazis. They also tugged on Nazi helmets as headgear. Young California surfers, blind to history, likewise demonstrated their rebelliousness by exchanging St. Christopher medals for swastikas. The swapping of sacred for profane angered their parents and split families. What made the fad even more bizarre was that the sharp edges of the swastika cut flesh during a wipeout. Soon non-surfers decided swastika wearing was a great fashion statement and bought loads of them. "Big Daddy" Ed Roth, the 275-pound supply sergeant for the Hell's Angels, sold 50,000 + of the "authentic" neckwear in no time at all. But his profits were miniscule compared to variety and jewelry store sales. In 1966, Ronnie Jewelry, Inc. (Rhode Island) produced 24,000 crosses a day for distribution. If the primary attribute of a fad is that its adoption not make much sense, then swastika wearing is a perfect example. The 1960s were too close to World War II and Nazi tyranny for baby-boom fathers to dismiss the fad lightly.

Not quite as dangerous as Russian Roulette but similar, pier roulette required a surfer to speed on a wave through concrete pilings covered with razor-sharp barnacles. The daredevil caught a wave close to the pier, then slid into the surging heart of the waterwall. When the wave began to curl, he cut across its face accelerating into the pilings. If he did not maneuver just right, flesh and board got ripped to shreds. Instead of being outlawed, pier roulette became an accepted part of some surfing contests.

Pypo- or piper-boarding arose out of necessity. The distress of no surf was eased somewhat by tossing a 28″ wide wooden disk in the foam at water's edge. A smooth layer of plastic coated the bottom of the board to make it glide. The pypo-boarder ran after the disk he had tossed and jumped onto it to skim over the water for close to 35 feet.

Fads in surfboard design became a growth industry. Every year new improved models came out as regularly as detergent. Different lengths, weights, and shapes caused nervous fits among jobless surfers. Their old boards were not good enough anymore. They feared the ocean would engulf them, laugh at them, spit them out on the beach. Some boards were better than others for "hot-dogging" (trick surfing), for "sliding" (riding almost parallel to the shore and the face of the wave), for "hairpin turns" (sudden reversals of direction), for "spinning" (turning the body rapidly in complete circles while riding the wave), for "head dips" (squatting on the board while sliding and putting the head in the water), and for "hanging five or ten" (extending the toes of one or both feet over the front end of the board without falling off).

A writer for *Holiday*, Carelton Mitchell, exposed his age and ignorance by asking a rhetorical question:

> What circumstances have combined to transform an ancient Polynesian pastime into an 'in' sport with sociological overtones; into an international cult having distinctive styles in dress and coiffure, and its own music, literature and motion pictures; into a way of life as separate from the community as a European gypsy encampment?

Arriving as it did in the mid-1960s, the surfing craze contributed to the dropout mentality espoused elsewhere in America. If a young person wanted to grow long hair and live close to nature, the beach was a great place to do it. Those who loved the beach but were not athletically inclined started another fad of the adventurous 1960s — nude bathing á la the South of France. Then there were the acolytes. Watching sets of waves roll to shore produced a hypnotic effect. The azure water lifting in swells, the glory of dawn and sunset combined to make for a religious experience. To heighten the transcendent feeling, smoking a little reefer did not hurt. (See also entry for *The Endless Summer*.)

# BIBLIOGRAPHY

Mitchell, Carleton. "The Fad and Fascination of Surfing," *Holiday*. 35 (May 1964) 122+.

Murray, William. "Hanging Five," *Holiday*. 42 (September 1967) 62-67.

"Pier Roulette—New Form of Surfboard Suicide," *Popular Mechanics*. 119 (February 1963) 127.

"The Surfer's Cross," *Time*. 87 (April 22, 1966) 81-82.

# The Topless Bathing Suit

The topless bathing suit had its genesis in a casual prediction made by fashion designer Rudi Gernreich. In a 1963 interview he noted that, "in five years every American woman will be wearing a bathing suit that is bare above the waist." While deliberating as to whether or not to produce such a suit, the Hess brothers department store in Allentown, Pennsylvania ordered a shipment. When other retailers across the United States also expressed an interest, Gernreich began making the suit in early 1964.

The garment raised a furor in many quarters as soon as it hit the stores. Some notable reactions included:

- In Dallas, the Reverend Ed Watt and a group of followers from the Carroll Avenue Baptist Mission picketed a department store displaying the suit in its window. The protest continued until the store removed the one topless suit being displayed; Watt, et al., had attracted so much attention to the suit that someone went in and bought it.
- The Republican party seized on it as a symbol of the "decadence" in America in order to gain support during an election year.
- In 1964, New York City Commissioner of Parks, Newbold Morris, indicated that women caught wearing the suit on beaches within his jurisdiction would be issued a summons for indecent exposure by police.
- The Vatican newspaper, *L'Osservatore Romano*, published an article in July 1964 devoted to the topless bathing suit which carried the headline, "The Ultimate Shame," and noted that wearing it "negates moral sense."
- In June 1964, the Soviet newspaper, *Isvestia*, termed the suit a sign of America's moral decay in an article entitled "Back to

Barbarism." "So the decay of the moneybags society continues," it stated.

Others chose to focus on the humorous side of the uproar. In July 1964, the suit was modeled by a four-year old in the San Francisco *Chronicle*. Jan and Dean recorded an album track, "One Piece Topless Bathing Suit," while The Rip Chords' cover on the Columbia label received notable radio play, hitting the *Billboard* Hot 100 charts in August 1964. Popular magazines such as *Life* featured pictures — albeit from unprovocative angles — as well as stories which documented the furor.

Moral considerations aside, many observers considered the garment — consisting of a double strap going over the shoulders which connected to a bottom piece reaching well above the navel — to be extraordinarily ugly; only three thousand of the suits were actually sold. However, the phenomenon netted Gernreich untold millions of dollars worth of publicity. He later noted that "I never dreamed it would go beyond the fashion business into sociology."

## BIBLIOGRAPHY

Alexander, Shana. "Me? In That! Topless Suits," *Life*. 57 (July 10, 1964) 54B-57.

"Barely a Bare," *Time*. 83 (June 26, 1964) 75.

Barry, L. "How Did Photographers, TV and the Press Meet the Challenge of the Topless Swimsuit?," *Popular Photography*. 55 (November 1964) 135-139ff.

Javna, John, and Gordon Javna. "Fashion; Scandals of the Sixties," In: *60s!*. New York: St. Martin's, 1983. p. 98.

# Trivial Pursuit

When Trivial Pursuit was introduced in the midst of the electronic video game craze, it appeared to be something of an anachronism. Rather than the "beep, bleep, buzz or zap" of its competitors, the game was played on a 20″ × 20″ multi-colored board adorned with a wheel-shaped pattern. The basic, or "genus," edition came with 1,000 cards, each containing one question on each of six general subjects: Geography, Entertainment, History, Art & Literature, Science & Nature, and Sports & Leisure. Players, ranging from two to twenty-four in number, would ask each other questions with a correct answer allowing the respondent to move and receive another question. Typical questions included:

- Who was Bram Stocker's most infamous character? (Dracula)
- What's a newly hatched swan called? (a cygnet)

The game was born on a rainy Saturday afternoon in Montreal in 1979 when two Canadian journalists, Chris Haney and Scott Abbott, challenged each other to a battle of wits at Scrabble. Then Haney thought, "Why not invent a game?" In less than one hour, they had designed the basic structure of what was to become Trivial Pursuit. After almost two years of research devoted to compiling a sufficient number of acceptable queries, the group—which now included Haney's brother John—was ready to test-market the game. The 1,100 units produced in 1981 all sold within a few weeks. A loan from a bank manager who had gotten hooked on the game made possible the production of 20,000 more units.

Word of mouth enabled the game to reach cult status in Canada. Selchow and Righter began manufacturing it in the United States in 1982, pushing retail sales to a total of roughly seventy million dollars by the end of 1983. Selchow and Righter executive, Hudson Dobson, noted "I have been in this business thirty years, and Trivial Pursuit is the biggest individual game I have ever had. It defies everything we've had before." And it continued to perform well into the mid-1980s; close to twenty million copies of Trivial Pursuit had been purchased by U.S. consumers, at prices ranging from seventeen to forty dollars, by the end of 1984. In addition, a host of spin-offs (e.g., the "Genus II," "Silver Screen," sports, music and bible editions) and competing versions began appearing at the height of the craze. Many international editions also hit the marketplace, beginning with Great Britain and Australia in 1983, followed by France, Germany, and Holland in 1984. F.A.O. Schwarz's Walter Reid predicted that the game would become "a long-term fad," not like Rubik's Cube, which wore off after nine months.

The appeal of the game appears to lie in (1) the pleasure of playing against people armed not with joy sticks but with arsenals of minutiae, and (2) the widespread reaction against video games where one experiences minimal human interaction (e.g., moaning, groaning, laughter). A sampling of customers during the height of Trivial Pursuit's popularity included the following testimonials:

- "Every couple we've ever invited over to play the game has bought it the next day." (Ruth Gordon, North Miami)
- "There's not a person in the entertainment business who hasn't heard of the game, played it or been hooked by it." (*Footloose* producer Craig Zadan)

Not all consumer reactions, however, have been positive. Within the broader field of trivia buffs, Cullen Murphy, in the September 1984 issue of *Atlantic*, noted that the answers approved by the game's creators have tended to penalize those who know too much. He offered the following evidence, culled from the basic edition:

- Lewis Carroll is credited with having "introduced Humpty Dumpty to the world" in *Through the Looking Glass* (1872), but the character appeared first in *Mother Goose's Melody* (c1803).
- "Who was Lyndon Johnson's secretary of defense?" Robert McNamara, of course, but what about Clark Clifford?
- "Who was the first black to star in a TV situation comedy?" Diahann Carroll is the given answer, disappointing fans of *Amos 'n Andy*.

- "What caused an adjournment of the 25th anniversary session of the United Nations General Assembly?" The given answer, Khrushchev's shoe pounding, in fact occurred during the 15th session.

Despite such complaints the game has continued to sell well through the decade, appearing to be on its way to classic status like Monopoly and Parcheesi.

## BIBLIOGRAPHY

Bruman, Carol. "A Rewarding Pursuit of Trivia," *Maclean's*. 96 (January 17, 1983) 36.

Corliss, Richard. "Pac-Man for Smart People: the Creators of Trivial Pursuit Roll Out a Sequel," *Time*. 124 (September 3, 1984) 76.

Frame, Randy. "Is Bible Knowledge Becoming Just Another Trivial Pursuit? Inspired by a Popular Board Game, Some Entrepreneurs Are Profiting from 'Bible Trivia,'" *Christianity Today*. 28 (October 5, 1984) 62-63.

"Hey, They Took My Trivia!," *Time*. 124 (November 5, 1984) 61. Reports on a lawsuit contesting the rights to Trivial Pursuit.

Hill, Phil. "Game's International Sales Aren't Trivial," *Advertising Age*. 55 (December 24, 1984) 18.

"Let's Get Trivial; the Hottest Board Game in America Has All the Answers," *Time*. 122 (October 24, 1983) 88.

Murphy, Cullen. "Foul Play," *The Atlantic*. 254 (September 1984) 16-18.

"Nothing Trivial About It," *Time*. 124 (August 6, 1984) 55.

"The Stunning Success of Trivial Pursuit," *Business Week*. (April 23, 1984) 51.

Tarpey, John P. "Selchow & Righter: Playing Trivial Pursuit to the Limit," *Business Week*. (November 26, 1984) 118-120.

"Trivia Games Spawn Second Generation," *Playthings*. 83 (May 5, 1985) 76-78.

"Trivia Mania," *Fortune*. 110 (November 12, 1984) 8.

# Tug-of-War

Two teams of burly men pull against each other from opposite ends of a thick rope in this contest of brute strength. The rope must be between 4″ and 5″ in circumference and at least 35 yards long to accommodate two eight-man teams. A piece of colored tape marks the halfway point on the rope; 6′6 3/4″ on either side of the center are two white tapes. On the ground three parallel lines correspond exactly to the three markings on the rope. With the rope pulled taut — center mark over its corresponding ground mark — and the hands of the nearest member of each team within 12″ of the outside white tapes, the contest begins. The idea is for one team to pull the other far enough forward for the opposition's white mark to cross the center ground mark.

In England, tug-of-war has been waged for centuries, and its battlefields have been various — indoors on a mat or outdoors across water and mud, over a pit, and the like. Retreating farther back in time, the ancient Chinese exhibited their brawn in rope-pulling matches as part of harvest gathering activities. Over the years, both sailors and soldiers, finding themselves equipped with rope and with time on their hands, naturally took to the sport. All this muscle splitting, sweating, and groaning usually occurred as group mood dictated. The sport was unorganized at any level much less an international one until it became an Olympic game.

Tug-of-war first appeared in the Second Olympiad, Paris 1900. Then, the Swedish-Dane team won with the United States second. In St. Louis 1904, American teams swept the first four places only to fall out of contention for medals in Athens 1906, won by a German team. London 1908 was all Great Britain as the home teams walked off with the three medals. In Stockholm 1912, Sweden repeated. And for the final year of Olympic competition in Antwerp 1920, Great Britain seized the gold.

Tug-of-war, with its dramatic straining after inches by stalwart men, their half-moon biceps bulging, should not have disappeared so quickly. In the Olympics, spectator boredom was minimal because the rule was whichever team pulled the other the furthest in five minutes won the victory. Even if the two teams were evenly matched and the action slow, it would be over with shortly. The time limit guaranteed that many teams would get to compete — some more exciting to watch than others. No longer an Olympic event, Americans lost interest in the sport which does, however, continue to show up at agricultural fairs, carnivals, fetes, and on college campuses.

## BIBLIOGRAPHY

Arlott, John, ed. *The Oxford Companion to World Sports and Games*. London & New York: Oxford University Press, 1975.
Wallechinsky, David. *The Complete Book of the Olympics*. New York: The Viking Press, 1984.

# The Mike Tyson-Robin Givens Affair

Celebrity couples have always been big box office. In this respect, 1988 proved to be a mother lode. As noted by Mike Lupica,

> Mark Gastineau and Brigitte Nielsen were joined in heavenly keister. And Wayne Gretzky gave up Canada for his actress wife; it was sort of a combination of the Duke of Windsor and Holiday on Ice. But nothing compared with the marriage of heavyweight champion Mike Tyson to Robin Givens, the lovely actress from *Head of the Class*. This was a fun couple the likes of which sports had not really known since . . . well, since when? Since Bo Belinsky married Mamie Van Doren?
>
> Since Jake and Vicki LaMotta?
>
> Mike and Robin's marriage was one made for our times, which means made for the tabloids. They probably should have tied the knot at a supermarket check-out counter.

Why did Americans — fed an almost daily dose of timely gossip via the media — keep a shameless vigil on the disintegration of their marriage? For starters, the activities of any heavyweight boxing champion would be major news in this era. But, more importantly, the couple's goings-on appeared to be a real-life soap opera, with a script written in Hollywood. The basic premise was guaranteed attention grabber: the sophisticated, beautiful television actress marries the street-smart pugilist from the wrong side of town. The tendency of observers to have strong feelings of one sort or another about the relationship, coupled with the widely varying reports surfacing with respect to events which transpired, served to keep the topic on the front page.

According to *People Weekly*, problems had surfaced in the marriage as early as the couple's honeymoon in the Bahamas.

Professional tennis player Lori McNeil, Givens' friend, was staying at the resort, and the three of them had been drinking in a hotel lounge. "Michael was drinking too much," says McNeil, "so me and Robin left. Michael comes after us and he breaks down the door. He starts throwing pitchers and glasses, and then he just sits down and watches television. We thought, 'Maybe it's over,' but then he grabs Robin and starts hitting her. Kicking her. I was screaming, and he turned and hit me, and my lip started to bleed. She's laying on the floor, and someone called security and there are eight or nine guys there and Michael takes off his shirt, is yelling, cursing, saying that they are going to have to deal with him."

By late summer of 1988 — following months of rampant rumor-mongering — Tyson's erratic behavior appeared to reflect some deeper problems, perhaps on the home front. In August, he was involved in a brawl in front of a Harlem clothing outlet with a former ring conquest of his, Mitch "Blood" Green. On September 4, while visiting an old friend in upstate New York, he ran his wife's BMW into a tree and was knocked unconscious. It was reported that this incident represented an attempted suicide.

The pivotal event in the marriage was Barbara Walters' interview with the couple for ABC's "20/20". Givens described the marriage as "Torture, pure hell, worse than anything I could imagine." Two days later Tyson — allegedly under the influence of thorazine during the Walters session — lashed back by hurling his furniture through the closed window of his New Jersey mansion and repeatedly striking Givens. Givens fled to the West Coast and initiated divorce proceedings shortly thereafter.

Givens — already discredited in the eyes of many due to the double-cross aspect of her "20/20" testimony — further hurt her cause by contacting celebrity divorce lawyer Marvin Mitchelson. The media had a field day blackening Givens' character. She was portrayed as a gold digger, under the spell of a domineering and manipulative mother, and not a particularly popular person while at college. Ultimately, Givens — appearing cowed by the unexpected outpouring of criticism — disavowed all interest in Tyson's money and quietly finalized the divorce (in the face of repeated rumors that the couple was working towards a reconciliation).

Tyson, while outwardly less hurt by the adverse publicity (evidently few expected the world heavyweight champion to be a choirboy), hardly emerged with his reputation unscathed. Although he was universally acknowledged to be a great fighter, he was loathed (even ridiculed) in many quarters as petty, cruel, physically abusive to women (he was quoted as telling a friend that Givens had been the recipient of the best punch he had ever thrown). Efforts by his promoter, Don King, to focus the public's attention upon the more noble and generous features of Tyson's character (e.g., his commitment to assisting culturally deprived youth) were only partially successful. As a result, it is probable that Tyson has thus far realized only a small fraction of his potential within the field of endorsements. Perhaps of greater significance, youths—especially inner city blacks—were denied a proper role model in the person straddling the single most visible promontory in the sports world.

## BIBLIOGRAPHY

"Divorced, Mike Tyson," *Time*. 133 (February 27, 1989) 69.

Gross, Ken. "As Wife Robin Givens Splits for the Coast, Mike Tyson Rearranges the Future," *People Weekly*. 30 (October 17, 1980) 60-61.

Gross, Ken. "A Life on the Brink," *People Weekly*. 30 (September 26, 1988) 86-91.

Gross, Ken. "Robin's Sad Song," *People Weekly*. 30 (December 19, 1988) 128-133.

Gross, Ken, with Victoria Balfour and Dan Knapp. "When Push Comes to Shove, Mike Tyson and Robin Givens Settled for a Split Decision," *People Weekly*. 30 (October 24, 1988) 56-58.

"Having Turned 'Iron Mike' into Molten Metal, Robin Givens Proves That Tyson is Ring-Ready," *People Weekly*. 29 (February 22, 1988) 32-33.

Jerome, Jim. "His Robin Flown, the Champ Pushes On," *People Weekly*. 31 (February 27, 1989) 30-35.

Jones, Robert. "A Couple of Knockouts; Mike Tyson and Robin Givens Are Hits in Two Different Areas," *Life*. 11 (July 1988) 26-31.

"The Lady and Her Champ," *Life*. 11 (March 1988) 7.

Lingeman, Richard. "A Whale of a Show: the Dukakis-Bush-Tyson-Givens Fight," *The Nation*. 247 (November 21, 1988) 513-514.

Lupica, Mike. "The Line on '89: Mike and Robin Together Again, and Other Future Shocks," *Esquire*. 110 (December 1988) 65-67.

McMurran, Kristan. "The Champ and the Vamp; Will Marriage to Robin Givens Be Harder on Mike Tyson Than Next Week's Fight with Spinks?," *People Weekly*. 29 (June 27, 1988) 64-69.

"Mike Tyson vs. Robin Givens: the Champ's Biggest Fight," *Ebony*. 44 (January 1989) 116-119.

"On the Ropes," *U.S. News & World Report*. 105 (September 19, 1988) 10.

"Seeking Divorce," *Time*. 132 (October 17, 1988) 65.

"Tyson: Last Scenes from a Marriage," *Newsweek*. 112 (October 17, 1988) 36.

Vader, J.E. "Back Off, Robin Bashers; a Few Words in Defense of the Villainous Robin Givens," *Sports Illustrated*. 69 (December 12, 1988) 108.

# Volleyball

Volleyball was invented in 1895 by William Morgan of the Holyoke (Mass.) Y.M.C.A. as an alternative to the monotonous program of calisthenics, indoor track, and other gymnasium activities during the winter. The sport flourished in the Far West and the Midwest almost from its beginning; Fort Wayne was a leading volleyball center, possessing 200 organized teams and more than 8,000 players among a population of 114,000 by the mid-1930s. During the Depression, it ranked near the top among recreational pursuits and was played at beaches and parks in the warm months as well as indoors to escape inclement weather. Over five million Americans played volleyball during this period, encompassing all age groups and members of both sexes.

The game owed its popularity to simple rules and its adaptability to the available space, time, and equipment. *The New York Times* noted at the time,

> It can be played during the noon hour outside the factory; it can be played on a roof, and in the back yard or in rural surroundings, where a fence takes the place of a net. If a fence is not available, a piece of rope will serve.

Despite the appearance of countless new recreational pursuits over the past half century, volleyball remains a popular participatory sport. In addition, it is beginning to make a mark as a spectator sport; ESPN has included both male and female volleyball matches as a regular programming item. In 1964, the game was included in the Olympic Games for the first time.

## BIBLIOGRAPHY

Anderson, Bruce. "Want to Make a Hit at the Beach? Pound a Yellow Redsand Volleyball," *Sports Illustrated*. 65 (August 25, 1986) 7.
Carey, John, and others. "Walleyball: a Sport is Born," *Newsweek*. 106 (July 8, 1985) 63. Delineates adaptation of volleyball to a walled court.

Elkins, Frank. "Big Volley Ball Vogue," *The New York Times Encyclopedia of Sports*, edited by Gene Brown. Volume 11: Indoor Sports. New York: Arno, 1979. p. 44.

Friermood, H.T. "Volley Ball in 1944," *Recreation*. 37 (January 1944) 548ff.

Kopit, A. "Thank You Annette Funicello," *Saturday Evening Post*. 239 (July 16, 1966) 74-77.

Kort, Michele. "How the Game is Played," *WomenSports*. 5 (October 1983) 42-43.

Kort, Michele. "Volleyball," *WomenSports*. 5 (October 1983) 33- 34. History of the sport.

McCallum, Jack. "For Pro Volleyballers, Life in the Sunshine is Clouded by Economics," *Sports Illustrated*. 63 (August 26, 1985) 19-22.

Monroe, K. "All Volley, No Thunder," *Nation's Business*. 38 (October 1950) 84.

Newman, Bruce. "Beach Bums No More," *Sports Illustrated*. 69 (August 1, 1988) 54-58. Discusses the large cash winnings being offered in beach volley ball competitions.

"Paddle Volleyball," *Recreation*. 46 (June 1952) 179.

Reed, J.D. "Beach Volleyball Nets Big Bucks; Once a Laid-Back Pastime, a Waterside Game Goes Major League," *Time*. 134 (August 28, 1989) 71.

Rogers, J.E. "Volleyball, Popular American Game," *Recreation*. 33 (December 1939) 502ff.

Schecter, Arnold. "Wallyball's Played Like Volleyball But Always on a Racquet-ball Court," *Sports Illustrated*. 56 (March 1982) 6.

Shewman, Byron. "Pro League: a Troubled Past," *WomenSports*. 3 (December 1981) 36-37.

"Smacquetball, Anyone?," *Changing Times*. 37 (September 1983) 8. Provides a look at recent racquetball and volleyball variants.

# "We Are Family":
# The 1979 Pittsburgh Pirates

The Pittsburgh Pirates, 1979 World Series winners, were a team in tune with the times. Although a solid first division club throughout the 1970s (known as the "Lumber Company" for their heavy hitting earlier in the decade), a series of concerted moves aimed at bringing a championship (e.g., high impact trades for quality pitching; the signing of a gregarious, eternally optimistic manager, Chuck Tanner) changed the Pirates into a more balanced, cohesive unit. Early in the 1979 campaign, the team adopted the then-popular disco song, Sister Sledge's "We Are Family," as an anthem in keeping with its boisterous camaraderie and high-spirited play, both on and off the field. The team leaders were two-time batting champion Dave Parker and the appropriately nicknamed Willie "Pops" Stargell, then in the twilight of a long, illustrious career which would land him in the Hall of Fame at Cooperstown. Stargell, in particular, served not only to keep the atmosphere relaxed in the clubhouse but to function as a diplomat to outsiders apt to be put off by tape decks blaring at top volume, flip quotes, and the players' exuberant wives—who challenged commentator Howard Cosell for top billing on ABC's World Series broadcasts.

The nation at large was introduced to "family" fever during October 1979 when the Pirates, emerging victorious from a tight pennant race, met the American League's Baltimore Orioles in the World Series. While the series was not played very artistically, it featured drama and dignity. Down three games to one, the Pirates stormed back to sweep the final three encounters with the thirty-eight-year-old Stargell hitting the winning homer in the final tilt. In the aftermath, President Jimmy Carter paid the ultimate accolade, noting that it was a shame that one of the teams had to lose.

The 1980s drastically changed the scenario. Disco retreated underground, Stargell retired, and many Pirate stars became embroiled in a drug scandal which severely taxed old friendships as well as team cohesiveness.

## BIBLIOGRAPHY

Axthelm, Pete. "Baseball's First Family," *Newsweek*. 94 (October 29, 1979) 89-91.

Fimrite, Ron. "Rising from the Ashes; Pittsburgh's Victory," *Sports Illustrated*. 51 (October 29, 1979) 61-62ff.

Lacayo, Richard. "The Cocaine Agonies Continue; Charges of Illegal Drug Use Touch Even Some Baseball Greats," *Time*. 126 (September 23, 1985) 62.

Quinn, H. "Boys of Shiver; Pittsburgh Pirates and the Baltimore Orioles," *Macleans*. 93 (October 22, 1979) 40ff.

Quinn, H. "Pops Won It For the Bucs," *Maclean's*. 92 (October 29, 1979) 44.

Seligman, D. "Bit of a Bet on the Pirates," *Fortune*. 100 (November 19, 1979) 41.

# Wrestlemania

Pro wrestling has entered into an economic renaissance in the 1980s, based upon a dazzling blend of larger-than-life characters and outrageous hype. The revival was due largely to the marketing genius of Vince McMahon, Jr. In 1982, he saw that the show business excesses and sheer spectacle of the pro wrestling world could be made to appeal to a generation raised on rock 'n' roll.

The genre had fallen upon hard times since the golden age of the 1950s, which featured colorful wrestlers such as Killer Kowalski, Whipper Billy Watson, Dick the Bruiser, and the Abruzzi Strong-boy, Bruno Sammartino, who reigned as World Champ for twelve years beginning in 1959. The audience for pro wrestling during this era was distinctly blue collar in nature, the composite picture of typical fans being that of tattooed men with criminal records and bleached-blond women with missing teeth. A standard joke among wrestlers on the circuit at the time was "What has 14 teeth and an IQ of 50? The first 10 rows at a wrestling match."

With the aim of broadening fan appeal across the socioeconomic spectrum, particularly among youth, McMahon began producing televised wrestling programs for syndication. He then sold them to cable networks and individual television stations, constructing a loose confederation capable of reaching eighty percent of the homes in North America. After succeeding his father as the head of the World Wrestling Federation (WWF), an organization supplying a substantial number of wrestlers for bouts around the globe, his cosmetic makeover of the genre proceeded in earnest. He began including popular music soundtracks on WWF programs, his wrestlers entered the ring with rock songs blaring through the arena PA systems.

McMahon and his cohorts received a substantial lift in 1984 when Cyndi Lauper began managing wrestler Wendi Richter and making appearances with her wrestling mentor, Captain Lou Al bano. Lauper's most memorable moment came at a WWF awards ceremony in December 1984 in honor of her "contributions to rock and wrestling." Bad guy wrestler Rowdy Roddy Piper kicked her in the face and smashed her trophy—a platinum record—over Albano's head. Lauper also served as pro wrestling's entree into the hallowed portals of MTV, then the hottest channel in North America.

Such publicity bonanzas led to the launching of "Wrestlemania," featuring a host of big-name performers, most notably a tag team bout in which Hulk Hogan and Mr. T defeated Piper and Paul "Mr. Wonderful" Orndorff. The card was witnessed by 20,000 fans in New York's Madison Square Garden as well as by more than one million spectators at 165 closed-circuit outlets in Canada and the United States. Billy Martin served as announcer, Muhammed Ali as a guest referee, and Liberace, using a small silver bell, acted as a guest timekeeper. Annual follow-ups to the extravaganza have been equally successful.

The WWF's competitors have also prospered. Its major rivals—the Minneapolis-based American Wrestling Association and the National Wrestling Alliance headquartered in Atlanta—joined forces to become Pro Wrestling U.S.A., which has also played to large crowds around the nation.

Critics—including doctors, educators, the clergy and parents—have assailed the genre on a wide number of issues:

- The cartoon-like violence has a coarsening effect on children.
- Sociologist Michael Smith feels it "exemplifies the need for simpleminded answers—black and white, good and bad, based on sexual and ethnic stereotyping, the Arabs, Nazis, Orientals, gays versus the Captain America types (see Table I). It reinforces underlying hostilities in a blatant, outrageous way."
- It cultivates an enjoyment of controlled anarchy—i.e., obvious rule breaking and a conspicuous lack of fair competition—which could lead to a susceptibility of the mob mentality and deception from manipulative power brokers.
- It indulges in fakery; e.g., freelance photographer Jeffrey Wasserman was close enough at Toronto's Maple Leaf Gardens to overhear two wrestlers choreographing their moves:

"One guy said, 'Is this hold comfortable?' Another guy said, 'Okay, I'm going to throw you now.'"

- Women—a weak draw as competitors—are portrayed almost exclusively in subservient roles. The ringside role of Miss Elizabeth as a cheerleader and gofer serves as a case in point.

---

Table I: The Cast of Characters—Good Guys vs. Bad Guys

---

Good Guys: Hulk Hogan, Andre the Giant, The Junk Yard Dog, Tita Santana, Sargeant Slaughter, Randy (Macho Man) Savage, Danny Boy Smith, Jesse "The Body" Ventura, Magnificent Muraca, Mr. T.

Bad Boys: Rowdy Roddy Piper, The Iron Sheik (an Iranian who became notorious during the American hostage crisis in 1980), Big John Studd, King Kong Bundy, Adorable Adrian Adonis (the most prominent of the gay impersonators).

---

Supporters have countered that pro wrestling provides an enjoyable recreation and a harmless release for aggression.

In the meantime, the WWF's media blitz continued to gather steam during the mid-1980s:

- CBS struck paydirt with the one-hour Saturday morning cartoon show, "Hulk Hogan's Rock 'n' Wrestling."
- Three weekly syndicated TV shows were being shown on 190 stations in North America.
- A ninety-minute special, "Saturday Night's Main Event," was being broadcast once per month in the "Saturday Night Live" slot on NBC.
- A sound recording, "The Wrestling Album," featuring such stars as Hogan and Piper singing "Tutti Frutti," "Land of a Thousand Dances," etc., became a best-seller.
- Numerous videotapes—including "WWF Grudge Matches" and six volumes of "The Best of the WWF"—also sold well.
- Following the example of rock performers, a wide array of merchandising tie-ins hit the market, including T-shirts, posters, hats and dolls.
- Numerous guest spots on TV variety and talk shows were filled by top wrestling stars.

All of this has added up to lucrative salaries for wrestlers like Hogan (aka bad guy Terry Boulder/Sterling Golden), whose career took off following an appearance as "Thunderlips" in the film, "Rocky III."

Pro wrestling has continued riding the crest of the big business wave into the 1990s, lining up behind God, Country, and Apple Pie. Hogan, ever conscious of his PR duties, admonishes his young fans to "eat your vitamins, say your prayers and train for your future." The public does not seem to mind the ambiguities of the genre. While college-age wise guys profess to like the kitschy aspects of it all, most fans simply enjoy the excitement and charisma of stars like Hogan. After all, as noted by Jeremy Tepper, editor of "Wrestling's Main Event," The Hulkster is just a really nice, oversized guy making a living the best way he knows how.

## BIBLIOGRAPHY

Glynn, Lenny. "Lesson from the Killer," *Maclean's*. 99 (May 19, 1986) 40. Profile of Wladek "Killer" Kowalski.

Gomez, Linda, and Theo Westenberger (photographs). "Mighty Wrestlers and Their Madding Crowds," *Life*. 8 (September 1985) 30-36.

Malanga, Steven. "This Hulk's for Sale; Not Quite a Sport, Not Exactly Theater, Professional Wrestling Has Nonetheless Grown Enormously Popular. A Licensing Program is Next," *Chain Store Age – General Merchandise Edition*. 61 (September 1985) 83-84.

Quinn, Hal. "The Man Inside Hulkmania," *Maclean's*. 99 (May 19, 1986) 39.

Scanlon, Kevin, with Nora Underwood. "Glitz, Glamor and New Fans," *Maclean's*. 99 (May 19, 1986) 38.

Wulf, Steve. "Their Idol," *Sports Illustrated*. 68 (June 20, 1988) 13. The young viewers of *Kid's Choice* have chosen Hulk Hogan as male athlete of the year.

# Yo-Yos

I can take a yo-yo and walk down the street up to a four-year-old kid and say, "What is it!" and he or she will say, "It's a yo-yo." Four years old. Maybe never played one, but knows what it is.

— George Malko

The yo-yo is a spool-like toy with a string attached to the axle holding its two halves together. It may be reeled up and let down by manipulating the string. The term is derived from the Filipino Tagalog for "comeback." Before anybody called it a "yo-yo," it was known as a "bandalore," "quiz," "l'emigrette," "l'emigrant," "coblentz," "incroyable," and, in ancient Greece, "disc."

Vases dating back to antiquity have been unearthed which depict Grecian youths playing with objects similar in appearance to the modern day toy. The National Museum of Athens possesses one of these discs, made of terra cotta. Since then, the yo-yo has experienced frequent revivals in popularity. The rage for the toy in France at the time of the 1789 Revolution inspired the playright Beaumarchais to insert a scene (XIII, Act III) addressing its virtues in his already successful masterpiece, *The Marriage of Figaro*. An 1891 edition of the English magazine, *Boys' Modern Playmate*, noted "About the beginning of the present century the 'bandilore' [sic] suddenly became a fashionable toy, under the name of 'quiz' and scarcely any person of fashion was without one of these toys."

In the United States, a large number of patents were issued for various improvements in the toy's design between 1866 and the late 1920s when Filipino immigrant Pedro Flores began producing a prototype of the modern yo-yo on the West Coast. The Flores yo-yo possessed a slip-string (rather than a fixed string) which not only permitted up and down movement, but would enable the yo-yo to "stick" or "sleep" when it reached the end of the string. Recognizing the toy's potential for success, Donald F. Duncan, the developer of the Good Humor Ice Cream franchise system, opened a

Flores yo-yo factory in Chicago in 1929 under the trademark of the "O-Boy Top." His marketing genius fueled a nationwide craze which peaked in 1932. Celebrities such as the Miss Universe title holder, baseball star Hack Wilson, and movie stars Douglas Fairbanks and Mary Pickford were photographed with the toy. Bing Crosby sang a yo-yo song. Aware that the toy had achieved a kind of national sport status in the Philippines, Duncan hired a flock of Filipinos to demonstrate and teach a growing repertoire of stunts (see Table I) to kids around the world.

World War II—with its lumber shortages and the preoccupation of newpapers with weightier matters—brought a halt to the popularity enjoyed by the yo-yo. The postwar years brought strong competitors into the field such as Cheerio, Good Manufacturing, and the Royal Top Manufacturing Company. Replicating the tried and true merchandising campaigns of the past—barnstorming demonstrations and contests, prominently positioned product displays in stores, and intensive media coverage—the yo-yo was hyped back into the forefront of public consciousness. In 1963 alone, the Duncan company—now located in Luck, Wisconsin and struggling to maintain its hegemony in the field—sold fifty-six million yo-yos. However, the popularity of the toy suffered a severe blow when Duncan was forced by creditors to declare bankruptcy in March 1965. After a lull of a couple years, prior associates of the firm parlayed the Duncan name, know-how, and distribution network into their own successful ventures, Festival and Flambeau Products, respectively. As a result, the yo-yo remains a constant, albeit less visible, fixture in the American toy scene, promoted in the 1980s by the likes of Tommy Smothers via the videocassette and TV talk show mediums.

Table I:
The Most Popular Tricks as Compiled By
Professional Demonstrator Barney Akers and
Executive Donald F. Duncan, Jr.

A. One Hand:

Spinner
Sleeping Beauty
Forward Pass
Rock the Baby
Walk the Dog
Loop-the-Loop
Overhead Loops
Around the World (forward; backward; double)
Breakaway
Over the Falls
Elephant's Trunk
Spank the Baby
Outside Loops
Interception (forward pass caught with the opposite hand)
Rattlesnake
Spaghetti
Buzz Saw
Behind the Bars
The Creeper
Spell Yo
Bouncing Betsy
Three-Leaf Clover
Dog Bite
Pin Wheel
Lindy Loop
Perpetual Motion
Lone Star
Two-Hand Star
Thread the Needle
Double Creeper
Arizona Cowboy
Dog Through the Hoop
Through the Subway
Skin the Cat

Punch the Bag
Hangman's Noose
Pickpocket
Elevator
Reaching for the Moon
Double or Nothing
Brain Teaser
Monkey Up the Tree
Penalty Shot
Manila Special
Hop the Fence
The Basket
Slap Shot
Crocheting
Barber Pole
Double Barrel Roll
Sky Ride, Sky Rocket
Home Run
Bow Tie
Eiffel Tower
Bank Deposit
Grasshopper
Changing Horses
Man on the Flying Trapeze
Ebb Tide
One-Handed Cradle

B. Two Hands:

Loop the Loops
Reach for the Moon & Punch the Bag
Around the World & Loop the Loops
Machine Gun
Rapid Fire
Ride the Horse
Criss Cross
Milk the Cow
Punch the Bag — Double
Double Outside Loops
Reach for the Moon & Ride the Horse

# BIBLIOGRAPHY

Allman, William F. "Physics on a String," *Science*. 5 (October 1984) 92-93.

"The Durable Yo-Yo: an Old Favorite," *Changing Times*. 37 (August 1983) 12.

Malko, George. *The One and Only Yo-Yo Book*. New York: Avon, 1978.

Pileggi, Sarah. "Praise Be, the True Wooden Yo-Yo Has Been Revived, and That's No Jive," *Sports Illustrated*. 57 (December 27, 1982) 15.

Sambrook, Clare. "Coke Bets 18m Pounds Sterling on Yo-Yo Craze," *Marketing*. (April 13, 1989) 2.

"Under the Children's Christmas Tree," *The New Yorker*. 58 (December 13, 1982) 112ff.

"Water Guns, Yo-Yos: Accent on Quality; Both Seasonal Categories Rely on Increased Promotions, New Licenses," *Playthings*. 81 (October 1983) 49.

"Water Pistol and Yo-Yo Market Concentrates on Innovation," *Playthings*. 80 (October 1982) 48-50.

Zuckerman, Edward. "Quest for the Perfect Yo-Yo," *Reader's Digest*. 130 (June 1987) 189-192.

# Index

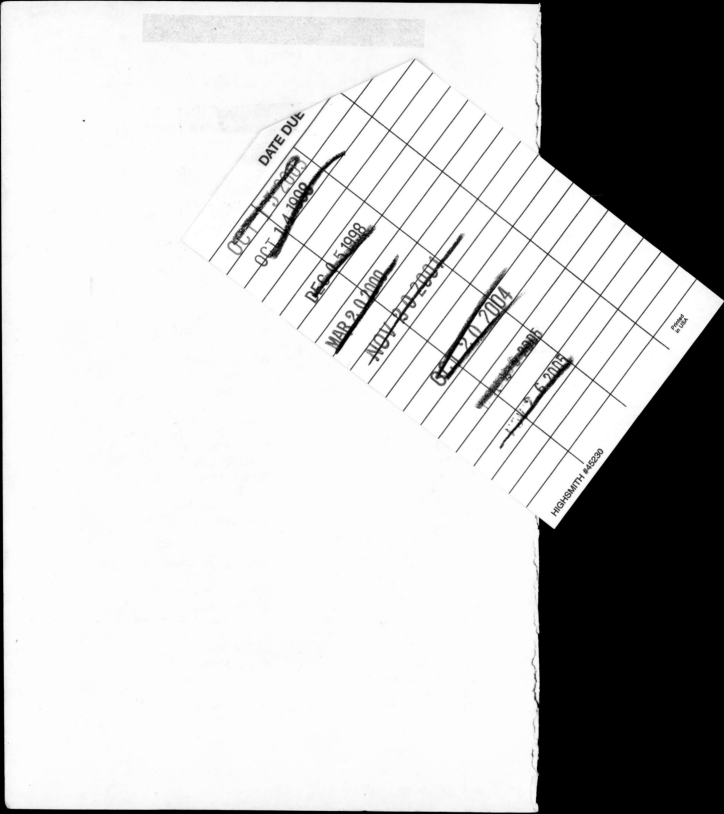

**DATE DUE**

OCT 2 3 2003

OCT 1 4 1998

DEC 1 5 1998

MAR 2 0 2000

NOV 3 0 2004

SEP 2 0 2004

NOV 1 5 2005